Remixing the Civil War

Remixing the Civil War

Meditations on the Sesquicentennial

Edited by Thomas J. Brown

The Johns Hopkins University Press
Baltimore

The Johns Hopkins University Press
2715 North Charles Street
Baltimore, Maryland 21218-4363
www.press.jhu.edu

Library of Congress Cataloging-in-Publication Data

Remixing the Civil War : meditations on the sesquicentennial /
edited by Thomas J. Brown.
    p. cm.
  Includes bibliographical references and index.
  ISBN-13: 978-1-4214-0250-5 (hardcover : alk. paper)
  ISBN-10: 1-4214-0250-5 (hardcover : alk. paper)
  ISBN-13: 978-1-4214-0251-2 (pbk. : alk. paper)
  ISBN-10: 1-4214-0251-3 (pbk. : alk. paper)
  1. United States—History—Civil War, 1861–1865—
Centennial celebrations, etc. 2. United States—History—Civil
War, 1861–1865—Historiography. 3. United States—History—
Civil War, 1861–1865—Art and the war. 4. United States—
History—Civil War, 1861–1865—Literature and the war.
5. Collective memory—United States. 6. Memorials—United
States. I. Brown, Thomas J., 1960–
E641.R45 2011
973.7—dc22   2011009986

A catalog record for this book is available from the British
Library.

*Special discounts are available for bulk purchases of this book. For
more information, please contact Special Sales at 410-516-6936 or
specialsales@press.jhu.edu.*

The Johns Hopkins University Press uses environmentally
friendly book materials, including recycled text paper that is
composed of at least 30 percent post-consumer waste,
whenever possible.

To the Lincoln Memorial

Authorized during the semicentennial anniversary of the Civil War, you remain the most fitting and proper model for observance of the sesquicentennial anniversary. Floating atop landfill, you are a marble illusion of timeless stability sustained by sunken steel pillars. Designed to demonstrate the continued value of memorial architecture in the age of print, you have flourished through a century of film. Your eclectic sampling of American citizenship brings together a wide variety of performances by tourists wandering through your chambers, orators standing on your steps, and crowds gathering before your façade. This volume humbly salutes the virtuosity with which you have for so long remixed the Civil War.

Contents

Illustrations

Remixing the Civil War

The Undead War

Thomas J. Brown

Robert Penn Warren declared in 1961 that "the Civil War is our only 'felt'
history—history lived in the national imagination." His explanation for the
enduring appeal of the conflict reflected his literary craftsmanship as well as
his historical vision. The war did not recede into the past like previous events,
Warren argued in *The Legacy of the Civil War*, because "that mystic cloud from
which emerged our modernity" permanently marked the beginning of the present. In transforming the shaky antebellum union into a nation, the ordeal had
established Americans' "most significant sense of identity, limited as that may
be, and the best and most inclusive hope for our future." The struggle had
introduced a potent industrial state with "a new sense of military and economic
competence" and nurtured a distinctive pragmatic style of thought. The defeated South had become a more coherent and insular region than the Confederacy ever was, sharing a "great alibi" that sheltered white racism and stunted
social progress. The overthrow of slavery had invested the rest of the United
States with a "treasury of virtue" that encouraged hubristic self-delusion.[1]
   Warren's alertness to such ironies illustrated the aesthetic viewpoint
that informed his more structural observations about the significance of

Civil War stories. Unlike the Revolution, which lacked "inner drama" in Warren's judgment, the psychological struggles of Lincoln and Grant and Lee and Jackson were self-divisions that mirrored the turmoil of the country and stirred the empathy of later generations. The importance of locality and community in the Civil War demonstrated a "right and natural relation of man to place and man to man" for a subsequently rootless American society. The twists and turns of the saga provided not only suspenseful excitement but also a field for contemplating the scope of human will and the force of destiny.[2]

This collection of essays takes the occasion of the Civil War sesquicentennial anniversary to reconsider the influential claims that Warren put forward at the centennial anniversary. Like Warren, the contributors focus on the ways in which the imaginative appeal of the war extends beyond the framework of professional scholarship. We draw this distinction not because we regard nonfiction literature as any less creative or important than the productions we discuss, but because colleges and universities maintain a self-sustaining momentum in intellectual attention to the Civil War that enjoys significant institutional autonomy even as it intersects with the broader culture. Doubtless other publications will survey new research.[3] In this book, students of art, literature, and history pool resources to offer a revealing perspective on contemporary America by examining other recent uses of the war.

Reassessment of Warren's argument begins with the premise he asserted so confidently. If the Civil War was "for the American imagination, the great single event of our history" in 1961, the evidence is not clear that it remains so in 2011. Roy Rosenzweig and David Thelen reported in 1998 that only a small percentage of Americans felt a connection to any aspect of the national past, in contrast with the many respondents enthusiastic about "petit narratives" of family history.[4] The finding was especially striking because Rosenzweig and Thelen conducted their survey at the end of a flurry of events bringing public attention to the Civil War. That surge began at the origins of the contemporary period in the early 1980s, when the basic framework of recent American society and politics consolidated at the outset of the Reagan administration. John Jakes's trilogy of novels about the Civil War and Reconstruction era spent seventy-four weeks on the *New York Times* bestseller list between 1982 and 1987 and spawned two of the most widely watched television miniseries of all time. Gore Vidal's *Lincoln* (1984) was a comparable commercial success in print and broadcast. The movies *Glory* (1989) and *Gettysburg* (1993) bracketed the immense popularity of Ken Burns's television documentary *The Civil War* (1990), which spawned a cable television series entitled *Civil War Journal*. James McPherson, Garry Wills, and David Herbert Donald found wide readership for original scholarship on the war. *Gone With the Wind* extended its astonishing record of persistent success, returning to the *Times* bestseller list in 1986 on the fiftieth anniversary of Margaret Mitchell's novel and again five years later amid the hoopla that surrounded the publication of Alexandra Ripley's widely distributed sequel, *Scarlett* (1991). Charles Frazier's *Cold Mountain* (1997) spent sixty-one weeks on the *Times* bestseller list.[5] Display of the Confederate battle flag became a burning political issue in several southern states. Despite this burst of activity, sociologist Barry Schwartz seconded the verdict of Rosenzweig and Thelen in a study that focused on the most durable element of the Civil War legacy, the stature of Abraham Lincoln. The cultural authority of Lincoln and all of the American past had eroded sharply since the early 1960s, Schwartz concluded in 1998. The Civil War still commanded a residual attachment, he acknowledged, but popular identification with the grand narrative had declined demonstrably.[6]

Warren's assertions about the uniqueness of the Civil War are now as debatable as his underlying claims about the scale of national interest in any phase of history. Perhaps he did not yet regard World War II as part of history in 1961, but that conflict is likely to remain the most formative historical event in the American imagination well after the last member of the so-called greatest generation passes from the scene. Setting aside other new challengers to the primacy of the Civil War, interest in the Revolution has narrowed the gap that Warren considered the starting point for understanding the importance of the sectional conflict. Of the ten top-selling nonfiction books published during the first decade of the twenty-first century that focused on either the Revolution or the Civil War, eight were about the Revolutionary era, which Warren deemed "too simple" to sustain attention.[7] Perhaps Americans have developed a more nuanced understanding of the Revolution; perhaps they have developed a taste for conflicts they consider clear-cut; perhaps a political conservatism claiming the mantle of the founders has achieved broad cultural influence; perhaps public indifference toward the past now manifests itself in random tides of fashion. Surely, the student of nonacademic interest in the

Civil War should no longer begin by taking the singularity of that interest for granted.

As this book abundantly demonstrates, the Civil War continues to attract remarkably rich imaginative engagement in many different venues of American culture and society. The wealth of recent art and literature related to the war required this volume to be selective in its coverage of new works. We focus primarily on the twenty-first century, although some essays address the previous two decades, and we aim to move the discussion of our topic beyond the well-examined examples of *Glory* and Burns's television documentary. We take up only one of the relatively few newer cinematic or broadcast interpretations of the Civil War, and we similarly pass lightly over references to the war in contemporary music.[8] We devote particular attention to initiatives of African Americans and white southerners, groups for whom the Civil War has long been regarded as a defining event. As a result we do not discuss fiction on the war and its preliminaries published during the last fifteen years by such important writers as Russell Banks, Geraldine Brooks, E. L. Doctorow, Dara Horn, Bruce Murkoff, Marilynne Robinson, Jane Smiley, and Stephen Wright.[9] Our exclusion of scholarship applies to forays into the Civil War by Roy Blount Jr., Adam Gopnik, and other wide-ranging authors of nonfiction.[10] We do not offer a comprehensive report on the observance of the bicentennial anniversary of Lincoln's birth, though we treat in detail the most significant aspect of that occasion. Nevertheless, this volume provides a much more thorough investigation of the current uses of the Civil War than any previous study. The essayists look at works of more than thirty artists and writers as well as three political and social movements that have invoked the war in different ways.

Such a range of material defies subordination to a single comprehensive interpretation. The authors have not attempted to develop a common thesis but instead present independent and sometimes divergent views of the current significance of the war. Those differences reflect not only the authors' judgments but also the variety of a contemporary culture in which Americans look toward the war from separate directions. The contributors find fresh examples for Warren's belief that "the 'inwardness' of the experience of the Civil War, in both personal and national terms," makes the event an inspiring point of historical reference.[11] The hero of *Cold Mountain* is even named Inman. Natasha Trethewey and Josephine Humphreys have updated Warren's approach to examine Civil War legacies of self-division for African Americans and Native Americans, as directors Ang Lee and Martin Scorsese have focused on conflicted German American and Irish American protagonists in the Civil War films *Ride with the Devil* (1999) and *Gangs of New York* (2002). At the same time, the essays show that the visibility of the Civil War in American culture today, including the most thoughtful manifestations, often reflects an interest in surface rather than depth and demonstrates the extent to which visual images have achieved ascendancy over stories.

This newer pattern has drawn little attention from previous commentators on the legacy of the Civil War. For example, discussions of the rising interest in the war during the 1980s rarely take notice of Robert Wilson's extravaganza *the CIVIL warS: a tree is best measured when it is down*, though the commission for the arts festival accompanying the 1984 Olympics in Los Angeles involved leading artists in a highly politicized conflict on a prominent stage. For all of its aggressive idiosyncrasy, Wilson's work anticipated some characteristic tendencies of Civil War interpretations during the following three decades. The subtitle of the avant-garde production typified a new interplay with the national canon of Civil War memory, aping Carl Sandburg's use of a folk aphorism as the title for the concluding chapter of his monumental Lincoln biography. The characters and action extended far beyond the mid-nineteenth-century United States and into the realm of directorial arbitrariness. Frederick the Great of Prussia was the main character in the section of the opera prepared in Cologne; Marie Curie, William the Silent, and Hercules figured in sections prepared in Marseilles, Rotterdam, and Rome. Wilson's research into the 1860s focused on pictures rather than events or characters. The work of Mathew Brady's studio was a primary inspiration, and the opera featured a poem by Pope Leo XIII about photography. Robert E. Lee delivered an aria while spinning weightlessly in a space capsule. Robert Penn Warren's inward-looking narrative of the Civil War was decidedly not the appeal of the event for Robert Wilson. Instead the war furnished a repertory of well-known, manipulable visual images that served as connective tissue in a theatrical performance without a conventional plot. "We come to the theater already knowing a story, so there was no need to tell a story," Wilson explained after his immensely successful collaboration with composer Philip Glass on *Einstein on the Beach* (1976), which provided the template for their work together on *the CIVIL warS*. The proposed epic was controversial. Plans for rock star David Bowie to deliver the Gettysburg Address in Japanese particularly troubled potential sponsors. The Olympic arts festival let the work go unpresented at Los Angeles for lack of funding, and the Pulitzer Prize board awarded no prize for drama in 1986 rather than accept a unanimous jury recommendation that the honor be given to a production of the Cologne section at the American Repertory Theater. But Wilson's collage offered a model for creative engagement with familiar Civil War material in a rumination on familial conflict.[12]

Even scholars interested specifically in recent Civil War cinema have failed to reckon adequately with Ross McElwee's *Sherman's March: A Meditation on the Possibility of Romantic Love in the South in an Era of Nuclear Weapons Proliferation* (1986), the most thoughtful film about the Civil War in the last twenty-five years. The conceit of the movie is that McElwee has received a grant to make a documentary film about the lingering regional impact of Sherman's invasion but instead decides, after his girlfriend dumps him, to wander toward his North Carolina hometown along the route of the march, mingling autobiographical and historical musings with new adventures. The picaresque send-up of the documentary genre challenges ideals of manhood and patterns of storytelling epitomized by Civil War tradition. McElwee contrasts himself with the passé virility of a Civil War military commander and contrasts his film with the passé monumentality of a Civil War equestrian statue. *Sherman's March* invites comparison with classic white southern interpretations of modernity as an exercise in wrestling with the legacy of the Civil War. McElwee's detour from his proposed documentary lacks the foreboding with which graduate student Jack Burden abandons his doctoral dissertation about Confederate casualty Cass Mastern in Robert Penn Warren's *All the King's Men* (1946). The elusiveness of historical truth is not a crisis for McElwee, and he roams across the antebellum ruins and twentieth-century strip malls of the South with amiable curiosity. His traumatic memories stem from witnessing a nuclear test explosion rather than any moral inheritance related to slavery or secession. Sherman's march is a time-burnished cultural narrative that the filmmaker cuts and splices into an intelligent, hopeful exploration of the themes promised in his subtitle.[13]

Wilson and McElwee were not the first artists to reconsider the Civil War from what might be described as postmodern perspectives. Flannery O'Connor's short story "A Late Encounter with the Enemy" (1953) and Larry Rivers's canvases of *The Last Civil War Veteran* (1959–1961) had parodied the reverential attitudes toward the war typical of the decade before the centennial anniversary and suggested that popular images generated by movies and magazines had displaced historical truth in defining the meaning of the past. But intellectual discussion of the role of history in contemporary culture intensified in the 1980s, coming to revolve most frequently around the influential arguments of Frederic Jameson and Jean François Lyotard that postmodern sensibility is incapable of historical understanding. Wilson and McElwee illustrate the extent to which the Civil War assumed a prominent position in American reflections on this debate. John Updike similarly chose the road to disunion as a setting for one of his most extended responses to the challenge of postmodernism, *Memories of the Ford Administration* (1992), in which a college history professor looks back at his failed attempts to marry the wife of the deconstruction expert on the faculty and write a life of James Buchanan. Updike's depiction of deconstruction is skeptical, though the passionate biographer agrees with his romantic rival that fictionalization is the only route to historical truth. Updike treats this impenetrability of the past with wistful resignation rather than the tragic grandeur that characterized the comparable observations of Warren or Faulkner. The collapse of the Buchanan biography and the collapse of the Buchanan administration are both anticlimactic. The failure to arrest the rush toward war during the winter of 1860–61, recounted at length in a concluding excerpt from the protagonist's unfinished manuscript, contrasts with the restoration of the historian to a reasonable approximation of conjugal happiness.[14]

The turn to the Civil War as storehouse of images, characters, and stories available for recycled manipulation has not been limited to the realm of high culture. As controversies over state displays of the Confederate battle flag spread across the South in the early 1990s, two African Americans in Charleston, South Carolina, formed the clothing company NuSouth around an emblem that reproduced the southern cross in the red, green, and black colors of the African liberation movement. Popular culture scholar Tara McPherson, the observer most alert to postmodern reconstructions of the sectional conflict, described NuSouth's design as a prime attempt to incorporate historical legacies of racial difference into a re-envisioned future of racial alliance, combining black and white standards in a venture that was both political and commercial. NuSouth did not last long as a business, and its failure to attract a market may well have reflected a collective judgment that the trademark emblem was more clever than compelling. McPherson is surely correct, however, that the NuSouth strategy of appropriation and remixing typifies recent uses of the past.[15]

-running television program *The Simpsons*, a triumph of contem-
rican cultural allusion, indicates the resonance of the Civil War
during the last twenty years. The comedy has mentioned Lincoln more often
than any other president. The most common motif in these references is
the sheer fame of Lincoln. He appears on pennies, on five-dollar bills, on
classroom walls, on Mount Rushmore, in the Lincoln Memorial. That stature
provides a springboard for parody. Miniature golf courses feature obstacles
in his image; Miss Illinois dresses as Lincoln in a beauty pageant; an immigrant convenience-store proprietor renames a child Lincoln to seem more patriotic.[16] These jokes lampoon the pieties of American hero worship, as does
the consistent description of Ulysses S. Grant as a bumbling drunk.

The emphasis of *The Simpsons* on Lincoln's cultural availability also provides context for a fascination with his assassination. Springfield news reporters announce the discovery, and soon the assassination, of a squirrel that resembles Lincoln. A Lincoln impersonator in a theater balcony shoots himself
in the head. Homer Simpson notes that Lincoln and Kennedy had the same
golf handicap, supplementing the widely circulated list of parallels between
the two presidential murders. Assassination becomes an extension not of politics but of celebrity, a fate suffered by John Lennon as well as John Kennedy.

The surge of interest in Lincoln's assassination, the climax of cultural availability, is one of the most striking reconfigurations of American priorities in
recent attention to the Civil War. Schwartz shows that attendance has declined over the last several decades at Lincoln's birthplace, boyhood home,
Springfield home, and tomb and has stagnated at the Lincoln Memorial but
has mushroomed at Ford's Theatre since the early 1980s. Robert Wilson's *the
CIVIL warS* was again a harbinger: its Lincoln was shot while watching *Gone
With the Wind* on television. Gore Vidal's *Lincoln* was conspicuous not only for
its detailed attention to the Booth conspiracy but also for a convergence between that plotline and the suggestion that the president, whom the novelist
presented to the reader from the perspectives of multiple observers without
entering into Lincoln's consciousness, was hollow at the core; Lincoln's genius
in *Lincoln* was his ability to be what others wanted him to be. Over the next
quarter-century the Lincoln assassination continued to feature prominently
in imaginative works like novelist Thomas Mallon's *Henry and Clara* (1994),
dramatist Suzan Lori-Parks's *America Play* (1994) and *Topdog/Underdog* (2001),
and film director Robert Redford's *The Conspirator* (2010) as well as two of the
three nonfiction Civil War books that spent the longest time on the *New York*

Times hardcover bestseller list during the first decade of the twenty-first century. A taboo subject in American humor from Mark Twain through Johnny Carson, the killing of Lincoln has become a commonplace theme in comedy. The online cartoon series *Hard Drinkin' Lincoln* (2000), written by a producer of *The Simpsons*, made the president "a loud, lewd, obnoxious guy in a big hat—the kind of guy you sit behind in a theater and just want to shoot." Every episode of the series featured an assassination of Lincoln.[17]

The most vivid depiction of presidential assassination as cultural appropriation is the Stephen Sondheim–John Weidman musical *Assassins*, which first opened off-Broadway in 1990 and won several Tony Awards for a 2004 production. The musical also served as a starting point for humorist Sarah Vowell's bestselling travelogue, *Assassination Vacation* (2005).[18] Lincoln is central to the show and to Vowell's book. The historical mélange of assassins and would-be assassins who make up the musical cast does not include Richard Lawrence, who fired two pistols at Andrew Jackson from close range in 1835. Nor does the cast include the assassin of Huey Long, for the show is about the institutionalization of celebrity governance in the office of the presidency. *Assassins* begins with Booth and Lincoln; the actor getting bad reviews unintentionally ensures that his victim will always get good reviews. Booth is the mentor to the other assassins in the group, many of whom have deep imaginative ties to the world of celebrity. John Hinckley sings his solo to a framed photograph of Jodie Foster. Squeaky Fromme and Sara Jane Moore look back nostalgically at the Charles Manson gang that murdered actress Sharon Tate as part of a twisted fantasy centered on obsession with the Beatles. The musical concludes logically with Booth and his fellow assassins convincing Lee Harvey Oswald to shoot John F. Kennedy, a president who epitomizes the convergence of politics and celebrity. *Assassins* is the story of an America divided not into classes or races or ideological factions but between the famous and the obscure. Booth is in danger of falling from the spotlight into the shadows, but he and the other assassins can achieve permanent fame with a gun. The beginning and ending anthem of the musical, "Everybody's Got the Right," emphasizes that the president is a public figure whom "everybody's got the right" to appropriate, or assassinate.

Like the Lincoln assassination, costumed reenactment of the Civil War is an important site of historical reflection in the contemporary American culture of homage. Reenactment marks a recent shift in the forms taken by popular interest in the war. The roots of reenactment reach back to commemorations organized by Civil War veterans, but the hobby began to take its current shape during the Civil War centennial—amid considerable controversy—and remained small in scale even after expansion during the centennial anniversary of the American Revolution. Only two thousand participants accepted an invitation to join in a costumed reenactment of the battle of Gettysburg in July 1976 despite the prospect of national television coverage. Another reenactment at Gettysburg five years later drew a similar crowd. But more than twelve thousand costumed reenactors appeared for the one-hundred-twenty-fifth anniversary of the battle in 1988, a figure that doubled in the next ten years.[19] Though connected to such trends as the introduction of costumed actor-guides at museums like Plimoth Plantation and the proliferation of Elvis impersonators and "tribute bands" imitating popular music groups, Civil War reenactment has secured its own distinct and prominent position in American culture. That visibility is the result not only of the number of hobbyists, which pales in comparison with the numbers of stamp collectors or model-railroad enthusiasts, but also the extent to which popular writers like Tony Horwitz and Elmore Leonard and numerous television satirists have identified the practice as a representative expression of contemporary American life.[20]

Although based on an ideal of authenticity ostensibly antithetical to postmodern appropriation, reenactment also takes a frankly subjective and non-narrative approach to historical interpretation. The reenactor's goal is a perceived experience of transportation across time, a privatized "period rush" achieved through careful attention to sights, sounds, smells, tastes, and textures rather than immersion in the moral or psychological depths of stories.[21] This individualization of historical meaning embodies one of the major themes most firmly associated with the Civil War today: the fragmentation of what many Americans understood in the early 1960s to be a unified mass culture. The Civil War buff has become a standard symbol of the national splintering into the pursuit of countless separate, sometimes bizarre, interests. Horwitz's *Confederates in the Attic* (1998) and Andrew Ferguson's *Land of Lincoln* (2004) both take the form of reports on an outsider's introduction to Civil War subcultures and, by extension, to a United States united by zealous devotion to personal passions. When Civil War relic hunter Sam White of Chester, Virginia, died in February 2008 in the explosion of a cannonball he was restoring, national news coverage described him as a paradigmatic American consumed by fascination with his hobby.[22]

Like the works of Robert Wilson, Ross McElwee, and John Updike, recent interest in the Lincoln assassination and costumed reenactment illustrates a tendency to approach the Civil War as a problem in the stability of cultural representation. The authority of the national saga now excites imaginations at least as much as the historical event itself. From this standpoint the crisis of the Union is hardly "the unwritten war," as Daniel Aaron paraphrased Walt Whitman. Perhaps the real war never did get into the books, or the statues or the movies, but influential versions of the Civil War nonetheless attract reflections that range from finding comedy in the murder of Lincoln to asserting the superiority of "living history." [23] Revision of the canonical texts is a typical strategy for engaging the received tradition. Alice Randall has reanimated *Gone With the Wind* in *The Wind Done Gone*, as has the Theatre of the Emerging American Moment in *Architecting*. Geraldine Brooks has returned to *Little Women* in *March*. DJ Spooky has reworked *Birth of a Nation*. Cindy Sherman, Sally Mann, and John Huddleston have revisited Civil War photographs. Kara Walker has riffed on *Harper's Pictorial History of the War*. Dario Robleto has fabricated Civil War relics. Similar concerns inform works often regarded merely as straightforward, emotionally charged narratives of the sectional conflict. *Glory* is a meditation on the current vitality of Augustus Saint-Gaudens's memorial to Robert Gould Shaw and the 54th Massachusetts Regiment no less than *Sherman's March* is a meditation on the relevance of Saint-Gaudens's equestrian statue of Sherman, though the two films advance different interpretations of the relationship between the era of monuments and the era of movies. Ken Burns's *The Civil War* is a hypnotic homage to photography in the age of Mathew Brady and reinforces period ballads with the ersatz nostalgia of the "Ashokan Farewell."

If the Civil War was for Warren in 1961 an event that lived in the American imagination, it is now an event undead in the American imagination, like the fictional figures of the Civil War era that have attracted much of the recent Hollywood investment in this particular past. [24] The war is not so much "our only felt history" as our most frequently rehearsed, most solemnly enshrined, most commercially exploited, and therefore most readily appropriated history. Warren's "mystic cloud from which emerged our modernity" has given way to the artificial lights of our postmodernity.

Although *Remixing the Civil War* addresses many different contemporary interpretations of the war, the remix format recurs throughout the book. The pattern appears in essays focused on political and social movements as well as essays focused on literary and visual representations of the war. C. Wyatt Evans's opening discussion of "the Lincoln-Obama moment" enriches recent scholarship on the politics of commemoration by offering direct analysis of the uses of historical memory in electoral politics. Moving well beyond the standard emphasis on those reputational entrepreneurs who have shaped the popular image of Lincoln since the 1860s, the essay looks at a doubling initiated but by no means controlled by Obama and opened by digital technology to rapid, multifaceted, "viral" development. In addition to updating familiar political mobilizations of the American past, the diffuse process drew on newer, more playful appropriations of Lincoln's image. As a result, the Lincoln-Obama phenomenon warrants comparison both with earlier campaign invocations of Lincoln and with Seth Grahame-Smith's semi-reverent bestselling novel *Abraham Lincoln, Vampire Hunter* (2010).

The next two contributions take up additional political and social movements that remix memory of the Civil War. Thomas Brown's essay on state displays of the Confederate battle flag stresses that enthusiasm for the southern cross illustrates a shift from a quasi-religious form of social identification, reinforced by such rituals as the observance of Confederate Memorial Day, to a consumer-based form of social identification, centered on the purchase of merchandise related to the Civil War only by an emblazoned emblem. The transformation of the flag into a marketing logo has caused the gender, religious, and class dynamics of disputes over the battle flag to differ sharply from the alignments that characterized the Lost Cause for decades after Appomattox. Meanwhile, the moral defense of Confederate soldiers has borrowed an explicitly post-Vietnam ideology. Mitch Kachun finds other discontinuities in the proliferation of Juneteenth observance since the mid-1990s, which collides with an earlier federal effort to commemorate the Thirteenth Amendment and also with locally based remembrances of emancipation. Even some communities with longstanding independent freedom festivals have imported the energetically promoted image of folk tradition associated across the country with the Texas holiday. Styles and values of commemoration have also changed in some ways, as celebration of cultural creativity has displaced a previous tension between festivals highlighting didactic reinforcement of social uplift and festivals highlighting hard-earned enjoyment of leisurely amusement.

Four essays focus on recent works of art and literature. Robert H. Brink-meyer Jr.'s survey of recent southern fiction finds few writers treating the Civil War as the decisive epic that Warren described. Black authors interested in history have devoted their primary attention to slavery, which has in some instances prompted powerful meditations on the war but has often produced fiction set firmly in the period before the firing on Fort Sumter. White authors have reversed the Homeric tradition by approaching the Civil War not as the *Iliad* but as the *Odyssey*, in Brinkmeyer's apt phrase. Brilliant as this work sometimes is, the novels rarely imagine the war as a communal regional narrative whether describing events in the nineteenth century or the shadow of the war in the contemporary South.

Remix strategies are particularly central in the essays that concentrate on visual and theatrical arts. Elizabeth Young points to the manipulation of photographic images in wartime visual culture as a precedent for recent work. Her essay invites the reflection that the Civil War flourishes in contemporary American culture not only because of the enduring political issues the war involved and the human costs it exacted, but also because the war was a signal event in the history of the immensely influential medium of photography. Gerard Brown juxtaposes satirical and earnest appropriations of Civil War representations in his discussion of conceptual artists Allison Smith and Dario Robleto. Smith's parody of Civil War reenactment and Robleto's adaptations of Civil War relics are excellent examples of work highly regarded within a particular discipline but little known to audiences interested primarily in current views of the war. W. Fitzhugh Brundage's essay on African Americans' recent uses of the Civil War ranges from visual arts, theater, and cinema to fiction and poetry. One of the strongest connecting threads in this work is a persistent cultural cross-referencing that builds on a black tradition of "signifying" that extends back to slavery.

The mashed-up Civil War found in these essays corresponds in technique to the substantive theme most clearly highlighted in this volume, the contemporary fluidity of formerly rigid social categories. National identity is a social category fundamentally implicated in the American model of civil war, as Robert Wilson underscored by proposing to present *the CIVIL warS* at an Olympic gathering of nations that had widely experienced violent disintegration and shared a long history of mutual conquest. The candid celebration of the entertainment industry and other global consumer structures in current attention to the Civil War suggests a post-national imagination at odds with

Really?

previous remembrance of the conflict. Gender is another social category long associated with warfare that has developed a new fluidity in the last several decades, including the increased acceptance of homosexuality that is one of the hallmarks of the contemporary period. The effort to add Lincoln to the list of eminent gay Americans has been a major form of interest in the Civil War era over the last fifteen years.[25] This book points out that renewed awareness of the Civil War as a mainspring of the American military tradition in the wake of the hostilities in Afghanistan and Iraq has brought further emphasis on the blurring of gender and sexual boundaries in the crisis of the Union.

Race is the formerly rigid social category most thoroughly problematized in this volume. Unlike nationality or gender, this category was in the forefront of Robert Penn Warren's thinking in 1961. But race has come to pervade representations of the Civil War in ways that Warren could not foresee amid the rising crest of the civil rights movement. He defined "the race question in the South" as the conflict between Jim Crow and the demand for racial equality, an approach appropriate for a centennial anniversary that shattered when a segregated hotel in Charleston, South Carolina, refused to accommodate a northern black delegate to the national assembly of the Civil War Centennial Commission. Decades later, the unfinished work of the civil rights movement continues to reshape American memory of the Civil War. In an effort to clarify that the sectional conflict revolved around the future of slavery, for example, Congress asked the National Park Service in 2000 to devote attention at battlefield parks to the origins and stakes of the war rather than maintaining a narrow focus on military tactics.[26]

But if the politics of morality plumbed by Warren remain unresolved and pressing, recent interpretations of the war often turn less on relations between social groups than on the subjective construction of individual racial identity. Many of the essays in this volume describe works that in different ways revel in the permeability of the color line. These emphases parallel Stephen Wright's dazzling novel *The Amalgamation Polka* (2006), which recounts young abolitionist Liberty Fish's wartime journey into the plantation heart of the South to confront his grandfather, a diabolical slaveholder who seeks to pervert and control racial instability by turning blacks into whites through chemical experiments and incestuous breeding. After vanquishing the villain, the hero cheerfully concludes that life "makes mongrels of us all."[27]

The instability of cultural representations and social categories is the motif that most consistently unites the separate contributions to this collection, but the authors address many additional features of the United States in the early twenty-first century. The volume repeatedly demonstrates that conflict between blue and gray serves as a field onto which Americans project partisan fervor in the blue-red era of competition between Democrats and Republicans. Contributors explore the complex relations between the American civil religion grounded in the Civil War and the evangelical mode in recent national politics. Several essays observe that pleas to preserve Civil War battlefields have become a standard expression of the cultural costs of commercial land development. These and other topics are defining characteristics of contemporary life that Warren did not imagine to be implicated in the legacy of the war.

❧

This book treats academic research as an enterprise institutionally committed to the importance of the Civil War in a way that precludes survey alongside other representations, but that compartmentalization implies the possibility of a deeper divide worthy of at least a brief concluding notice. Warren saw no such schism in 1961, the year after C. Vann Woodward dedicated *The Burden of Southern History* to the poet and novelist, and *The Legacy of the Civil War* plausibly indicated that Woodward, David Donald, Kenneth Stampp, Allan Nevins, and other leading experts shared Warren's understanding of the war.[28] Fifty years later, research specialists called on to analyze the lasting appeal of the war routinely echo Warren's emphasis on the narrative traction of the conflict even though writers, artists, and broad-based political movements have pointed toward alternative explanations since at least the 1980s.[29] The outstanding works of Civil War scholarship that have earned a position on the *New York Times* bestseller list during the first decade of the twenty-first century have in original and important ways stressed themes that Warren considered central a half-century ago: the making of modernity, the establishment of national identity, the consolidation of the white South, the emergence of pragmatism, the drama of personal struggle, the delineation of contingency, the call of stories.[30] Perhaps even the most widely admired scholarship no longer follows lines of development closely related to other popular and penetrating interpretations of the past. Idiosyncratic pastiche does not transfer easily to the norms of academic research.

But recent work also suggests opportunities for renewed synergy between scholarship and other creative genres. Specialists in the Civil War era have shared in the broader interest in instabilities of racial, gender, and national identity, and they have devoted increasing attention to topics previously shunned by academic historians, such as the Lincoln assassination. Scholars have also experimented with parallels to the stylistic forms that have characterized Civil War art and fiction since the 1980s. Stephen Cushman's *Bloody Promenade* (1999) relies on a subjective first-person narrator who lives in the part of Virginia at which Union and Confederate armies fought the Battle of the Wilderness. He rambles authoritatively over the field, mingling past and present with a bookish version of the charm exhibited by Ross McElwee in *Sherman's March*. Christopher Benfey's *A Summer of Hummingbirds* (2008) is organized around visual imagery no less than Robert Wilson's *the CIVIL warS* was, and shares a comparable if less idiosyncratic inclination toward impressionistic collage. Benfey's study is at the same time a learned analysis of the impact of the war on American lives and ideals.[31]

One of the most important developments in Civil War scholarship during the last twenty years and most dynamic lines of connection to the trends described in this volume has been the surge of writing about representations of the war in popular culture. David Blight's *Race and Reunion: The Civil War in American Memory* (2001), probably the most influential academic interpretation of the Civil War published in the last decade, shares with many leading non-academic interpretations a fascination with the war waged in community ceremonies, bestselling literature, and other public venues before and after Appomattox. For Blight, as for Kara Walker and DJ Spooky, the pages of *Harper's Weekly* and screenings of *Birth of a Nation* are crucial battlefields of the war. While *Race and Reunion* reconstructs and illuminates a political debate over issues explicitly at stake in the sectional conflict, other recent scholarship has explored the Civil War and its aftermath as a dramatic example of the complex relations between mass-produced imagination and lived personal experience. Alice Fahs, Nina Silber, and Amy Murrell Taylor, for example, have each written brilliantly about the public and private implications of the ubiquitous comparison of the war to a family crisis, the point of departure for Robert Wilson, Ross McElwee, and John Updike.[32]

Students of the Civil War will only be able to assess the most promising avenues for scholarship in making use of the past when they know more about the other forms of interpretation circulating in contemporary American culture. This collaborative effort seeks to inform that evaluation.

CHAPTER ONE

The Lincoln-Obama Moment

C. Wyatt Evans

On February 10, 2007, Senator Barack Obama announced his presidential bid from the steps of the Old Statehouse in Springfield, Illinois. To most observers the choice of time and place was obvious: Abraham Lincoln's birthday was a few days away, and in 1858 Lincoln announced his run for the U.S. Senate from the very same spot. Indeed, Obama invoked Lincoln twice in the course of his short address. The first time was in speaking of the "impossible odds" Americans faced in overcoming the nation's ills. Obama reflected that in a previous era of national adversity, Lincoln "had his doubts. He had his defeats. He had his setbacks. But through his will and his words, he moved a nation and helped free a people. It is because of the millions who rallied to his cause that we are no longer divided, North and South, slave and free."[1] The second time was in the peroration, when Obama offered his listeners a series of short phrases invoking familiar images of who Lincoln was. These included the rangy midwesterner and self-made man, the eloquent speaker, the Great Emancipator, and the selfless man of principle who labored to bind up the nation's wounds.

With this speech Obama awakened the collective memory of Abraham Lincoln for his listeners. As the late Merrill Peterson demonstrated fifteen years ago, the images Obama used have long been stock components in mainstream America's memory of Lincoln.[2] The specific shape this memory has assumed and the words and images used to invoke it have varied greatly according to time and circumstances. For Obama, the memory he gave voice to was influenced by his racial identity, his political outlook, and his commitment to the prophetic tradition in American politics: it emphasized Lincoln's role in furthering the nation's democratic ideals and preserving the Union.[3] Over the next two years—in speeches, interviews, and campaign trail "town halls"—Obama would refer to Lincoln at regular intervals. The references ranged from simple mentions, to invocations like the above, and reflections on Lincoln's influence in Obama's political development.

At one level it seems fair to say that Obama's use of Lincoln was just good politicking. Most presidential candidates appeal to historical figures. That Obama engaged in this practice more wholeheartedly than his contemporaries does not alter the basic similarity. There are several factors, however, that belie this view. The most important is simply that the appeals to Lincoln were not his alone. Although Obama initiated the Lincoln talk, his output was quickly overtaken by that of the mainstream press, scholars, public intellectuals, artists, and grassroots commentators. Ranging from speeches, articles, cartoons, images, and commentary on the blogosphere, the association of Obama with Lincoln became a phenomenon of the 2008 campaign. One explanation for this outpouring is that Lincoln provided Americans with a framework for understanding Obama. According to this argument, journalists draw on collective memory to help frame complex stories for their readers. Obama's racial identity and newcomer status to national politics made him an "atypical story" for many Americans. By referring to familiar historical figures, including Lincoln, journalists were able to connect Obama to a familiar past.[4]

While useful, this framing thesis does not fully explain the phenomenon's significance in American politics and culture. It was significant for three reasons. First, the sustained appeals to Lincoln and his era marked the return of history to Democratic political discourse. After a long hiatus, during which the Republican Party exercised a near monopoly on telling the story of the nation's past, the left grabbed the story back. Second, the raising up of Lincoln in a national political contest marked his return to active commemorative status. Although Lincoln has long served as a national icon, and is routinely invoked on ceremonial occasions, his relevance in active political contests has eroded since the civil rights era. Sociologist Barry Schwartz argues that Lincoln's image has suffered from fading prestige and "benign ridicule" in our "post-heroic" era.[5] The revival of Lincoln the Great Emancipator and democratic prophet during the 2008 campaign disproved, for a time at least, Schwartz's thesis. Third, as the two preceding points suggest, the Lincoln-Obama phenomenon demonstrated the ever-changing and dialogical character of collective memory. Lincoln's return to the political mainstream was made possible by Obama's racial identity and the conservative party's relative neglect of Lincoln in recent decades. Obama's initial acceptance by white voters helped revive the civil-rights-era memory of Lincoln as the Great Emancipator, prophet of democracy, and Savior of the Union.

This essay considers the origins, production, and effects of the Lincoln-Obama phenomenon. Based on a variety of Lincoln-Obama texts gathered through online searches, it does not attempt an exhaustive analysis of all the extant material. As this paper was being written, words and images linking the two men (or denying the linkage) were still being produced. But an initial assessment is possible. It promises to tell us much about the influence of historical memory in a specific presidential election and more generally about the functioning of memory in politics. In addition to determining the phenomenon's significance, this essay is above all interested in the question of production. What makes memory work in a political setting? Intentionality; the role of speechwriters, journalists, historians, and other public persons skilled at deploying historical references; the role of existing collective memory structures; popular manipulation of these structures; matters of identity and fortunate coincidence—all of these elements contributed to promoting Lincoln's memory and the associations with Obama. The result was a dynamic mélange in which no single element held sway for long.

Consider the graphic images associating the two men. Following Shepard Fairey's "HOPE" poster, the election's most recognizable image was Ron English's *Abraham Obama* composite portrait. In a May 2009 Q&A session, English explained how in early 2008 the Obama campaign contacted several West Coast street artists including Fairey and himself to create art that would appeal to younger voters. Fairey's iconic poster drew on the social realist school, while English was inspired (and encouraged by the campaign) "to do something positive" in lieu of his usually sardonic "popaganda" aimed at big business and Republican politics. When asked what inspired his composition, the artist replied, "Obama pretty much had the same experience as Lincoln had, and no one seemed to have argued with his abilities. Then I realized there were similarities between these two skinny guys from Illinois." English's portrait adapted Mathew Brady's wartime photo of Lincoln, already familiar to the public in numerous guises including the visage of the seated figure at the Lincoln Memorial. Intentionally or not (and from English's statements it appears he was mainly concerned with the technical challenge of merging the two men's facial features), English used an established image of Lincoln that symbolizes his status as national patriarch.[6] After merging the images and tinting multiple copies in rainbow hues, he disseminated the portrait over the Internet. It gained greater publicity when English mobilized his troupe of street performers to tour major cities and install posters in public places.[7]

A campaign button issued shortly after Obama's February 2007 announcement featured the same Brady portrait. But in a clever twist Lincoln is shown wearing an "Obama in 2008" T-shirt with Obama's portrait printed on it.[8] Editorial cartoons also invoked the sixteenth president and his Illinois heir-apparent. The campaign and election witnessed a revival of Lincoln political cartoons. A rough count of newspapers and magazines indicates thirty or more featuring a Lincoln-Obama theme ran during the campaign and post-election period, with the bulk appearing right after his nomination and victory in the general election.[9] Many of these cartoons made use of the Lincoln Memorial and its seated patriarch to highlight the parallels between Lincoln and Obama or to portray Obama's nomination and election as culminating historical events. One favored treatment had the marble patriarch "fist-bumping" with Obama, a play on the celebrated "dap" between Michelle and Barack Obama once his primary victory was sealed. A second used the Memorial as a backdrop to depict the progression from Lincoln to Martin Luther King Jr.'s August 1963 address to Obama's nomination.[10] Two magazine covers appearing shortly after Obama's election featured stylized renderings of the same theme. The *New Yorker* depicted the Lincoln Memorial at night from the far end of the Reflecting Basin, lit from within and shone down upon by an illuminated "O." *Newsweek* showed Obama—depending on one's visual

Obama for President 2008 campaign button. Photograph
by Carol Harrison

interpretation—either casting a shadow of Lincoln or "channeling" Lincoln,
who stands behind him.[11]

These images were produced by professional artists and distributed through
mainstream media channels. The use of the Lincoln Memorial especially invoked the memory of Lincoln as a national patriarch and champion of civil
rights. However, the deployment of these iconic images was no guarantee
against alteration and subversion. In the case of English's *Abraham Obama*
portrait, the multiple silkscreened images were disseminated rapidly over the
Internet and modified on a few occasions to present anti-Obama messages.
In a few locales billboard displays were painted over to depict Obama as a
Muslim warrior.[12] In June 2008 the conservative religious website First Things
placed *Abraham Obama* alongside Warner Sallman's iconic "Head of Christ"
(1941) portrait—modified with Obama's facial features.[13] The intentions were
clearly satirical given the First Things anti-Obama stance and the image title,
"Messiah Abe Obama." Following George McGovern's statement that Obama
was "a second Lincoln," the conservative website freerepublic.com posted a

photoshopped version of Alexander Gardner's daguerreotype of Lincoln at Antietam. Playing on the right-wing belief that Obama was a crypto-Muslim, the altered image placed Obama's head on Lincoln's body and inserted word balloons for the two figures standing next to him. Civil War spymaster Allan Pinkerton was made to say "Funny—I don't recall the Emancipation Proclamation saying anything about beheading the infidels," while General John McClernand mused, "Swear allegiance on the Kooran—what the hell is a Kooran?"[14] An editorial cartoon posted to a gun reloaders' website in January 2009 depicted Obama with exaggerated facial features, dressed in a top hat and frock coat, delivering an adulterated version of the Gettysburg Address.[15] All of these counter-images were produced and disseminated in online forums.

Other grassroots images were positive. The Tagyerit political blog sponsored a "Bush Bashing Pumpkin Contest" in 2008 that featured two carved jack-o'-lanterns depicting Lincoln and Obama. Captioned "Lincoln & Obama: The Boys from Illinois," this blogger made the connection between Lincoln and Obama in terms of their Illinois origins, their concern for civil rights, and their relative inexperience in public office when they ran for the presidency.[16] Other grassroots Internet offerings included silkscreened T-shirts, coffee mugs, and the prognostications of a medium whose collage juxtaposing Obama's face with Lyman Trumbull's was intended to show that Obama is the reincarnation of the Civil War senator from Illinois.[17]

These grassroots productions relied less on iconic imagery to make their points and showed more variety, whether or not supporting the Lincoln-Obama connection. The mainstream artists' reliance on the Lincoln Memorial and the portrait of the wartime Lincoln emphasized iconic images, supporting the opinion of historians that the monument functions as an important memory site in contemporary America.[18] The memorial's depiction in cartoons and illustrations clearly appealed to the civil-rights-era memory of Lincoln by depicting Obama's nomination and election as the historic culmination of the progress toward full democracy supposedly initiated by Lincoln. Historian Scott Sandage has argued that civil rights activists transformed the monument through an intentional "politics of memory" beginning with Marian Anderson's 1939 concert. Against its original conception as a monument to white consensus and nationalism, black leaders' ritual tactics made the memorial a moral pinnacle "from which to exhort America to finish what Lincoln called 'the great task remaining before us.'"[19] The mainstream Lincoln-Obama imagery reaffirmed this vision. It was only at the grassroots level that oppositional imagery appeared, and even this imagery did not take direct aim at the memory of Lincoln as a civil rights champion.

With a few exceptions the phenomenon's written and spoken production also appealed to the memory of Lincoln as a prophet of democratic fulfillment and racial justice. This textual production included the candidate's statements, copy produced by professional journalists (including interviews with public figures), essays and editorials by historians, and online forums that discussed the linkages between Obama and Lincoln. There were three phases to its production. After a brief flurry following Obama's initial announcement, phase one began in earnest following the Iowa caucuses in late December 2007 and continued through the primary contest. Phase two began in early June 2008 and had two peak moments, the period of the nominating convention and immediately following Obama's victory in the general election. Phase three began after the November election and persisted through the inauguration in January 2009. While the first phase sought to establish the linkages between the two men through historical analogy and comparison, the second abandoned historical analysis for the soaring rhetoric of American political panegyric. The third intensified the search for comparisons and analogies, and in the opinion of critics became excessive in the months leading up to the inauguration. Especially near the end of the phenomenon's lifespan, the voices of dissent established a presence in mainstream venues, unlike the skeptical images.

Historians, both academics and others whom the public considers vested with the authority to interpret the past, played an important role in this textual production. Indeed, historians' involvement in the 2008 campaign appears to have been exceptional. The joint endorsement organized by Georgetown professor Michael Kazin in late November 2007 was described as "unusually early and specific" and drew both criticism and praise from other scholars.[20] While mentioning Lincoln, the statement's main focus was the global and governmental crisis and Obama's perceived qualifications to serve as president. In the weeks that followed three historians spoke out on the candidate, and the work of historical comparison began. In mid-December, filmmaker Ken Burns declared for Obama. For Burns, the crucial similarity between Obama and Lincoln involved their perceived candor and genuineness. His remarks to reporters stressed authenticity and vision as necessary qualities; he emphasized the importance of electing "someone who is able to suggest a future that isn't so completely tied to the past."[21] Following the New Hampshire primary, Joseph Ellis endorsed Obama in the *Los Angeles Times*, noting that Obama's appeals to a unified electorate rang historically true and were "in accord with the most heartfelt and cherished version of our original intentions as a people and a nation."[22] Writing in the same newspaper a week later, Sean Wilentz took issue with Ellis' analysis, accusing Obama and his supporters of exceeding Reagan zealots in distorting the historical record. Wilentz's criticism centered on the Obama campaign's attempts to minimize its candidate's lack of experience by comparing him to past greats who, it argued, similarly lacked experience. "These comparisons distort the past beyond recognition," Wilentz stated. He contrasted Obama's historical sensibility to that of John F. Kennedy, "who won a Pulitzer Prize for a work of history."[23] These early statements clearly reflected individual political preferences. They also demonstrated how the discourse of historians contributes to the mobilization of collective memory in political settings. All three situated Obama in historical context, whether supporting his candidacy or not. They did so by referring to important values including authenticity, vision, and political traditions, or to familiar events such as Kennedy's presidency.

As the primary contest intensified, so did the references to Lincoln. Journalists as well as historians contributed to this discourse. *Vanity Fair* editor Todd Purdum's lengthy biography in the magazine's March 2008 issue distinguished between the various memories of Lincoln. Purdum chose to pass over the "holy Lincoln of hagiography, and the melancholy Lincoln of martyrdom," to focus instead on Lincoln's "steely ambition" and "cold political calculation" in his closing comparisons to Obama. *Rolling Stone* editor Jann Wenner's endorsement of Obama in the same month ended in more conventional iconic fashion: "Like Abraham Lincoln, Barack Obama challenges America to rise up, to do what so many of us long to do: to summon 'the better angels of our nature.'"[24] Indicative of Obama's increasing references to Lincoln, when he spoke at Cooper Union at the end of March, journalists covering the campaign placed bets on how many times he would mention Lincoln. He did not, although those introducing him did. [25]

During this first phase, even Obama's major rival for the Democratic nomination got tangled up in the Lincoln-Obama phenomenon. On the eve of crucial primaries in late April 2008, Hillary Clinton challenged her opponent to a series of "Lincoln-Douglas" style debates in the key state of Indiana. Clinton's campaign manager noted the holding of the original debates one hundred and fifty years earlier in neighboring Illinois and observed that she had no doubt "Senator Obama, who hails from that great state, understands how valuable and vital these national conversations were to the heart of America." Obama's campaign declined the offer.[26] While minor from a political standpoint, the episode sheds light on the mobilization of collective memory in politics. The Clinton campaign's decision to challenge its opponent using the historical memory Obama unquestionably controlled appears a questionable tactic. Clinton's managers may have judged it a worthwhile gambit given her eroding delegate count and her skill in debating. Had the debates been held and Clinton prevailed, her campaign might have struck a "memory coup" by claiming a portion of the historical narrative claimed by Obama. But except in especially contentious cases, it is doubtful that any candidate or party has successfully usurped a rival's hold on a historical figure or event. John Kerry's losing battle in 2004 with Republicans and the Swift Boat Veterans for Truth over the memory of the Vietnam War is a recent case in point. Although the Civil War and Abraham Lincoln remain contentious points in our history, the only interpretive challenges during the 2008 campaign came from conservative quarters, but none of them attempted to reclaim Lincoln.

Historian Garry Wills's "Two Speeches on Race," published on May 1, 2008, compared Lincoln's Cooper Institute Address to Obama's March 18, 2008, speech in which he responded to the controversy sparked by his pastor Jeremiah Wright. Obama's speech and Wills's essay marked the high point in the phenomenon's narrative side. Obama achieved it by not mentioning Lincoln at all. His eloquent address invoked the nation's founding ideals, his personal history, and the historical experiences of all Americans—black, white, and immigrant. He concluded with the touching story of a young white campaign volunteer and her elderly black co-worker.[27] Wills found Obama's oratorical performance Lincolnesque in tone. Both politicians "used a campaign occasion to rise to a higher vision of America's future. Both argued intelligently for closer union in the cause of progress." Lincoln and Obama, Wills concluded, argued against the politics of fear. Without denying the somber chapters of our national history, both sought out what Lincoln termed "the better angels of our nature."[28] This analysis and references to iconic statements provided the mainstream phenomenon's fullest articulation during its formative phase: Obama was Lincoln's successor in the American prophetic tradition.

The mundane comparisons of Illinois residence, physical gangliness, inexperience in politics gave way to this deeper political message. Obama's stock rose in the face of a serious campaign challenge, and so did Lincoln's. For the first time in modern American politics, the sixteenth president became significant for immediate political reasons as his statements and values were mobilized in a political campaign. Furthermore, the linkage to race was essential in the memory of Lincoln that Wills invoked. The occasion of Obama's speech—his pastor's inflammatory racial statements—and Wills's title underscored the extent to which the calling forth of Lincoln was tied to the perception of Obama's racial identity and the meaning this identity attached to Lincoln.

Once Obama gained the primary victory, the theme of historic culmination took over, and political panegyric replaced historical analysis. Speaking at the Democratic National Convention, former vice president and presidential candidate Al Gore compared the nation's present situation to the Civil War. He noted Lincoln's "powerful ability to inspire hope in the future at a time of impasse. He was known chiefly as a clear thinker and a great orator, with a passion for justice and a determination to heal the deep divisions of our land. He insisted on reaching past partisan and regional divides to exalt our common humanity." Now, Gore continued, the nation faced "a mandate from history to launch another new beginning. And once again, we have a candidate whose experience perfectly matches an extraordinary moment of transition."[29] The historical vision Gore offered in this speech was replicated in the political cartoons mentioned earlier. This second phase was evocative, triumphant, and dealt in the highly figurative language of prophetic politics and the American civil religion. It marked the high point of the Lincoln-Obama

Doonesbury, June 26, 2008 © G. B. Trudeau 2008. Reprinted by permission of Universal Uclick. All rights reserved.

phenomenon, mixing powerful political rhetoric with the groundswell of popular feeling that accompanied Obama's nomination.

What followed next was an interlude. Obama and his supporters made limited use of Lincoln during the general election campaign. Nor did journalists, historians, or cartoonists, continue to invoke Lincoln in discussing the election. Phase three began shortly after Obama was elected and continued up to the inauguration. This phase was characterized by increasing attempts on the part of journalists and some historians to match the circumstances of Obama's election with Lincoln's a century and a half earlier. This memory work was also encouraged by the preparations for the upcoming bicentennial anniversary of Lincoln's birth. Even without Obama's victory, the activities of the Abraham Lincoln Bicentennial Commission (ALBC) and output of the "Lincoln industry" guaranteed increasing attention to the sixteenth president.

After Obama's victory at the polls, websites and online discussion forums waxed eloquent on the historic dimensions of Obama's election and the similarities to Lincoln and his times. A YouTube video titled "Mysterious Obama and Lincoln Destiny" narrates the similarities between the two men, asserting Lincoln made "freedom the law," and Obama made "freedom a reality."[30] The nation's media played a leading role in promoting comparisons and analogies with numerous articles, blogs, and cable news commentary. A sampling of titles includes "Obama Looks to Lincoln" (*Newsweek*), "Can Lincoln's Playbook Help Obama in the Years Ahead?" (CNN), "Prospects For An Obama 'Team of Rivals' Uncertain," (*USA Today*), "Obama's National Security 'Team of Rivals,'" (*Christian Science Monitor*), and "Obama as Lincoln" (*Washington Times*). The "team of rivals" analogy marked the apogee of the post-election Lincoln-Obama discourse, as the president-elect made his cabinet selections. The references to historian Doris Kearns Goodwin's award-winning study of Lincoln's cabinet, lauded by Obama in a post-election interview, also revealed a shift in emphasis. Now it was Lincoln the pragmatist, the politician able to build consensus across factions, who was celebrated.[31]

Not everyone agreed with the analogy. Some journalists and conservative commentators criticized the focus as excessive. Historians also weighed in, with some contributing to the elaboration of parallels while others pointed out the inherent difficulties in aligning two distinct personalities and historical situations. Speaking on CNN shortly after the election, Eric Foner cautioned,

"People ought to calm down a little about these comparisons." Lincoln and Obama faced "entirely different situations, worlds, political systems. There aren't I think a lot of exact direct lessons one can or should necessarily try to learn from Lincoln."[32] Other historians shared Foner's skepticism, but their voices were submerged beneath the media's desire to package the Obama story with the catchy "rivals" analogy.[33]

The stronger objections to equating Obama with Lincoln came from the conservative corner, and this time the criticisms were not limited to grassroots forums. Conservative commentators objected on two main grounds. Some denied the associations on the basis that "Obama was no Lincoln." Speechwriter and columnist Peggy Noonan sounded this note as far back as 2005, when Obama first publicly expressed his admiration for Lincoln. Writing in the conservative *National Review*, political blogger Jonah Goldberg noted the inappropriateness of the comparisons, given Obama's lack of record, and remarked that even granting the analogy, returning to Civil War–like conditions was hardly to be desired. Lincoln, after all, "unified the country at gunpoint and curtailed civil liberties in a way that makes President Bush look like an ACLU zealot."[34]

The other tack took issue with the post-election comparisons on ideological grounds. Also writing in the *National Review*, historian Allen Guelzo's "Our Lincoln: Obama He Was Not," was a rebuttal to Eric Foner's similarly titled piece in the leftist *Nation*.[35] Guelzo emphasized Lincoln's essential conservatism, "preserving the old against the new." At the core of Lincoln's conservatism, Guelzo argued, stood the Declaration of Independence. Lincoln understood its "created equal" principle as a natural law doctrine. It did not imply "radical egalitarianism . . . Lincoln's notion of equality was about leveling up, not whittling down."[36] Guelzo portrayed Lincoln as a strict interpretationist and free market advocate, and he invoked a different set of images of who Lincoln was, stressing the self-made man and free-labor advocate. Two other conservative commentators sounded this version of Lincoln during this period.[37]

At the vernacular level the reaction against the Lincoln-Obama analogies assumed a harder edge. A commenter on freerepublic.com wrote, "Well, he may end up presiding over another civil war . . . but that's about where the similarities stop. Lincoln was an intelligent, humble, self-made, and selfless man. Obama is none of those." In other cases, the association was to Obama's disadvantage by invoking the conservative memory of Lincoln as a tyrant who violated the Constitution and American civil liberties. Earlier in the same thread, a poster with the tag "BGHater" wrote: "Wow. More Fed power. Imprisonment of reporters and protesters." The drift of the freerepublic.com thread was decidedly anti-Obama but not decidedly pro-Lincoln. His legacy as the Great Emancipator certainly did not work in his favor. What predominated was the image of Lincoln as the fomenter of a disastrous war and initiator of big government. At the gun reloaders' website, the invocation of Lincoln's memory was even harsher. A lengthy post from a writer in Michigan garnered two approving replies and sounded many of the keynotes of grass-roots neo-conservatism: Lincoln's freeing of the slaves was political opportunism; federal intervention to end slavery was "a giant case of big brother." The comparisons between Obama and Lincoln were not that far off, this blogger concluded, for "no other election in history split this country as badly as this one." The opposition to civil rights and big government, and yearning for communal wholeness, articulates one brand of right-wing political thinking. And the assertion that Lincoln opposed slavery for politically opportunistic reasons coincides with the contemporary academic assault on Lincoln led by economist Thomas DiLorenzo and editor Lerone Bennett Jr.[38]

Most significantly, the conservative opposition to the Lincoln-Obama analogies did not place an effective claim on Lincoln's memory. The appeal to Lincoln as advocate of natural rights and free markets could hardly compete with the inspirational appeal of the Great Emancipator and national unifier. Nor did Republican speakers make a concerted attempt to challenge this liberal vision, evidence of Lincoln's lost standing in conservative circles.

Even without an effective conservative counter-memory, the Lincoln-Obama phenomenon had run its course by the inauguration in January 2009. Although the references to Lincoln continued unabated, they no longer served the same political purposes; Lincoln returned to his former status as a venerated and commodified but politically inactive ceremonial icon. In mid-January 2009, *Publishers Weekly* reported the release of an estimated sixty new titles bearing on some aspect of the sixteenth president's life, including twenty-seven children's books.[39] By early March, Amazon.com listed nearly one hundred titles, new or re-issued. A raft of media coverage was devoted to Lincoln in newspapers, magazines, cable television, e-zines, and online blogs. ALBC member Harold Holzer noted that Obama's election and emulation of Lincoln turned "the Lincoln Bicentennial into a national preoccupation instead of an obligation."[40] The inauguration was organized around the bicentennial theme.

Obama duplicated Lincoln's rail journey from Springfield, Illinois, to Washington in early 1861, and he spoke at the Lincoln Memorial the evening before the inauguration ceremony. The order of ceremony included using the same bible as had Lincoln for the swearing-in; the state luncheon featured a "Lincoln-inspired menu" of seafood stew, roasted pheasant, and cinnamon apple sponge cake.[41] Even Holzer, who played a leading role in promoting the bicentennial ceremonies, acknowledged the president-elect might have stretched the limits with his Lincoln tributes.[42]

಄

Despite fizzling at the end, at its prime the phenomenon provided a powerful narrative about the past that helped Americans place the Democratic contender's candidacy in historical perspective. With the possible exception of Teddy Roosevelt, no other candidate over the last century has invoked a single historical figure as intensively, or prompted so much response by writers, artists, and grassroots sources.[43] The closest modern equivalent is Ronald Reagan, who offered to the American public an inspiring account of the national story. Reagan's paeans to the "city on a hill," Thomas Paine, and heroic settlers, resonated with many people seeking a renewal of optimism and an end to the criticism of American institutions. The historical memory he offered was effective—politically and rhetorically—regardless of the accuracy of Reagan's version of history.[44]

The comparison to Reagan highlights the Lincoln-Obama phenomenon's single most important political consequence: the return of history to Democratic Party discourse. Beginning with Reagan's election in 1980, Republican politicians controlled the story of the nation's past for the next twenty-eight years. Although presidents from both parties routinely appeal to historical events in ceremonial speeches—referred to as epideictic rhetoric by communications scholars—the rough and tumble of campaign oratory has been another matter.[45] The Democratic invocation of the past has been anemic compared to that of its rival. The nomination acceptance speeches of Al Gore and George W. Bush in 2000 highlight the difference. Gore made no references to historical figures, and the historical memory he appealed to was the fraught memory of Vietnam and the 1960s. Bush, however, made some twenty-six references to historical figures (including Franklin Roosevelt) and evoked the heroic age of World War II.[46]

The difference between parties is due to several causes, and includes the liberal self-perception of being the "party of the future," and a reluctance to appear overtly religious. The impact on campaign rhetoric is substantial. America's most persuasive political speech form, the political jeremiad, derives its powerful effect by invoking the past to renew belief in the nation's providential destiny.[47] Over the past generation, Republican candidates have mastered this formula and, regardless of their personal religious viewpoints, speak freely of God and the nation's destiny under God. Adding to liberal rhetorical and collective memory woes is the problematic character of the liberal past. The New Deal legacy—long the cornerstone of left historical identity—has fallen into disrepute. The 1960s have been recast as a period of violence, disorder, and hedonistic excess—all taking place under Democratic auspices. These limitations may explain the liberal penchant for social-scientific methods to solving the "vision thing," as they may be perceived as value-neutral and future-oriented. Witness the popularity of linguist George Lakoff's "framing paradigm" during the 2004 election cycle.[48]

Nonetheless, there was a time, as Michael Kazin and others remind us, when liberal politicians did speak the language of faith.[49] Through the formula of the political jeremiad, their appeals to divine destiny also permitted fulsome appeals to the nation's historical memories. Then as now, these successful invocations were conditioned by racial, religious, and political contexts. At the turn of the last century, William Jennings Bryan could speak of faith, the nation's heritage, and progressive reform without risking contradiction. To a lesser extent, so could Kennedy sixty years later. It is unlikely today that a white candidate could invoke Lincoln as effectively as did Obama and his supporters; it is equally doubtful that a white liberal candidate could express his or her religious beliefs at length without risking criticism from the secular left. Barack Obama's successful invocation of Lincoln, and the echoing of his appeals by many other voices, lay in his racial identity and his professed religious faith. But black voters did not need the memory of Lincoln to vote for Obama. Previous African American presidential candidates Jesse Jackson and Al Sharpton made no effort to appeal to his memory despite their racial identity and strong allegiance to the black evangelical tradition. Indeed, Jackson and Sharpton are among several black leaders who have dismissed Lincoln's role in freeing the slaves.[50] However, there is a sense in which black voters did need Lincoln's memory. As Sandage has noted, black leaders during the early civil rights era "regarded public appeals to Lincoln and national memory as the only symbolic language available to them to communicate with white America."[51] Although this formula broke down in the late 1960s, Obama's attraction to Lincoln is the carryover of this tradition. It explains the Lincoln-Obama phenomenon's depth and reach. As the nation's first successful black presidential candidate, Obama benefited from the political struggles of the previous generation. He benefited symbolically from their successful effort to shape the memory of Lincoln for the civil rights cause. The historians, journalists, artists, and grassroots supporters who contributed to the Lincoln-Obama phenomenon invoked a memory of Lincoln familiar to the American public, and more particularly to a significant segment of the white voting public. They also benefited from the generation-long effort of historians to return slavery and race to a central place in the history of the Civil War.

Ironically perhaps, the Lincoln-Obama phenomenon was facilitated by the conservative-sponsored return of religious discourse to the public sphere, and the Republican Party's abandonment of Lincoln as its principal political avatar. Public contestation over Lincoln's memory, which marked a previous era, has lessened. Although differences of opinion regarding the Lincoln legacy persist, the debate over what he stood for has been relegated to the margins of our political discourse. The emancipationist memory of Lincoln has endured since its revival during the civil rights era, and no mainstream conservative spokesperson would dare gainsay it. The conservative "anti-Lincoln" tradition is now relegated to online discussion forums, digitally edited images, and the occasional book. For many conservatives Lincoln remains the savior of the Union and national demigod, while for others he symbolizes the perceived tyranny of big government and civil rights. In terms of active political usage, it is this second tradition that holds sway in conservative circles. Mainstream Republicans pay reverence to their founding father on ceremonial occasions, but his political usefulness has eroded. His fall from grace in conservative circles was signaled by the renaming of the Lincoln Day Dinner as the Reagan-Lincoln Dinner. The most dramatic act has been the erection under Republican sponsorship of the World War II Memorial. Its placement at the end of the Reflecting Pool obstructs the formerly untrammeled sightline from Washington's monument to Lincoln's marble shrine.

We may speculate on the extent to which Obama and chief political consultant David Axelrod calculated Lincoln's symbolic usefulness in realizing their campaign strategy. Axelrod has been credited with revolutionizing modern presidential campaigning with his use of new media and grassroots voter mobilization. Prior to Obama, the former journalist gained repute for his work on behalf of African American political candidates; his particular forte has been persuading white voters to support black candidates.[52] However, to grant the Obama campaign too much intentionality in summoning Lincoln's memory fails to acknowledge the phenomenon's group dynamic. The campaign's Lincoln talk and commissioned images were matched by texts and images from other sources. The grassroots effusion cannot be solely credited to the artful designs of political consultants. Second, Lincoln and Obama depended on the other for their successful mutual evocation. The revival of images of an emancipationist, prophetic, and unifying Lincoln depended on Obama's racial identity. The memory of Lincoln helped place Obama in historical context. It helped voters understand how Obama fit into the pattern of our political life as a nation and underscored the historic nature of Obama's candidacy. This selected memory of Lincoln reassured voters that Obama fit within the American political tradition and challenged them to fulfill the democratic promise by electing the nation's first president of African descent. It also relied on an existing structure of memory, the civil-rights-era memory of Lincoln physically embodied in the Lincoln Memorial. Nonetheless, the phenomenon's last phase sends a mixed signal regarding Lincoln's staying power in American political memory. The inauguration period, despite the sincere and genuine tribute paid to Lincoln on the imminent occasion of his bicentennial year, also saw the return of the commemorative "inertia" and commodification that marks his contemporary image.[53] And so, while the texts and images making up the Lincoln-Obama phenomenon showed that Lincoln's memory still holds an inspirational, moral, and politically useful appeal with the American people, the excessive analogies and appeals of the last phase saw Lincoln return to the trivialization Schwartz holds is characteristic of his postmodern image.

There is one final twist to the story. At the same time Obama and millions of Americans were paying tribute to the nation's sixteenth president on the occasion of his birthday, a very different narrative about the American past was coming to dominate the political airwaves. The Tea Party movement, which now traces its origins to Mary Rakovich's one-woman protest against Obama's bailout plan and CNBC commentator Rick Santelli's televised tirade on the floor of the Chicago Board of Trade, has successfully leveraged the event after which it is named for political purposes.[54] A loose coalition of groups, the movement invokes the celebrated incident from the American Revolution to rally opposition to government spending. The groups' organizational methods are intensely grassroots and include an active Internet presence, local mobilization, and festive demonstrations featuring costumed Indians and patriots.[55] Originally non-partisan and focused on fiscal issues, the Tea Party evolved in the months following Obama's inauguration to become the frontline movement opposed to everything associated—rightly or wrongly—with the new president. This agenda included health care reform, illegal immigration, abortion, economic recovery programs, the mortgage bailout, and financial support for the nation's banks. Following incidents of racism at some Tea Party events, its leaders attempted to distance the movement from the more radical elements of this opposition, including those who deny Obama's right to hold office because of where he was born (the so-called "birthers").[56] From its spontaneous local origins, the Tea Party has become a populist conservative juggernaut. It sponsors an annual 9/12 march on Washington to present congressional leaders with a "Contract from America." It supported selected candidates in the 2010 midterm elections and is poised to influence the Republican nomination in 2012. Indicative of the movement's growing pull was Republican hopeful Sarah Palin's keynote address at a national convention organized by the Tea Party Nation in February 2010.[57]

Even more dramatic was the August 28, 2010, mass demonstration at the Lincoln Memorial organized by FOX News host and Tea Party advocate Glenn Beck. Taking place on the forty-seventh anniversary of Martin Luther King Jr.'s "I Have a Dream" speech, the "Restoring Honor" rally, with its message of honor and religious values, attracted an estimated 87,000 people (disputed by Beck and conservative bloggers, who claim that a half-million or more "activists" attended). Featured speakers included Sarah Palin, who declared that "we must not fundamentally transform America, as some would want" but rather reaffirm the nation's founding principles and the legacy of its great leaders including Washington, Lincoln, and King. The event was described at glennbeck.com as a "non-political event that pays tribute to America's service personnel and other upstanding citizens who embody our nation's founding principles of integrity, truth and honor."[58] Beck's previous record and statements on FOX News indicate his motives were not quite so pure. He has accused Obama of being a racist, claims that progressives have "co-opted" the civil rights movement, and told his listeners last spring "this is the moment, quite honestly, that I think we reclaim the civil rights movement . . . We are on the right side of history. We are on the side of individual freedoms and liberties and, damn it, we will reclaim the civil rights moment. We will take that movement because we are the people that did it in the first place."[59] The rally produced a reaction among civil rights advocates and liberals. Al Sharpton accused Beck of "hijacking the dream" and led a counter-rally entitled "Restore the Dream" from Dunbar High School in Washington to the Mall. Interestingly, Sharpton came out in defense of Lincoln's civil rights record.

yuck

Political movements mobilize memory to achieve their ends. The Tea Party is fascinating for the speed with which it developed, for what it reveals about conservative Americans' preferred historical memories, and for its impact on the contemporary memory landscape. If we consider that in early February 2009, Abraham Lincoln still held America's commemorative attention, the Tea Party's rise to prominence shortly afterwards amounts to nothing less than a collective memory upset. The Boston Tea Party has inspired anti-tax protesters in the past, and the popular memory of the event suits the movement's purposes admirably: a group of intrepid patriots steals aboard ships of the English East India Company disguised as Indians and dumps cargo of tea overboard. The salient points of this memory narrative include popular protest (including a good dose of popular political theater) and anti-government action. Contrast this formula to the themes of democratic fulfillment and historic culmination expressed by the Lincoln-Obama phenomenon at its zenith to see how far the memory landscape shifted in a very short time. This grassroots conservative movement is now mobilizing—in addition to the Tea Party—the memory of 9/11 and the Lincoln Memorial, appropriating the latter for conservative ends. While the counter-ralliers' accusations of racism may be overstated, there is no doubt that Beck and his supporters attempted to turn the established memory of King's speech and of Lincoln as emancipator and national unifier on its head. What they did constituted a masterfully ironic, even facetious, manipulation of the Memorial and the dominant civil-rights-era memory of Lincoln there enshrined. Whether or not this episode signals the return of the public contestation over Lincoln's memory is questionable. Beck is not universally admired among conservatives or even within the Tea Party movement. Conservatives have made no effort to reclaim Lincoln for their own, as his legacy contains elements inimical to contemporary conservative ideology.

How this will all play out in the next presidential election cycle remains to be seen. To indulge in the obvious pun, is the conservative commemorative counterattack a tempest in a teapot or does it represent something enduring? Will Obama and his supporters re-invoke the memory of Lincoln? If so, the presidential campaign may witness two competing narratives of the American past, one devoted to the founding generation, and the other to Abraham Lincoln and the memory of the Civil War. The version of Lincoln that best appeals in this case will likely differ from the memory of the Great Emancipator, democratic prophet, and unifier that resonated so well on the historic occasion of Obama's first election. It may be Lincoln's ability, as several historians have argued, to urge people forward by appealing to the past that proves most useful to the Democratic contender.[60] Change, or the fear of change, as Sarah Palin's comments and the tenor of the "Restoring Honor" rally testify, is the kernel of the radical conservative opposition. One thing is certain. The Lincoln-Obama phenomenon proved the Democratic Party's ability to marshal historical discourse for political advantage. Since Obama's inauguration, conservatives have regained the initiative in directing the story of the nation's past. Obama and his strategists are too caught up in current issues to pay much attention to history. There are even indications the forty-fourth president may be less willing to learn from his predecessors than he led us to believe.[61] Obama's grassroots supporters also seem quiescent, preferring either to counter the history offered up by conservative operatives like Glenn Beck or to linger in the waning rays of the Lincoln-Obama phenomenon's post-election glow. Liberal commentators as well as scholars and political strategists would do well to remember its influence during a critical period of our national political life. Lincoln's evocation hit a collective memory "sweet spot," that proved Americans will yet respond to a version of the past that emphasizes our obligations to one another and the nation's democratic promise.

CHAPTER TWO

The Confederate Battle Flag and the Desertion of the Lost Cause Tradition

Thomas J. Brown

The surge of protest against state displays of the Confederate battle flag at the turn of the millennium posed a fundamental challenge to American habits of remembrance. In the years since New York City patriots pulled down an equestrian statue of George III to celebrate the Declaration of Independence, public attention has rarely focused on the deliberate retraction of earlier acts of commemoration. Many milestones and heroes have slipped into oblivion, but the process has less often involved repudiation than the corrosive force of time and the substitution of other memories. More typical than the fate of the George III statue has been the career of the monument that the South Carolina legislature erected in 1766 to William Pitt in gratitude for his role in the repeal of the Stamp Act. Although dedicated to the understanding that the colonists were, in Pitt's phrase quoted in the inscription, "true sons of England" whose differences with Parliament might be resolved amicably, the tribute remained in the central intersection of Charleston until 1794. Removed because complaints about the obstruction of traffic added weight to a flutter of enthusiasm for the French Revolution, the statue soon assumed a new place of honor in front of the Orphan House, an inadvertently apt site for the

abandoned public memory that American independence may have been unnecessary.[1] Attacks on the Confederate battle flag struck at a commemorative shadow that has not softened as readily as public remembrance of the
British Empire. These emotionally charged campaigns suggested that some memorial gestures warrant more explicit rejection than the accretion of community indifference that is the lot of so much American commemoration.

Conflict over the Confederate banner heated up across the South during
the late 1980s and reached apparent exhaustion by the early twenty-first century. Florida eliminated an array of historical flags on the capitol plaza that
featured the second Confederate national flag. Mississippi voters in a 2001
referendum defeated a proposal to remove the southern cross from the state
flag. Georgia in contrast adopted new designs for its state flag in 2001 and
2003. Alabama removed a Confederate banner from the state house dome in
1993 and installed a different military standard in a display with the three
Confederate national flags at the Confederate monument on the capitol
grounds. South Carolina similarly lowered the unbordered, rectangular Confederate naval jack from the Columbia dome in July 2000 and raised a white-
bordered, square version of the southern cross, used by many units in Lee's
army, in front of the capitol at the state monument to the Confederate dead.

The most vigorous and revealing of these struggles, the controversy over
the Confederate flag in South Carolina presented a remarkable grassroots debate over collective memory. In the decade leading up to the removal of the
flag from the dome, the Columbia daily newspaper *The State* published well
over a thousand letters to the editor and guest editorials on the issue in addition to hundreds of columns by staff or syndicated writers and news stories
about public opinion. Citizens' engagement escalated through three successive
peaks. The first period of intensive concentration began with the legislative
consideration of a proposed Heritage Act in the spring of 1994 and lasted
through the Republican primary election in August 1994, in which a record
turnout of voters urged the party to keep the flag atop the capitol. Republican
governor David Beasley opened a second major phase of debate in November
1996 by calling for passage of the Heritage Act in the first gubernatorial address to be televised statewide in thirteen years. The ensuing flurry of discussion subsided in the first few months of 1997, after the House of Representatives blocked Beasley's proposal. The state branch of the National Association
for the Advancement of Colored People (NAACP) launched the third and most
absorbing round in July 1999 by securing approval at the national NAACP

convention for a boycott of travel and tourism in South Carolina. In the next twelve months, *The State* published well over four hundred guest editorials and letters to the editor about the flag, in addition to scores of regular columns and news stories. The newspaper rarely appeared for two consecutive days without an opinion piece on the issue until Citadel cadets changed the Confederate flags at the state house on July 1, 2000, pursuant to legislation modeled closely on the Heritage Act proposed six years earlier. Public debate continued more sporadically afterward under the prodding of NAACP sanctions that remained in place in April 2011 on the sesquicentennial anniversary of the firing on Fort Sumter.

The depth of passion in South Carolina surprised nobody. "Let's face it," sighed one legislator. "We're still fighting the Civil War."[2] Countless commentators noted the persistence, or obstinacy, of the first state to secede from the Union and the last to take down the rebel flag. Champions of the flag fervently insisted that they were preserving a longstanding Confederate "heritage," and their adversaries complained that nostalgic reverie paralyzed the state. "Wake up, Rip Van Winkle. We lost," jabbed one letter to *The State*. Academic analysis has similarly tended to assume that debates over the Confederate flag pitted "traditionalists" against modernizing critics. A book-length study of the controversy in South Carolina reports that the groups that rallied around the flag were "direct descendants" of the Lost Cause movement that pervaded southern culture for more than a half-century after Appomattox, now working through different organizations and responding to the fresh challenge of a multicultural society but emotionally and intellectually faithful to an inherited bond with the Confederate past. The leading scholar of the Confederate flag similarly concludes that its defenders' political muscle shows that "the traditional South is not disappearing any time soon."[3]

The image of old wine in new bottles fairly describes the reversal of South Carolina political parties' racial profiles and electoral fortunes. The controversy made Confederate honor the political property of the Republican Party, the organization that the Lost Cause had in no small part cohered to defeat during Reconstruction and its aftermath. Legislative machinations over the flag fit within a broader story of the consolidation of Republican dominance in a former Democratic stronghold of the white South. Factional alignments and personal rivalries within the party strongly influenced the flow of events, as did more structural considerations like the use of race in the drawing of legislative districts. The Republican invitation to voters in the August 1994 primary to express an opinion on the flag was a particularly straightforward use of the issue for party-building purposes.[4]

Beyond the most obvious racial politics of the flag, however, the claim for continuity from the Lost Cause era to contemporary defense of the southern cross fails to recognize important shifts in the foundations and uses of Confederate memory. The raising of the flag above the South Carolina state house in March 1962 reflected its recent emergence in a popular culture of recreation and consumption starkly different from, and in some ways antithetical to, the memorial culture of the Lost Cause. When state display of the flag came under attack, its defenders could not rely on the gender, religious, and class structures that had sustained earlier Confederate commemoration. To the contrary, those established patterns of white southern social organization more often characterized the mobilization against the flag, which was in large part an exercise in collective remembrance of the civil rights movement of the 1950s and 1960s. The moral defense of the battle flag on the basis of common soldiers' individual integrity similarly paralleled the Lost Cause glorification of Confederate heroism less than it drew on American tributes to Vietnam veterans. Shaped by the powerful contemporary currents of mass consumerism and the legacies of the civil rights movement and the Vietnam War, the millennial rally around the flag differed diametrically from the anti-commercial critique of modernity that had dominated the Confederate image from Appomattox through the Southern Renascence. The most vital form of Confederate commemoration now projected a disintegration of traditional social institutions into an atomism best exemplified by the consumer marketplace.

❦

The Confederate battle flag at the end of the twentieth century stood apart from the dense memorial framework joined to it at the beginning of the century. Flag defenders sometimes claimed that the attack on the flag was the first step in an assault on all public remembrance of the Confederacy. Letters to *The State* warned that flag opponents "won't stop their crusade until every school and street named for a Southern hero has been renamed, every Confederate monument demolished, every Confederate grave desecrated, and flying the flag declared a hate crime." No such expansion of targets even began to take place. One leading critic of the flag laughed that "you'd have to tear down half the state." An isolated local call for removal of the Confederate monument in Walterboro in 1997 attracted little attention or support.[5] The monuments and place names across South Carolina had long ago lost the potency that might merit serious protest. Champions of Confederate memory struck a more resonant chord when they worried that the flag was not their first but last line of defense. One supporter called it "the only visible thing we have to show for the sacrifices our ancestors made," though the capitol grounds alone offered monuments to Confederate soldiers, Confederate women, and Wade Hampton, a magnolia tree planted as a memorial to Robert E. Lee, carefully preserved and highlighted evidence of Sherman's attack on Columbia, and a marker pointing out the position of the state house on the Lee Highway.[6]

Charleston attorney Samuel W. Howell IV situated the unique vitality of the flag in the most poignant comparative context. Howell wrote in March 1997 that he would gladly agree to removal of the flag from the state house if South Carolina revived Confederate Memorial Day with the energy and earnestness the occasion had once inspired. Government offices and businesses would close; citizens would decorate monuments and graves; soldiers would parade; public leaders would deliver orations. But that world of Confederate remembrance had long ago disappeared. Even in Charleston, where several thousand citizens had gathered annually at Magnolia Cemetery for decades after the war to hear the ritual reading of Henry Timrod's ode and join in other Memorial Day exercises, attendance had dwindled by the early 1950s to about one hundred participants, "mostly elderly ladies wearing the Stars and Bars of the Confederacy like a shibboleth."[7] Unable to restore his ideal of community, Howell chose to take his stand behind the battle flag like another thwarted Charlestonian, the hero of DuBose Heyward's novel *Peter Ashley*.

The impulses that placed the southern cross atop the South Carolina state house in March 1962 differed dramatically from the traditions followed to the end by the aging women in Magnolia Cemetery. As John Coski has chronicled, the divergence of the battle flag from other forms of Confederate remembrance originated on southern college campuses. In the 1920s, Coski reports, chapters of the Kappa Alpha Order—a student fraternity founded in 1865 at the school where Robert E. Lee presided—began to sponsor dances that "assumed the characteristics of modern 'retro' fads." Confederate flags festooned halls in which students in gray uniforms drank mint juleps with young women wearing vintage dresses. *Gone With the Wind*, also a flapper appropriation of the Lost Cause, added to the popularity of these Old South balls after publication of the novel in 1936 and release of the film in 1939, by which point intercollegiate athletics were becoming a forum for more fervent and enduring *sports and military displays of masculinity* (handwritten margin note)

display of the battle flag. The ironic, mildly rebellious undercurrents to college students' use of the banner as a party decoration recurred when the flag entered another realm of white youth culture, the segregated United States armed forces. Noticeable numbers of white southern servicemen used Confederate flags in World War II for pranks tweaking military authority and nostalgic efforts to identify with home. The trend peaked a few years later in a nation-wide Confederate flag fad that mixed mischievous incidents with lasting incorporation of the emblem into commercial and recreational settings. Tracks affiliated with the National Association of Stock Car Auto Racing quickly adopted the flag as a logo after the establishment of NASCAR in 1949, recognizing that the emblem perfectly fit the image of white southern moonshining speedsters that the racing series sought to promote.[8]

This revitalization of the Confederate battle flag infused it with new political potential. The second Ku Klux Klan, founded in 1915 by a young man who closely followed popular culture, had devoted no particular attention to the southern cross. But the Klan revival that began in the late 1930s often used the flag to symbolize its fidelity to Confederate principles. John D. Long, a thirty-seven-year-old lawyer serving his first term in the South Carolina legislature, sponsored a resolution in March 1938 that installed the battle flag alongside the state and federal flags behind the speaker's desk in the House of Representatives. Long's initiative celebrated the triumph of a record-breaking filibuster staged by southern Democrats in Congress to block federal anti-lynching legislation that the NAACP had conspicuously supported by repeatedly flying outside its New York City offices a black banner which announced that "A Man Was Lynched Yesterday." The prominence of the battle flag in the Dixiecrat presidential campaign of 1948 marked its maturation as a symbol in mass politics. College students carried the banner into the nominating convention of the National States' Rights Democratic Party, and the Dixiecrats' extensive use of the battle flag during the campaign reinforced the youthful image projected by presidential nominee Strom Thurmond. Together with the broader flag fad of the early 1950s, the Dixiecrat example ensured that advocates of "massive resistance" to the racial integration ordered by the Supreme Court in *Brown v. Board of Education* would turn to the Confederate banner to express their defiance. John D. Long, now a member of the South Carolina Senate, sponsored a successful resolution in April 1956 to drape the battle flag alongside the federal and state flags in the chamber of the upper house on the last day of a legislative session that a newspaper reporter described as "dominated by one note—maintain at all costs segregation in the public schools of South Carolina."[9]

By the Civil War centennial, the southern cross was a common feature of white student life, mass consumerism, and segregationist politics. Some white southerners rued the transformation of the flag, much as many Americans expressed reservations about the new practice of reenacting Civil War battles in which men had died gruesome deaths. When a textile manufacturer reported booming sales of a beach towel that replicated the battle flag in February 1958, the South Carolina legislature adopted a resolution deploring the towel as "a veiled attack, parading in the garb of legitimate advertisement, on the valor, courage and sacrifice of the Men in Gray." The legislature made it a criminal offense to sell merchandise imprinted with a representation of a Confederate flag or "publicly mutilate, deface, defile, defy, jeer at, trample upon, or cast contempt" on a Confederate flag. The statute did little to impede the distribution of souvenirs and other commercial ephemera during the Civil War centennial, which promoters welcomed as "one of the most mouthwatering marketing situations to come along in years." The federal Civil War Centennial Commission (CWCC) encouraged the robust exercise of free enterprise as essential to a popular and fiercely anti-communist festival, but even eighty-year-old CWCC chairman Ulysses S. Grant III complained on his arrival in Charleston for the anniversary of the firing on Fort Sumter that "I don't believe some of the advertising I've seen is carrying out the heritage your forefathers fought for."[10]

The United Daughters of the Confederacy (UDC) committed itself to turning back the waves of popular culture, only to marginalize the organization through its futile efforts. Although its influence in white southern society had peaked a few decades earlier, the UDC remained by far the largest and most powerful Confederate commemorative organization when it denounced use of the battle flag by "college groups" as well as "political groups" shortly after the Dixiecrat campaign. The flag fad of the early 1950s quieted this insistence on restriction of the flag to ceremonial uses, as the popularity of the Confederate emblem delighted many UDC members. With the arrival of the Civil War centennial, however, the UDC firmly endorsed the principle that the sanctity of the emblem precluded its use in many settings. The national convention adopted a flag code in 1961 that prohibited incorporation of Confederate flags in "clothing of any kind," including athletic uniforms, or in any merchandise "designed for temporary use and discard."[11] The guidelines were hopelessly ineffectual in preventing the southern cross from appearing on bathing suits and women's underwear during the Civil War centennial. The battle flag had become defined by a proliferation far beyond the boundaries that the UDC deemed consistent with respect for the emblem.

John A. May, the legislator responsible for installing the battle flag above the South Carolina state house, personified the newer approach to Confederate remembrance. Flamboyantly styling himself as "Mr. Confederate," May sometimes wore a Confederate uniform in the capitol, where he represented Aiken County in the House of Representatives off and on from 1935 through 1966. On other occasions he dressed as "a walking Rebel exhibit," in the words of an acquaintance of the early 1960s, replete with battle flags on his necktie, tie clasp, and cuff links.[12] In addition to collecting Confederate knickknacks and memorabilia, May played an active role in the invigoration of the Sons of Confederate Veterans (SCV), the younger and historically feebler sibling of the UDC. A moribund organization with only one thousand members and one thousand dollars in the treasury on the eve of the Supreme Court decision in *Brown v. Board of Education*, the SCV had begun to develop into a substantial enterprise for the first time under the guidance of Mississippi arch-segregationist William D. McCain, the adjutant-in-chief of the organization from 1953 to 1993.[13] During the Civil War centennial May suspended his law practice to immerse himself in his work as national commander-in-chief of the SCV and chairman of the South Carolina Confederate War Centennial Commission. For the ceremonies opening the centennial observance in Charleston in April 1961, he wore a top hat, gray suit, and brightly colored vest emblazoned with the southern cross.[14]

May would have attracted attention at the Charleston ceremonies regardless of his costume, for his position on the South Carolina commission placed him at the center of the controversy that dominated the gathering, the storm that had erupted when the segregated Francis Marion Hotel refused to host a black member of the New Jersey delegation to the national assembly of the CWCC. May vehemently defended the Jim Crow policy of his state in the confrontation, which attracted extensive national publicity in the weeks leading up to the meeting. Shortly after the Kennedy administration resolved the impasse by moving the federally sponsored meeting to the Charleston naval base, May arranged with a state administrator to add the Confederate banner to a flagpole atop the state house portico in recognition of the festivities that would begin in the next few days. May also supplied a battle flag to several fellow legislators and socially prominent Charlestonians who sneaked onto Fort Sumter in the dark of night and raised the standard in time for the exact anniversary of the first Confederate shots at 4:30 on the morning of April 12. As white southerners continued to rail against White House handling of the hotel dispute, May took a leadership position in the Confederate States Centennial Conference (CSCC) that met in downtown Charleston while the depleted national assembly of the CWCC convened at the naval base.

The coalition of southern states remained an important vehicle for negotiation with the federal commission when the new CWCC leaders appointed by Kennedy began plans to focus on commemoration of the Emancipation Proclamation. At a meeting of the CWCC and state commissions in Washington in early February 1962, May presented a CSCC resolution protesting any initiative "that could, or would, be considered by any section of our nation as propaganda for any cause that would tend to reopen the wounds of the war." Upon returning to South Carolina he promptly introduced a legislative resolution on February 14 calling for addition of the Confederate battle flag to the pole on top of the state house dome that had been refit for the display of the United States and South Carolina flags five weeks earlier. The House of Representatives immediately approved, punctuating its endorsement with a resolution that praised May's work as chairman of the state commission and the regional CSCC. Both measures soon sailed through the Senate, and the battle flag was installed above the dome before the end of March 1962.[15]

May's initiative was more akin to the placement of a bumper sticker on the state house than to an extension of the prevailing American flag culture. Popular treatment of the U.S. flag in the early 1960s revolved around a rigid set of ceremonial and ritual practices, including recitation of the Pledge of Allegiance, singing of "The Star-Spangled Banner," and protocols for handling and display of the national banner set forth in the flag code formulated in 1923 and endorsed by Congress in 1942. Schools and military units taught that reverence for the American flag was essential to good citizenship. Ironic appropriations of the stars and stripes comparable to the uses that had recently popularized the southern cross were rare, which was part of the satirical appeal of the Confederate flag in settings like the armed forces. In 1958 the Museum of Modern Art even declined to acquire Jasper Johns's coolly detached pop art icon *Flag* (1954–55) because the trustees feared that the work "would offend patriotic sensibilities." American veneration of the flag was the very heart of what Robert Bellah famously identified in 1967 as a "civil religion" also centered by the Gettysburg Address, Memorial Day, and Arlington National Cemetery on sacralization of the vast bloodshed of the Civil War.[16]

White southern passion for Confederate military banners had played an important part in forging the distinctive American flag culture during the Civil War, but placement of the southern cross atop the capitol dome in 1962 did not reproduce nineteenth-century sentiments. Kitsch imprinted with the battle flag continued to abound. State senator Earle E. Morris Jr. attracted brief notice in 1965 by decrying the "commercialization and abuse" of the flag, and sympathetic newspaper reports indicated that "protests have been arising spasmodically throughout the South recently as the flag becomes a decoration for a score of trinkets and articles of clothing." The legislature did not approve Morris's proposal for a commission to study the problem, however, and the initiative mostly illustrated the extent to which South Carolinians had forgotten that the state had extended the protections of the U.S. flag code to Confederate flags in 1958.[17] Law enforcement officials evidently made only one effort to enforce those restrictions, predictably in response to the burning of a Confederate flag by a University of South Carolina student at a protest held on Lincoln's birthday in 1969 in support of a request by African American students that the school administration ban the display of the flag and the singing of "Dixie" on campus. Even on that occasion, however, authorities declined to prosecute the student on the basis of the patently unconstitutional statute and furnish a forum for further challenge to the Confederate aegis.[18] Without the benefit of the legal, ritual, and educational practices that had fostered American respect for flags since the Civil War, the Confederate battle flag generated supporters in the quarter-century after the centennial partly through racial politics but also through the presence of the emblem on T-shirts, baseball caps, and shot glasses and in entertainments like sporting events or performances of the southern rock band Lynyrd Skynyrd. For example, the popular television comedy *The Dukes of Hazzard* (1979–1985), which revolved around a pair of happy-go-lucky good old boys, prominently featured a Dodge Charger nicknamed "General Lee" and emblazoned on the roof with the southern cross.

The consumer foundations of the Confederate battle flag in the late-twentieth-century controversy were epitomized by the most prominent South Carolina champion of the flag, state senator Glenn McConnell of Charleston. An attorney by training, McConnell started a new career in the late 1980s as the proprietor of CSA Galleries. The shop carried a wide variety of Confederatethemed merchandise, much of which featured the southern cross. Most reminiscent of the Lost Cause were prints of Civil War scenes that broadly imitated the pathos of the less expensive prints widely circulated a century earlier, though brandishing Confederate battle flags much more frequently. The southern cross also appeared on key chains, beer steins, ashtrays, and a dizzying assortment of other wares. For the womenfolk, CSA Galleries offered dolls and memorabilia based on *Gone With the Wind*. And converging with McConnell's avid participation in Civil War reenactment, the shop sold simulated Confederate uniforms and accompanying reproductions of accoutrements from the 1860s.[19] As reenactors came to dominate the meager attempts to develop a ceremonial culture around display of the southern cross in response to the intensification of protests, their prominence underscored Confederate flag supporters' substitution of recreation and consumerism for the quasi-religious authority of American flags. Reenactment is a hobby in which the purchase of historically accurate gear defines "authenticity" and underlies participants' claim to honor the men and women of the Civil War era. Consumption becomes reverence.[20] That mode of commemoration would shape debate no less than the racial theme of commemoration when flag defenders mobilized against demands for removal of the southern cross from the dome of the state house.

Like the practices reinforcing enthusiasm for the Confederate battle flag, the grounds of opposition to it shifted from the Lost Cause era to the late twentieth century. Hostility to Confederate commemoration rested for decades on disapproval of the proslavery rebellion against the United States. After the war against Nazi Germany and the civil rights movement of the 1950s and 1960s, objections tended to focus more often on the Confederate commitment to racial bondage than secessionists' disloyalty to American democracy. The observation that "you cannot separate slavery from the flag, bottom line" remained the single most common historical argument against state display of the flag in the debates at the end of the century. The NAACP boycott resolution of 1999 pointed to it as the first reason that South Carolina should not honor the flag. Many white South Carolinians agreed, "The cause for which our ancestors fought, although with great courage and valor, was evil." Professional historians engaged in the protest focused almost exclusively on the Confederate determination to preserve slavery.[21] But the millennial struggle against the flag also drew on newer sources of momentum, for it invoked remembrance of the civil rights movement as well as remembrance of the Civil War. Attention to the South Carolina that raised the battle flag in the 1960s instead of the 1860s brought the controversy into the realm of many citizens' personal recollections and provided opportunities to interlace individual and regional experience. This emphasis broadened the appeal of the campaign while clarifying that the challenge to Confederate commemoration did not extend beyond the flag.

The latter approach contrasted with the earliest recorded protests against state display of the battle flag, which took place in the first legislative session in which African Americans returned to the General Assembly after seven decades of exclusion. Representative I. S. Leevy Johnson, one of three African Americans elected in 1970, and his fellow members of the Richland County delegation conducted public hearings in July 1972 on a proposal to remove the battle flag from the capitol. The president of the Columbia YWCA stressed that the flag "connotes the subjugation of minority groups, the idealization of slavery, and the unwillingness to be governed by the constitution of the United States." The president of the state branch of the NAACP urged removal of the flag as a unifying measure in the current social tumult, noting that "the people who fought under that flag fought more militantly than any revolutionary force in the country today to divide this nation." The head of the South Carolina Council of Human Relations endorsed the initiative as consistent with Governor John West's announced intention to eliminate vestiges of discrimination in the state. Newspaper reports of the hearing do not indicate that the speakers dwelled on any use of the battle flag by more recent opponents of civil rights.[22]

In the major phase of the flag controversy, the frame of historical reference was more complex. Public memory of the Civil War had received fresh stimulus from the movie *Glory* (1989) and Ken Burns's television documentary series *The Civil War* (1990). But public memory of the civil rights movement had truly begun to crest. The campaign to establish a holiday honoring Martin Luther King Jr., which achieved success on the federal level in the mid-1980s and in every state except South Carolina by 2000, was the most conspicuous of countless initiatives. Other milestones included the television documentary *Eyes on the Prize* (1987), the movies *Mississippi Burning* (1988) and *Malcolm X* (1992), the dedication of Maya Lin's civil rights memorial in Montgomery (1989), and the opening of the National Civil Rights Museum in Memphis

(1991). Commemorations in South Carolina repeatedly revisited the *Briggs v. Elliott* school desegregation litigation initiated in Clarendon County and consolidated at the U.S. Supreme Court with *Brown v. Board of Education*, the integration of all-white state universities, and the Orangeburg Massacre of 1968.

Memory of the civil rights movement added two important arguments against the Confederate battle flag to the call for repudiation of proslavery secession. South Carolinians did not need to know about John A. May's role in the contentious Civil War centennial to infer that the installation of the flag atop the state house was "an act of defiance by politicians against an emerging civil rights movement." Many participants in the debate deemed legislators' motives in the 1960s more disturbing than disunionists' motives in the 1860s. "I would rather be ignorant of what the Confederate flag stands for [in Civil War history] than to be ignorant of why it was put up," maintained one reply to the argument that the Confederacy had formed to defend states' rights.[23] The situation in South Carolina was in this respect much like that in Georgia, which had incorporated the southern cross in the state flag during a legislative session devoted to planning resistance to *Brown v. Board of Education*, and in Alabama, where Governor George Wallace had raised the battle flag above the capitol in April 1963 when U.S. Attorney General Robert F. Kennedy visited Montgomery to discuss the integration of the University of Alabama. The only state that did not modify its display of the battle flag at the turn of the millennium, Mississippi, had added the southern cross to its state flag in 1894.

Condemnation of the battle flag as an artifact of resistance to the civil rights movement also emphasized the use of the symbol by extralegal white supremacists. Mobilization against the flag gained region-wide momentum in 1987 from a dramatic reminder of the iconic mass protests of the 1960s, a widely publicized confrontation in Forsyth County, Georgia, in which more than five thousand white reactionaries, some waving Confederate battle flags, harassed approximately twenty thousand marchers for calling attention to the exceptionally disturbing racial record of that community. A few weeks later James Clyburn of the South Carolina Human Affairs Commission, the principal anti-discrimination agency in the state, renewed the demand for removal of the Confederate flag from the capitol dome. In March 1987 the NAACP southeast regional conference called on South Carolina, Alabama, Georgia, and Mississippi to discontinue official use of the southern cross. The protests stressed that the battle flag was an emblem of anti-integrationists. Clyburn indicated that African Americans would much rather see the stars and bars atop the state house than the southern cross. State senator Kay Patterson, who had led efforts to remove the battle flag from the legislative chambers of the capitol since his election to the House of Representatives in 1974, suggested the same substitution in an address to the Sons of the Confederate Veterans. For African Americans, Patterson reported, the battle flag symbolized "the Klan activity, the muggings, the hangings from trees, the shootings and killings." The readiness of black leaders to accept state display of the first national flag of the Confederacy marked a shift from the earlier emphasis on the shadow of slavery. At the peak of the South Carolina debate, flag opponents circulated an image that depicted a hooded Klansman with the southern cross at the state house, again suggesting that violent resistance to civil rights had more polemical traction than the violence of slavery.[24]

Identification of the battle flag with extralegal white supremacism did not focus exclusively on the civil rights era. Some contributions to the debate associated the flag with the entire history of white terrorism since secession. That violence had not disappeared at the end of the twentieth century. David Beasley's television address in November 1996 responded in part to the burning of thirteen black churches in South Carolina during the past five years and a recent incident in which three young African Americans had been shot by two Klansmen returning from a Confederate flag rally.[25] But the center of gravity for the many references to the Klan was not in the distant past or in the present but in the bloody death struggle of the Jim Crow order. A newspaper reporter for the Charleston *Post and Courier,* after traveling throughout the South to find shared themes in the various flag controversies, concluded that "the battle flag was waved by the Ku Klux Klan during the 1950s and 1960s, back when the Klan was more prone to murder than marching. To the people who remember those horrible years, the argument that the flag has nothing to say about race is a hard sell."[26] To the considerable extent that it focused on the Klan rather than the Confederacy, the protest against the flag resembled the affirmation of the civil rights movement signaled by the 1993 reopening of FBI investigation into the 1963 bombing of the Sixteenth Street Baptist Church in Birmingham, Alabama, which led to the convictions of Thomas Edwin Blanton and Bobby Frank Cherry in the first years of the new century.

Flag protesters' invocations of the civil rights movement were incomplete and in some ways unsatisfying. Identification of the Klan as the chief antagonist of racial progress highlighted the denial of basic human dignity to African Americans and the courage with which they transcended violence. But that emphasis isolated resistance in a set of extremists thoroughly disdained in the contemporary United States, situating the civil rights movement in a past embodied by archaic opponents of law. Attention to state legislators' motives for placing the battle flag on the state house focused on a legacy of legally sanctioned discrimination. But this narrative tended to attribute progress to the federal government, rather than local grassroots activism, and implied that the movement ended with the achievement of legal equality. Neither link between the Confederate flag and the civil rights movement directed attention to the economics of racial injustice. The flashbacks to famous events of the 1960s affirmed public consensus about racial harmony without opening questions that remained deeply controversial.[27]

The two most elaborate rallies against the flag in South Carolina vividly presented the campaign as a commemoration of the civil rights movement. The anniversary of Martin Luther King Jr.'s birthday in January 2000 provided the occasion for the largest social protest in state history. A crowd estimated at 46,000 people gathered at the capitol to support removal of the flag from the dome as a continuation of King's legacy, an argument that many critics of the flag had made in recent years. The rally called national attention to South Carolina as both the only state to fly the Confederate flag from its capitol and the only state that had not made King's birthday a holiday. In April 2000, Charleston mayor Joseph Riley led a group of marchers from Charleston to Columbia to protest the flag less than one month after President Bill Clinton and luminaries of the civil rights movement had participated in a well-publicized thirty-fifth anniversary partial retracing of the 1965 march from Selma to Montgomery. Riley's trek from Marion Square to the state house covered more than one hundred miles and lasted four days. Newspaper coverage stressed that "King Day at the Dome" and the "Get in Step" march were extraordinary fusions of past and present in which veterans of the civil rights era remembered their experiences for younger listeners.[28]

Echoes of the civil rights movement also influenced the defense of the flag. Racial conservatives joined in denouncing violent white supremacism and complained that the Klan had "hijacked" the Confederate emblem, though pro-flag rhetoric did include a good deal of raw resentment over advances in the status of African Americans. Many flag supporters argued that display of the southern cross was a fitting price to exact for public expression of black collective consciousness and pride. "Let the blacks have Martin Luther King Jr. Day, and let whites have our flag," proposed a typical letter to *The State*. Similar demands for exchange focused on the proposal to place a monument on the capitol grounds devoted to the history of African Americans, an idea included in the initial draft of the Heritage Act and authorized separately by the legislature in July 1996. "We have given and we have given, and why can't you?" asked one Republican legislator.[29] More sophisticated variations aimed to borrow rather than deplore the legacy of the civil rights movement. These arguments claimed that the white descendants of Confederate veterans shared a common past just as African Americans did. "The kind of genocide inflicted on the ancestors of our black citizens by the Yankee slave traders and ship owners is not that much different from the cultural genocide still being waged against the South," asserted one flag advocate. Defense of the flag was accordingly an appeal for cultural pluralism. "At what point in the Palmetto State do we realize we have a diverse heritage?" pleaded state senator John Courson, an architect of the Heritage Act. Flag critics needed to learn "toleration and an appreciation for differences," agreed Glenn McConnell, who played a key role in piloting authorization of the African American History Monument through the legislature and chaired the commission that supervised the project through the dedication ceremony in March 2001. Some polemicists maintained that King surely would have supported the Confederate battle flag on this basis.[30]

The Heritage Act adopted in 2000 bowed to the attacks on the flag based on remembrance of the civil rights movement while standing firm in commemoration of the Confederacy. The removal of the flag from the capitol dome to the soldiers monument distinguished the tribute from the gesture of the early 1960s and anchored the flag more securely in the Civil War era. The legislation also sought to dissociate the state display from the Klan by substituting a square battle flag for the more readily available rectangular banner ordinarily used by Klan members. Like flag defenders' attempts to turn allegations of racial bigotry on their opponents, the Heritage Act revealed the commemorative priorities of the contemporary South. Celebration of the civil rights movement was a more powerful orthodoxy than celebration of the Confederacy by the turn of the millennium. In many ways, the culture of remembrance that mobilized against the flag inherited the orthodox traditions of Confederate commemoration rather than the supposed heirs to the Lost Cause who rallied in defense of their logo.

❈

The Lost Cause helped to define norms of gender, religion, and class in the white South for more than fifty years after Appomattox. Remembrance of the Confederacy intertwined with fundamental social institutions of family, church, and social hierarchy to shape the distribution of power. Hardly a monolith, that tradition sustained considerable debate among competing advocates of Confederate memory, whose creative differences yielded a variety of significant voluntary organizations, community rituals, and works of art and literature. The anti-flag campaign at the end of the twentieth century reconstituted important parts of this cultural formation even as it differed diametrically from the Lost Cause precedent on the fundamental subject of race relations. The defense of the flag, in contrast, resembled the Lost Cause almost solely in its racism. Rejecting the communal bonds through which Confederate commemoration had once thrived, flag champions envisioned an atomistic society in which individual consumers determined the value of the common past much as buyers set the price for any commodity.

No feature of the Lost Cause distinguished it more thoroughly in the judgment of its adherents than the central role of women. White southern women took the lead in forming organizations like Ladies' Memorial Associations and the UDC, supervising the interment of fallen soldiers in Confederate cemeteries across the South, establishing widespread observance of Memorial Day, sponsoring the construction of countless civic monuments, founding museums for the display of Confederate artifacts, publishing fiction and nonfiction accounts of the war and Reconstruction, and other initiatives. These ventures served many different purposes for the participating women. Some ends were quite conservative, such as reinforcement of the patriarchal family through salutes to male valor. Other ends were more daring, including women's use of Confederate commemoration to participate in political debates during the pre-suffrage era and challenge prevailing ideals of manhood and womanhood.[31]

Women's role in the flag controversy differed sharply from the pattern established in the Lost Cause. Women played leading roles in the campaign against the flag, sometimes from positions dramatically removed from the earlier reliance on Confederate remembrance as an outlet for engagement in public life. Gilda Cobb-Hunter, minority leader of the state House of Representatives, and Paula Harper Bethea, board chair of the state Chamber of Commerce, demonstrated that black and white women now wielded authority formerly monopolized by men. Women responded to continued gender discrimination by attacking rather than promoting Confederate commemoration. One letter to *The State* described the flag as "a painful reminder of the injustices I have suffered as a woman as a result of the 'good ol' boy system.'" Women acting more consistently with older gender roles also spoke out against the flag. Mary Simms Oliphant had guarded the Lost Cause flame for decades in a series of updates to her grandfather William Gilmore Simms's history of South Carolina, which public schools in the state continued to use into the 1980s. Oliphant's granddaughter reported in 1994 that she had inherited her grandmother's custodial reverence for history but not her interpretation of the war. As history clearly showed that the Confederacy had fought for slavery, the battle flag belonged in a museum.[32]

The most notable revision of the Lost Cause model of voluntaristic domesticity involved Jamie Renda, a suburban Republican descended from a slaveholding family that included a Confederate captain. After watching a Disney television movie about the civil rights movement with her young daughters on the eve of Martin Luther King Jr.'s birthday in 1999, Renda decided to become active in the campaign against the flag. She formed an organization called United 2000 designed to serve as a nonpartisan clearinghouse for different groups interested in removal of the flag from the state house dome. United 2000 took the leading role in organizing the King Day at the Dome rally in January 2000, a spectacular example of the extent to which the onetime constituency of the UDC now mobilized against the flag in remembrance of the civil rights movement.[33]

Conversely, women played little part in the defense of the flag. The UDC, which dwarfed the SCV in membership and influence for three-quarters of a century, surrendered its longstanding role as the leading Confederate commemorative organization. By the turn of the millennium the SCV claimed to have somewhat more than the approximately 25,000 members of the UDC, and the men's group was much more geographically concentrated and energetic. The UDC sometimes claimed that its charter precluded the group from intervening in political disputes, though the founding generation of women had participated in highly politicized controversies over commemorative initiatives. When invited to do so, UDC leaders ignored the supposed ban but tended to endorse compromise. UDC president general June Murray Wells, a Charlestonian, declared in January 2000 that she wished the state house displayed the stars and bars because it encompassed the women and children of the Confederacy while the southern cross merely represented the men in the army. The tepid support of the leading women's commemorative organization typified the overall gender gap in the flag debate. A 1999 public opinion poll showed that women were much more likely than men to favor removal of the flag from the capitol dome. Although women comprised only one-fourth of the identifiable authors of unpaid contributions to the flag debate in *The State* from 1991 to July 2000, they wrote well over half of the letters and guest editorials that explicitly called for removal of the flag not only from the dome but also from the state house grounds.[34]

Defense of the flag spurned the institutional legacy of Lost Cause women. The central element of that legacy at stake in the flag controversy was the Confederate Relic Room in Columbia, founded by the local UDC chapter in the 1890s. Although contemporary American culture offered many examples of museums fusing memorial and educational goals, including the National Civil Rights Museum, flag champions loudly rejected the suggestion that the Relic Room could effectively substitute for display of the flag at the state house. "Encasement means entombment," chanted McConnell. "The flag will not be taken down and put in a museum and forgotten about. That is not going to happen, period," vowed Courson.[35] This stance underscored that the banner atop the capitol dome was a fungible, routinely replaced commodity rather than a historic artifact like the several dozen Confederate banners already owned by the Relic Room.

Flag defenders' contempt for museums also reflected distrust of the broader educational enterprise in which white southern women had placed faith in the early twentieth century. The UDC had counted on schools and museums as well as youth groups like the Children of the Confederacy to perpetuate reverence for the cause and had closely monitored the process. Flag defenders moaned that "if the school system would tell what really happened during the war instead of pumping this garbage about slavery into kids' heads, this issue wouldn't even be brought up."[36] But they did not try to restore the earlier mechanisms of remembrance. Sporadic calls for a Confederate History Month comparable to Black History Month generated little interest. This set of priorities was pragmatic. Flag defenders' interpretation of the Civil War commanded little support among educators at any level. One of the public officials who took a strong stand against the flag was the South Carolina superintendent of education, the only woman to hold a position elected on a statewide basis. Beyond an awareness of the academic forces that closed the schoolhouse door to the Confederacy, flag defenders' claims to accurate historical understanding drew on an ideal of self-education divorced from the intergenerational institutions the UDC had supported. Letters to the editor in support of the flag, which often accused opponents of historical ignorance, indicated that the exemplary citizen did not learn historical truth in school but in the leisure time of the adult individual, through books and archives deliberately neglected by the dominant forces in society.[37]

Flag defenders' gender strategies abandoned Confederate veterans' patriarchal response to feminism. Veterans had tried to assert male authority and virility by sponsoring monuments to Confederate women and by making the selection of attractive young female sponsors a central part of Confederate reunions. Flag champions did not style themselves as husbands or fathers but only as sons who inherited Confederate identity without the power to propagate it further. Metaphorically located in the nuclear family throughout the Lost Cause era, Confederate commemoration was in the flag controversy rhetorically centered on the sterile homosocial realm of the army. Addresses often compared flag defenders to Confederate soldiers. McConnell urged supporters to "stand and fight at the dome." "This is our 'summer of '64,' " the state SCV commander told members at the peak of debate. The posture of combative masculinity proved crucial to the passage of the Heritage Act, which divided the coalition that called for removal of the flag from the dome. When the Black Legislative Caucus and the NAACP announced their opposition to the substitution of a Confederate flag display at the soldiers monument directly in front of the state house, Republicans seized the opportunity to frame the measure as defiant resistance to the boycott through which the civil rights organization had brought pressure to bear on the legislature. "I'm simply not going to be bullied anymore," declared House speaker David Wilkins as he exhorted party members to vote for the measure.[38] This pugnacity presented a more instinctual, less socially engaged model of manhood than the ideals that women or men had promoted in the Lost Cause era.

Religion was a second vital feature of the Lost Cause that was more typical of the millennial attack on the southern cross than its defense. The battle flag had been the foremost site for the sacralization of Confederate memory during the Civil War. In the years after Appomattox, white southerners developed a vast set of Confederate symbols, shrines, rituals, myths, and venerated heroes. This cultural formation not only served fundamental moral and spiritual purposes associated with religion but also intertwined with the strategies of particular religious institutions. Ministers ranked among the most influential promoters of the Lost Cause. Interpretation of Confederate experience played an important part in denominational development in the postwar South, including the perpetuation of regional divisions in white Protestant evangelical churches.[39]

Religion was similarly central to white southerners' late-twentieth-century opposition to the flag. The call by the annual conference of the United Methodist Church for removal of the southern cross from the dome helped to mark the transition from intermittent public discussion of the issue to full-scale debate. David Beasley's reopening of the question in November 1996 built on his broader effort to mobilize white evangelical Christian voters and expand the place of religion in public life. Beasley reported on his prayers, quoted the Bible, and urged his television audience to "show Judeo-Christian love that will bring the races closer together and teach our children that we can live together in mutual respect."[40] Though he failed to sway some key elements of his party, the governor correctly anticipated the response of organized religion. More than six hundred white and black ministers endorsed his appeal. Scores of letters supporting removal of the banner from the dome agreed that "the Bible instructs us on how to handle the flag issue." Beasley called the debate "the most spiritually uplifting experience in this state in my lifetime."[41]

The religious mobilization against the flag did not correspond exactly to the ecclesiastical underpinnings of the Lost Cause any more than women's role in the campaign reproduced pre-suffrage gender models. The sacralization of Confederate memory had centered on rituals and symbols. The sacralization of civil rights memory in the flag debate emphasized recognition of sin in social relations. Reconciliation of the races was now a key step in the reconciliation of humanity to God. But both religious uses of remembrance featured ministers in prominent roles that advanced denominational interests and built on a tradition of interaction between history and theology in the white southern imagination.

Despite that regional pattern, religion formed almost no part of the defense of the flag. Only sixteen ministers signed the clerical petition in support of the display on the dome. Even the few pro-flag ministers often concentrated on secular arguments.[42] A scattering of polemicists stood by the old-time argument that the southern cross was the Christian symbol of a Christian army that fought for a holy cause. State senator Arthur Ravenel tried the backhanded reasoning that "if God didn't want that flag up there, he'd of let lightning strike it," perhaps unaware that a lightning bolt had demolished the Confederate soldiers monument in 1882. The overwhelming bulk of pro-flag commentary on the subject denounced "pseudo-religious posturing." "The church should concern itself more with saving souls instead of creating new areas of division and controversy within the state," asserted a typical letter.[43] Flag defenders plainly included many devout Christians, a significant percentage of whom doubtless favored a vigorous religious influence in public life. Attorney general Charlie Condon was merely the most prominent and politically opportunistic flag champion to compare the allegedly anti-majoritarian protest against the Confederate standard with the allegedly anti-majoritarian protests that had restricted group prayer in public schools.[44] But the southern cross could not reverse secularization when flag defenders regarded state display of the emblem as strictly a secular matter. If women's desertion of Confederate commemoration ripped out the heart of the Lost Cause, the rupture with the churches destroyed its soul.

The white southern class order had been the backbone of the Lost Cause. Like the gender and religious patterns of Confederate commemoration, its class implications were varied and have invited different scholarly interpretations. Some studies have stressed planters' efforts to restore their social dominance; some studies have described the Lost Cause as the legitimation of an emerging industrial and commercial leadership; some studies have highlighted the attempts of urban women to form a bourgeoisie through the establishment of organizations like the UDC. Much of this work observes that the Lost Cause inscribed an ideal of deference in white southern culture comparable to the command structure of the army. The primary hero of Confederate remembrance, Robert E. Lee, personified the conflation of social and military rank, a metaphor reinforced in South Carolina by admiration for Wade Hampton. Alternative readings have seen moments in which prescribed hierarchy relaxed into an inter-class harmony. The Lost Cause offered no cultural support, however, for antagonism toward white southern elites. Soldiers in arms may have grumbled about "a rich man's war and a poor man's fight," but the Lost Cause had little room for such dangerous sentiments.[45]

The flag debate clearly associated class privilege with opposition to the display on the state house dome. Some assertions of this pattern were remarkably blunt, though no social or economic data illuminated the relative status of flag critics and defenders. A dean of Bob Jones University and member of the state Republican executive committee observed: "When you ask people what they think when they see the flag up there, they say, 'Beer-drinking ignorant rednecks.' Is that what flag supporters are trying to preserve?" Another political conservative reported that at flag rallies "you'll find belt buckles outnumber teeth three-to-one."[46] Conversely, the campaign against the flag drew on strong support from powerful business interests and placed corporate executives in symbolic positions of leadership. Presidents and board chairmen of the largest companies in the state were the plaintiffs in a lawsuit organized by the mayor of Columbia that sought to follow the strategy that had succeeded in Alabama by challenging the legislative authorization for the display at the state house.[47] Family history was another significant venue for hierarchy in the debate about heritage. Flag critics were much more likely than their adversaries to base authority to speak for South Carolina on an ancestry that boasted not only a record of Confederate service but also claims to inheritance of high social status. Letters and guest editorials calling for relocation of the flag came from contributors who described themselves as the descendants of Huguenots, slaveholders, nineteenth-century political leaders, and Confederate generals, field officers, and surgeons. No defender of the dome relied on similar credentials.[48]

Class structure in the attack on the flag often took the form of pride in a tradition of white gentility. An eighth-generation state resident argued "it is time to put an end to the notion that being a South Carolinian is equivalent to driving a pickup truck with the Confederate flag and rifles on the rear windshield. Let us show the rest of the country what the majority of us really represent: gentility, grace, and dignity." "No gentleman would expose a symbol that caused such pain and anger in his neighbors," agreed a schoolteacher. Many letters pointed to manners rather than morality as a reason to take down the flag. One contributor underscored the distinction by calling on readers to remember childhood lessons to "at least pause and pretend to care about other people." Flag critics enlisted the Lost Cause paragon of white southern gentility, Robert E. Lee, in support of their cause. "Can we not learn from genuine heroes like Lee . . . to put good manners ahead of this exclusive and peculiar pride?" asked one of many debate participants who maintained that Lee would have opposed a commemoration that upset community harmony. A guest editorial reported that "there is no doubt he would politely ask that his flag be lowered." Other arguments invoked the authority of Hampton for the same position.[49]

Flag supporters occasionally protested the conscription of Lee and "socially demeaning" newspaper descriptions of participants in flag rallies, but they largely ceded superior class standing to their opponents. The turn-of-the-millennium flag defense differed from the self-image put forth in 1972 by a South Carolinian with "reasonable wealth" and "a nice home" who beseeched "the black minority, the marijuana minority, the poor, the jobless, the food stamp people, the general do-gooders, to please leave the darned flag alone."[50] Later flag champions continued to identify African Americans as their main nemesis but now went on to rail against hostile elites, including business elites, media elites, religious elites, academic elites, and the political elites like U.S. Senator Strom Thurmond and seven other former governors who supported the call for removal of the flag from the dome. "This is a case of the people vs. the leaders," said McConnell. "I'm going to stick with the people." Hecklers at an anti-flag rally warned that protesters who burned the flag would go to "hillbilly hell."[51] Some flag defenders delighted in flouting the genteel decorum that their opponents sought to establish. Arthur Ravenel referred to the NAACP in a public address as the "National Association of Retarded People" and not only refused to apologize to the civil rights organization but protested that "I made a rhetorical slip, and they want to lynch me for it." Like McConnell's warnings of "cultural genocide," Ravenel's brash appropriation of the lynching image figured flag supporters as a highly vulnerable group despite their claims to speak for a majority of voters.[52]

Flag defenders' vision of the Confederate army bore little resemblance to the band of gentleman privates admired by Mary Chesnut or the marble tablet that the UDC installed in the state house in 1897 to honor the four socially prominent standard-bearers of Gregg's 1st South Carolina Regiment killed at Gaines Mill while carrying the regimental colors. The Confederate army consisted of "poor farmers defending their homes," reported Condon. McConnell told the same television audience that "96 percent of the people in South Carolina did not even own slaves," which almost doubled the actual percentage of white residents belonging to non-slaveholding families in 1860. No one who expressed enthusiasm in *The State* for display of the flag atop the dome acknowledged descent from a slaveholding family. To the contrary, many grandchildren and great-grandchildren of Confederate soldiers expressly denied any connection to the master class and denied that elites made up any significant portion of the army.[53] Flag supporters shared little of the Lost Cause fascination with the Confederate high command. When relocation became inevitable, they immediately rejected the suggestion that the equestrian statute of Wade Hampton would be a suitable place for the battle flag. That opposition turned primarily on the greater visibility of the soldiers monument in front of the state house but also reflected the conviction that the Confederate saga centered on private soldiers from humble social backgrounds rather than powerful generals. Such an approach did not point out that the ladies of the South Carolina Monument Association had asked their sculptor to base the depiction of a private soldier on a photograph of General Stephen Elliott, a socially privileged lowcountry planter.

Prominent flag partisan Clyde Wilson warned in January 1997 that if South Carolina removed the Confederate banner from the capitol dome the state would abandon the cultural distinctiveness necessary to produce literature, manners, "or anything else except consumption and triviality." The debate over the flag shows instead that the campaign to remove the southern cross from the dome relied on much the same traditions through which the Lost Cause had contributed to regional creativity in the late nineteenth and early twentieth centuries. The embrace of the civil rights movement transformed and re-energized these gender, religious, and class patterns in a configuration that Fred Hobson has described as "the white southern racial conversion narrative." Opposition to the Confederate battle flag expanded onto a public scale the defining regional story of self-perceived progress from bigotry to enlightenment pioneered by white southern autobiographers like Grace Lumpkin and James McBride Dabbs in the late 1940s and early 1950s. Attachment to the southern cross took its place among the racial sins for which ordinary white citizens atoned in conversions that turned on remembrance of the civil rights movement rather than participation in it. Eugene Downs's letter to *The State* neatly encapsulated the narrative. "When I was a boy, I had a Confederate flag on my bedroom wall," Downs recalled. "I was very proud of it. And as much as it shames me now to admit it, I—reflecting the sentiments of others—was happy when Dr. Martin Luther King was assassinated. I have since learned that Dr. King was a great man. But I know the source of reverence for the Confederacy. It is racism." The most substantial expression of this genre was the "King Day at the Dome" rally, initiated by a Confederate descendant, whose account of her youth focused on the standard childhood racial sins confessed by Hobson's authors, the perpetration of pranks on African Americans and use of the epithet "nigger." The plea for redemption of South Carolina that Jamie Renda traced to the television movie *Selma, Lord, Selma* was a cultural production as remarkable as the dedication ceremony for the South Carolina Soldiers Monument held at the same location in 1879.[54]

Wilson's fears notwithstanding, commitment to the battle flag was more closely associated with "consumption and triviality" than opposition to the banner. Separated from all foundations of the Lost Cause except for self-conscious whiteness, contemporary Confederate commemoration was also isolated from a non-elite white southern creative tradition that from the era of Huck Finn through the era of Elvis Presley had drawn on racial heterodoxy as well as religious and gender patterns antithetical to the pro-flag campaign. Beyond the display atop the dome, Confederate commemoration remained heavily dependent on the marketplace. The most noteworthy spillover of the pro-flag campaign was legislative authorization of the sale of state license plates emblazoned with the southern cross, an official identification of the citizen as consumer. In May 2000 the Republican legislature instituted a state holiday on Confederate Memorial Day in exchange for future recognition of King's birthday, but the public response was feeble. Only ten of the forty-six counties in the state adopted the holiday during the next five years. Few schools or businesses observed the occasion. Attendance at ceremonies in Columbia and Charleston attracted small crowds comparable in number if not in demographic composition to the gatherings of elderly women who had foreseen the end of the Memorial Day ritual at Magnolia Cemetery in the early 1950s. The SCV, the core of participation in the attempted renewal of Memorial Day, continued to honor the Confederacy more vigorously through the purchase of car decals, logo clothing, and other merchandise.[55]

Isolated from Lost Cause traditions, the southern cross fell from the capitol dome in the face of the shared memory that most deeply excited white and black South Carolinians at the end of the twentieth century, celebration of the successful civil rights movement of the 1950s and 1960s. But the decision to continue display of the banner on the state house grounds did not simply express a residual popular respect for the Confederacy reinforced by Republican political calculations and enthusiastic consumerism. The shift of the battle flag to the Confederate soldiers monument also drew support from the shared memory that Americans associated most darkly with social alienation: the specter of the Vietnam War.

The millennial defense of the battle flag abandoned the moral premises of the Lost Cause as well as its social foundations. Jefferson Davis outlined the original values of Confederate commemoration in 1878 when he told a Memorial Day gathering in Macon, Georgia, that "heroism derives its lustre from the justice of the cause in which it is displayed." The former president warned his fellow admirers of Confederate soldiers not to "impugn their faith by offering the penitential plea that they believed they were right." Davis insisted that the South *was* right to secede and fight the Civil War. The dozens of Confederate monuments dedicated throughout South Carolina from the 1860s into the 1920s demonstrated the consistency with which the Lost Cause followed these precepts. The inscriptions on three county monuments echoed Davis by quoting the same verse of poetry: "The world shall yet decide, / In truth's clear, far-off light, / That the soldiers who wore the gray and died / With Lee, were in the right." Other monuments used different formulations to assert the justice of the Confederate cause. Many of the monuments specifically identified concepts of "state sovereignty" and "constitutional liberty" on which Confederate claims to remembrance rested. The monument in Clarendon County, for example, proclaimed that Confederate soldiers took up arms "to defend cherished principles of civil rights."[56]

Davis's emphasis on soldiering as political action matched the dominant framework of American military commemoration in the century after the Civil War. Called upon to honor men who had fought and died in the moral quagmire of World War I, for example, Americans tended to depict doughboys as crusaders striving to save the world for democracy or to end all wars, in contrast with the European allies' stark remembrance of suffering and death. As recent scholarship has emphasized, many northerners in the decades after Appomattox wove a respect for Confederate gallantry into a powerful narrative of sectional reconciliation that obscured the ideological stakes of the war. But because many other northerners, particularly Union veterans, maintained that valiant treason was nonetheless reprehensible, the northern narrative of sectional reconciliation drew not merely on a valorization of all veterans but on an identification of the Confederacy with legitimate decentralizing and anti-modern elements in American politics and culture. White southerners similarly clung firmly to the political predicate for martial heroism. The Confederate monument in a federal forum like Arlington National Cemetery might assert only that rebel soldiers fought "in simple obedience to duty as they understood it." Outside of such problematic settings, however, white southerners usually remembered Davis's admonition. In an address delivered to the South Carolina Senate in 1957, for example, Senator John Long observed that "no cause is lost whose principle is right." The Senate unanimously adopted a resolution proposed by Long declaring that "this Flag symbolizes the divine cause of human freedom for which our forefathers fought" and that "the Battle Flag of the Confederacy inspires our dedication to the resurrection of truth with glorious and eternal vindication."[57]

Davis's approach to Confederate commemoration aligned squarely with American remembrance of the dominant military landmark in twentieth-century public memory, World War II. The example of Nazi Germany provided an undisputed illustration that soldierly commitment and competence could not bring honor to the adherents of an evil cause. That precedent featured prominently in the millennial debate over the battle flag. Many letters to *The State* argued that South Carolina should furl the standard of the proslavery republic as Germans had repudiated the banner of Aryan supremacy.[58]

Although quick to contest the identification of the Confederacy with slavery and reject the Nazi analogy, flag defenders did not demonstrate the same ideological zeal that pervaded John Long's 1957 speech or the inscriptions on Lost Cause monuments. To be sure, polemicists repeated and sometimes updated the well-worn claims that the Confederacy represented a historical alternative to the expansion of the federal government. The southern cross thus became the banner of tax relief. The Lincoln administration sought to "enslave all men under an all-powerful central government," wrote one flag defender, as "anyone earning a paycheck is reminded when he sees the federal withholding taxes."[59] But pro-flag politicians seldom focused on such claims even when they heartily shared a post-Reagan disdain for government and especially the federal government. Aware of the commitment to slavery expressed in such documents as the South Carolina ordinance of secession and the Confederate constitution, the chief defenders of the flag defined the Confederate cause not in terms of southern policy but in terms of the supposedly apolitical experiences of individual soldiers. McConnell rejected substitution of a Confederate national flag for the southern cross because "the soldiers' flag is the battle flag, not the governmental flag." The meaning of the southern cross had been defined "at Gettysburg, at Chancellorsville, at Secessionville, at Fort Sumter and in the *Hunley*," not at the South Carolina secession convention in Columbia and Charleston, the drafting of the Confederate constitution in Montgomery, or the meetings of the Confederate government in Richmond.[60]

The attempt to distinguish soldiers from the government that enlisted them drew directly on the Vietnam War commemoration that escalated shortly before the Confederate flag controversies. Movies, television programs, and books about Vietnam proliferated rapidly in the fifteen years after the fall of Saigon. Communities across the country built monuments to Vietnam veterans. The Vietnam Veterans Memorial dedicated on the National Mall in 1982 was the most widely seen and passionately discussed non-cinematic work of art unveiled in the United States during the last two decades of the twentieth century. As Patrick Hagopian has recently charted, in this negotiation of collective memory the faction that sought to depict American intervention in Vietnam as "a noble crusade" made little headway. Public remembrance instead focused overwhelmingly on the ordeal of the individual soldier, epitomized by the iconic list of names on the wall in Washington. Taking its cue from the emergence of post-traumatic stress disorder as a medical diagnosis for the continued suffering of Vietnam veterans, commemoration centered on a quest for "healing" of the nation as well as the individual survivors. The public wound in need of healing was, in most accounts, an estrangement between civilian society and Vietnam veterans who were angered by the extent to which elites had avoided combat service, the protests that American military intervention in Southeast Asia was immoral, the suspicions that substantial numbers of soldiers had participated in atrocities like the My Lai massacre, the eventual abandonment of the effort for which so many Americans had suffered and died, the failure to provide veterans with adequate medical treatment or social services, and the reports that soldiers returning from Vietnam often met with derision rather than gratitude from civilians. Commemoration acknowledged the integrity and sacrifices of American soldiers but mostly declined to justify the presidential and Congressional decisions to go to war.[61]

Vietnam remembrance provided a template for defense of the Confederate battle flag at the turn of the millennium. "I think you ought to be able to honor people who thought they were doing their duty without honoring the cause they fought for," observed southern intellectual John Shelton Reed. "That's the compromise we've reached on Vietnam. There are people who think that was an evil, imperialistic war, but I don't see them protesting the Vietnam

[handwritten margin note: war's causes vs support for troops]

Memorial."[62] Similar expressions of sentiment in South Carolina far outnumbered arguments that Confederate soldiers had nobly represented decentralized government or a pre-modern ideal of community. "I'm proud of the men who fought for their beliefs with blood, sweat and tears," declared a letter to *The State* that typically saw no need to discuss the content of the soldiers' beliefs. Some participants in the debate specifically indicated that display of the flag, if not necessarily on the capitol dome, reflected a "justifiable pride" in soldiers' commitment even though the collective cause that brought them to the battlefield was morally wrong. Suggestions that commemoration should express a public evaluation of that cause prompted warnings to "remember how the Vietnam veterans were treated." After the United States invaded Iraq in March 2003, supporters of the southern cross again pointed to state display of the Confederate banner as a promise that the American public would not decline to honor soldiers who fought in a highly controversial war.[63]

Defense of the battle flag also resembled the Vietnam model of remembrance more closely than the Lost Cause precedent in other important ways. Flag advocates' self-identification with a Confederate army comprised almost entirely of nonslaveholders built on the class tensions surrounding the Vietnam War and its most transformative institutional legacy, the all-volunteer military. Supporters of the Confederate flag "are the ones who have fought in every war this country has engaged in for the last 40 years," seethed a letter to the Charleston *Post and Courier* in 2003. "There is a very harmful battle being waged right inside the borders of this country. It is the open hostility that is being promoted against the average blue-collar working guy and it needs to be addressed, and stopped." The image of a working-class homage to a working-class army differed sharply from the Lost Cause claims of universal white southern mobilization in support of the war. Commemoration in the post-Vietnam War era also ended the Lost Cause boasts of Confederate martial prowess, which John Long illustrated in 1957 when he called the battle flag "the symbol of the only nation known to history whose soldiers wore themselves out whipping and chasing the armies of the enemy and thus lost a war by utter exhaustion and collapse." Later admirers of the battle flag occasionally alluded to the accomplishments of the Confederate army, but like Vietnam War memorials, flag advocates tended much more frequently to base tributes on soldiers' courage through suffering and death. Assertions of battlefield superiority had lost standing in American culture, and defeat no longer needed to be explained away. One disabled veteran wrote that South Caro-

linians should remember Confederates along with all other military personnel or else the state would signal that soldiers must "win at all costs, because if
you lose, your memory and sacrifices will be swept into the garbage." The point
to emphasize was simply that Confederate soldiers, like their Union counter-
parts, had served, suffered, and died. When legislative discussion turned to
alternatives to the dome display, McConnell directly appropriated the rhetoric
of the Vietnam Veterans Memorial by calling for a "healing pool" lined with
statues of Civil War soldiers reminiscent of the figures by Frederick Hart installed near Maya Lin's therapeutic wall in Washington.[64]

The shift of the southern cross to the state monument to the Confederate
dead linked the banner to the manifestation of the Lost Cause tradition most
frequently cited by flag defenders, William Henry Trescot's inscription on the
1879 memorial. The connection was in some ways appropriate. Writing in the
shadow of Reconstruction, Trescot had worried that a forthright statement of
the continued white southern commitment to Confederate principles would
risk renewed enforcement of the federal victory. Instead he emphasized the
loneliness of the soldiers who had suffered "IN THE DARK HOURS OF IMPRISON-
MENT, / IN THE HOPELESSNESS OF THE HOSPITAL, / IN THE SHORT, SHARP AGONY OF THE
FIELD" and who now lay "BURIED IN REMOTE AND ALIEN GRAVES." But these images
set up Trescot's fundamentally sentimental resolution that the soldiers "FOUND
SUPPORT AND CONSOLATION / IN THE BELIEF / THAT AT HOME THEY WOULD NOT BE FOR-
GOTTEN."[65] The installation of the battle flag in July 2000 contradicted this
nineteenth-century climax. Championed as the symbol of the army alone—
not the Confederate republic or its civilian society—the flag instead offered
the twenty-first-century conclusion that in their crisis the Confederate soldiers
stood by themselves. Isolated from the domestic institutions of the Old South,
they were images of alienation as complete as the pervasive depictions of American soldiers separated from all authority and support while on nightmarish
patrols in the jungles of Southeast Asia.

The reliance of the Confederate flag defense on post-Vietnam shifts in
American military commemoration was a good deal grimmer than the origins
of contemporary flag enthusiasm in consumer and recreational practices, but
both impulses shared a pronounced social atomism. The abandonment of
Jefferson Davis's insistence on the justice of the southern cause detached flag
defense from political responsibility at the same time that Confederate commemoration departed from its earlier grounding in gender, religious, and class
relations. Flag champions dissolved the Civil War, like the Vietnam War, into

as many private wars as there were soldiers, into whose inner experiences nobody else could enter with full understanding. Commemorative judgments were in this situation the sum of individual assessments rather than the expression of communal ideals. "How people view this flag is like how they view beauty. It is in the eye of the beholder," explained a flag supporter.[66] If Confederate memory had not thereby become "the essence of anarchy," as Lincoln called secession, defense of the flag had surely moved far from the Lost Cause tradition.

♞

"We did what General Lee should have done at Gettysburg. We flanked on them," crowed McConnell after the legislature moved the flag display to the soldiers monument over the objections of the Black Legislative Caucus and the NAACP.[67] The analogy was in some ways curiously inapt, for flag admirers were on the defensive during the millennial controversies, not on the attack as Lee had been in his invasion of the North. Flag supporters had followed tactics that Lee ably illustrated against many Union charges: sharp counterpunching, followed by a sidestep to more defensible ground. But McConnell's comparison was in another sense inevitable, for it came directly from the movie *Gettysburg* (1993), a commercially successful adaptation of Michael Shaara's novel *The Killer Angels* (1974) that sympathetically depicted Civil War soldiers on both sides of the battlefield. McConnell's choice of a historical precedent reflected not only the influence of Hollywood on even a passionate Civil War buff but also flag defenders' discontent with tradition. Lee represents in *Gettysburg* an inability to leave inherited models behind. He sees his current military situation through a reliance on the example of Napoleon and a faith that southern soldiers will most likely succeed at Gettysburg by fighting as their regional culture has taught them to fight, in a gallant charge. He therefore fails to follow the prescient advice of General James Longstreet, who recognizes that the Civil War has begun to anticipate that archetype of modernity, the Western Front, and that long-cherished southern ways are doomed.

McConnell similarly endorsed artifice and rejected tradition in an intramural disagreement among flag admirers that followed the relocation of the southern cross to the soldiers monument. Made of cotton, like many Confederate standards of the Civil War era, the new banner clung to its flagpole rather than catching the breeze. The colors also tended to run after rainstorms. Noting that "pink stars aren't seemly," McConnell ordered the substitution of a nylon flag. Visibility was more important than verisimilitude for the retailer of reproductions. When Courson insisted on representation of Dixie as the land of cotton, not the land of synthetic fibers, the flag supporters compromised on a silk-cotton blend.[68]

In these incidents McConnell epitomized a desertion of Lost Cause tradition, a desertion that had shaped enthusiasm for the flag ever since college fraternities introduced Old South balls during the Prohibition era. The cutting edge of that impulse remained consumerism and recreation, which continued to provide lively venues for flag debates in South Carolina after legislators left the issue behind. Rabid flag advocates who felt betrayed by the Heritage Act immediately found a new champion in barbecue entrepreneur Maurice Bessinger, who hoisted immense Confederate battle flags above his nine Piggie Parks in the Columbia area on the same day that the southern cross came down from the capitol. The substitution of the chain restaurant for the state house was consistent with a commemorative campaign that had already severed most of the Lost Cause institutional moorings. For the next several years, the Piggie Parks became the pre-eminent South Carolina forum for public expression of opinion about Confederate commemoration. Columbia diners unwilling to endorse Bessinger's views informally boycotted his restaurants despite the excellent reputation of his barbecue. Pro-flag diners patronized the enterprise.[69]

Like disappointed defenders of the dome, opponents to the continued display of the flag at the capitol expressed their dissent in recreational and consumer arenas. Intercollegiate sports became the main field of resistance to the Heritage Act, as the NAACP tourism boycott evolved into a policy adopted by the National Collegiate Athletic Association and leading regional athletic conferences not to hold basketball tournament games, football bowl games, or several other lucrative types of championship events in South Carolina while the state continued to display the flag on the capitol grounds. The world of college sports, in which the battle flag had won much of its popularity during the mid-twentieth century, became the leading forum for appeals to remove the banner from the pole near the soldiers monument. The most sustained public debate of the issue in the first decade of the new century followed a remark by the University of South Carolina football coach that the legislature should remove the flag from the capitol grounds.[70]

Institutions of government played a minor role in the continuing controversy after passage of the Heritage Act. Ministers occasionally conducted anti-flag vigils at the capitol as they had in the 1990s. An African American who called himself the Reverend E. X. Slave carried out a direct protest in April 2002 by propping an extension ladder against the flag pole and setting the flag ablaze while dressed in a black Santa Claus costume. But the legislature devoted little attention to the issue, though twenty-two of the twenty-six African Americans in the House of Representatives in 2000 had voted against the Heritage Act. This hesitancy reflected in part the difficulties encountered by the millennial campaign to move the flag, now compounded by the diminished availability of an attack based on remembrance of the civil rights movement and the increased availability of a defense based on popular support for soldiers regardless of the cause for which they fought. Some of the most determined opponents of the flag display, including several African Americans who voted for the Heritage Act in the Senate, evidently concluded that in its new position the flag would gradually become as ineffective in inspiring enthusiasm for Confederate principles as the soldiers monument had long ago become.[71]

Whether the flag disappeared altogether from the capitol grounds in another extraordinary act of repudiation or merely faded into public neglect, the shift of the debate from government to barbecue and sports underscored the displacement of traditional social institutions and modes of commemoration in contemporary promotion of Confederate memory. In arguing that rampant exploitation of the Confederate emblem could deepen reverence, flag admirers had to some degree anticipated the trajectory of the United States flag. Modest commercial appropriations of the stars and stripes gave way in the last third of the twentieth century to much bolder and more pervasive use of the American flag for a wide variety of purposes. The notion that wearing even the most informal leisure clothing emblazoned with a flag logo might express patriotism, as defined by the consumer, became a commonplace. The Museum of Modern Art eagerly added Jasper Johns's *Flag* to its permanent collection in 1973. But the overall pattern still differed significantly from the Confederate precedent. Traditional cultural practices reinforcing respect for the United States flag remained stringent in many ways, and a primal identification of the flag with violent death continued to be renewed. The terrorist attacks of September 11, 2001, prompted a marked reassertion of the quasi-religious veneration of the flag. The designer Ralph Lauren generated large revenues by selling casual apparel decorated with the stars and stripes, but he also helped to fund a thoroughly conventional shrine at the Smithsonian Museum of

American History for display of the preserved standard that had inspired Francis Scott Key to write "The Star-Spangled Banner" during the War of 1812.[72]

Much closer was the parallel between the Confederate battle flag and its fraternal twin, the state flag of South Carolina. Both banners were products of secession. The South Carolina legislature adopted the design proposed by fire-eater Robert Barnwell Rhett Jr. for the standard of the self-proclaimed sovereignty on January 28, 1861, a few days before the opening of the Montgomery convention at which Rhett's fellow South Carolina radical William Porcher Miles began his ultimately successful campaign for adoption of the St. Andrew's Cross as the ensign of proslavery Christianity.[73] An invocation of South Carolina memories dating back to the Revolutionary War, the white palmetto tree and crescent on a field of blue expressed from the outset the martial resonance that the southern cross added after Confederate commanders adopted it. Like the southern cross, the palmetto and crescent served as a banner for many South Carolina units in the Civil War, and into the 1890s it remained sufficiently associated with the sectional conflict for the legislature to consider a proposal to change the field to purple in recognition of the blood that Confederate soldiers had shed. Routine official use defined the banner for most of the twentieth century, beginning with a 1910 statute that provided for its display at government buildings. At the end of the century, however, the state flag became "downright trendy and definitely marketable." The palmetto and crescent appeared on an astonishing array of merchandise, including many items for upscale consumers. State residents frequently purchased banners to fly from their homes or boats. A journalist reported that the palmetto and crescent ranked with the lone star of Texas as the "most embraced" state emblem. Nowhere else in the United States did commercial appropriations of a flag comprise a larger part of what might plausibly be called a collective identity. That enthusiasm rarely touched on the Civil War origins of the state flag, and at least one retailer speculated that the controversy over the southern cross had spurred interest in a visually striking but less ideologically problematic banner. Surely more influential was the immense popularity of such corporate symbols as the Nike swoosh and the Apple apple.[74]

The transformation of the South Carolina flag from a separatist standard into a marketing phenomenon neatly counterpointed the removal of the Confederate battle flag from the capitol dome under pressure of a tourism boycott. In the business jargon of the day, the state had protected its brand. For South Carolina now was a brand more than it was "a soul" constituted by "a rich legacy of memories," as Ernest Renan famously defined the sort of nation that secessionists had hoped to establish and the Lost Cause had tried to perpetuate.[75] Tourism was the largest industry in South Carolina, and the dominant form of livelihood reflected an appetite for popular images that characterized the era as thoroughly as the production of staple crops had once fostered cultivation of the land. Confederate commemoration, long the most sacred part of the state legacy of memories, offered a preview of the transition from nineteenth-century romantic nationalism to a post-national pattern of allegiance. Reinvented by consumerism well before Dick and Mac McDonald built their first set of golden arches in 1953, the southern cross had eventually achieved a global circulation and retained considerable currency even after the millennial reassessment. The model of social relations defended by the proslavery republic had collapsed in the Civil War, but the model of social relations pioneered by the Confederate battle flag in the twentieth century was on the rise at the sesquicentennial anniversary of the war. Although the winds of history had not blown as Henry Timrod predicted in "Ethnogenesis," a chastened South Carolina strained to catch "the softened breeze" in the logo that fluttered atop the state house.

CHAPTER THREE

Celebrating Freedom

Juneteenth and the Emancipation Festival Tradition

quite a transition

Mitch Kachun

The convergence of the sesquicentennial of the American Civil War and the bicentennial of Abraham Lincoln's birth calls our collective attention to an important turning point in American history. Of all the marks left behind by these iconic touchstones, perhaps none has had the profound impact of emancipation. From the moment Lincoln's January 1, 1863, Emancipation Proclamation declared free all Confederate-held slaves, African Americans celebrated their liberation. They have been at it ever since. Yet today, if Americans have any knowledge at all about celebrations of the end of American slavery, their reference point is often Juneteenth. The term is a contraction for June 19th, the date in 1865 when Major General Gordon Granger landed his troops at Galveston, Texas, and announced that slavery in that former Confederate state was ended and that all African Americans were free. Black Texans have celebrated Juneteenth more or less continuously since 1865, and in 1980 the state of Texas designated Juneteenth an official state holiday.

Only Florida and Oklahoma joined Texas in officially recognizing Juneteenth prior to 2000, but the holiday has experienced a remarkable explosion of popularity since the start of the new century. With the addition of Mississippi in 2010, at least thirty-six states at this writing list Juneteenth as an official holiday, though most do not close government offices. In addition, hundreds of communities large and small across the United States now observe Juneteenth regardless of official governmental recognition, and several organizations are promoting the celebration, with one attempting to establish "Juneteenth National Freedom Day" as an official national holiday. These organizations often identify Juneteenth as "the oldest nationally celebrated commemoration of the ending of slavery in the United States" or "the oldest African American holiday."[1]

Such statements are open to debate. When blacks in Texas first began celebrating Juneteenth in the nineteenth century, their use of that date was an anomaly limited to Texas and parts of surrounding states. Occasional efforts to spread the tradition to other regions proved futile. In the 1880s, when a handful of transplanted Texans tried to instigate Juneteenth celebrations in northern Alabama and western Tennessee, they were gently ridiculed in the local press. Emancipation celebrations in that region were usually held on January 1, marking the date of Lincoln's 1863 Proclamation.[2] One virtually unique site of a short-lived transplantation was Covert, Michigan, a small town near the Lake Michigan shore where a number of local blacks had served in United States Colored Troop units in Texas and organized Juneteenth celebrations in Covert in the 1870s. After a few years, however, residents there reverted to their earlier tradition of celebrating emancipation on the First of August.[3]

Northern African Americans and many white abolitionists had celebrated on the First of August since the late 1830s, commemorating the date in 1834 when Great Britain abolished slavery in its West Indian colonies. West Indian emancipation was seen as a momentous step forward in the march of freedom, and a portent of the eventual abolition of slavery in the United States. After American slavery did end, African Americans used many different dates to commemorate the event; most of these—like Juneteenth—had local or regional significance. Blacks in the North and Midwest often continued to celebrate on the First of August. Many communities observed the January 1st date of Lincoln's 1863 Proclamation or the September 22nd date of his 1862 Preliminary Proclamation. African Americans in southern Virginia often celebrated April 9 as "Surrender Day," to mark General Robert E. Lee's surrender at Appomattox, following the logic that Lincoln's pronouncement had no real effect as long as Confederate armies were in the field. Richmond blacks celebrated April 3rd, the date in 1865 that United States troops took control of the former Confederate capital. Other examples abound, and sometimes the reasons for a particular date seem to have vanished from memory over the years. Often the stories from the South suggest that a particular date, like Juneteenth, related to the arrival of either Union troops or the news of emancipation.[4]

This proliferation of dates is one reason that late-nineteenth-century African American activists had difficulty joining together to lobby for one single date for an official national holiday commemorating the end of slavery, though some did try at different times. Black divisions aside, the postwar white sectional reconciliation and pervasive white racism presented even more enormous obstacles for any national Emancipation Day holiday movement.[5] Blacks continued their own local and regional observances into the twentieth century, though some communities did so more consistently and more enthusiastically than others. Aside from a brief flurry of national interest—and several large commemorations—surrounding the semi-centennial of emancipation between 1913 and 1915, African Americans' enthusiasm for commemorating emancipation waned significantly through most of the twentieth century.

Many black commentators at the time questioned the very basis for commemorating emancipation in the first place. A January 1913 editorial in the *AME Church Review* prescribed a new direction for blacks' relationship with emancipation and with their history. The editor argued that it was not appropriate, "either in jubilation or self-praise, to be counting the milestones of our progress or enumerating our material wealth or intellectual gains." Black Americans in 1913, he said, "had been wandering for these past forty years in the wilderness of political serfdom and drinking the bitter water . . . of Jim Crowism. Within the next fifty years there must come to the Negro a new emancipation . . . from social degradation, industrial and commercial exclusion, political inequality and all discrimination based on race and color." Ever conscious of the importance of posterity, he recognized that, "fifty years hence the Negroes of this generation will be reviewed by our children's children." Contemporary leaders, he contended, must "fully emancipate ourselves" to earn the respect of future generations.[6]

If the editorialist did not call for the complete abandonment of emancipation celebrations, these festivals of freedom were indeed dwindling. "By the 1920s," one historian of blacks in western Michigan has noted, "the . . . festive protest parade [on August 1] ceased to occur." In 1924 an editorial from the *Norfolk Journal and Guide* called attention to "a steady decline in attendance upon Emancipation Day observances." Street parades still attracted "a creditable crowd," numbering as much as several thousand people, but "speeches and recitations appropriate to the occasion" no longer held people's interest. His language echoed that of the *AME Church Review* editorial from a decade before. "[T]he Negro of the latter day," he claimed,

> is . . . not interested in celebrating emancipation from chattel slavery. In the first place any reference to American slavery fosters into his imagination a picture of the abhorrence of the times. In the next place he realizes that there is yet so much to be done to break the bonds of economic slavery, proscription of opportunity, injustice before the law and denial of citizenship rights, that his attention is focused more upon gaining a newer emancipation.[7]

A 1929 call to "End Emancipation Day Celebrations" from Gary, Indiana, made a similar point. Noting the numerous different dates celebrated every year, the writer suggested that "this lack of uniformity and agreement on a day to celebrate is merely one of the inanities of such a celebration." "Emancipation day celebrations have a habit of leaving us too well satisfied. We get drunk on words," glorifying the progress of the race when that progress was often difficult to see. He also implied that a new emancipation was needed to make the old one seem real. It was still sadly the case, he wrote, that "many Negroes who live in Mississippi and other places will never know that they are 'free' unless they accidentally drop around where one of the celebrations is in progress. . . . The sooner the Negro forgets that he was once a slave, the better. The sooner he quits celebrating the day when one white man took him away from another, the better." Not all who opposed celebrations, or called for more complex understandings of race history, were quite so ready to completely dissociate from the slave past, but most expressed some version of the idea that "we are emancipated but in many ways we are as yet not free." By 1930 even the space of the celebrations themselves was no longer as free as it once had been. In Warrenton, Georgia, blacks had planned to invite Benjamin J. Davis, radical leftist editor of the Atlanta *Independent* newspaper, to be orator of the day. Unhappy with that choice, local whites put pressure on the sheriff, who "felt it his duty to tell the 'niggers to call it off.'" The celebration did not take place.[8]

The lack of a single date to commemorate was only one of the obstacles to the creation of a national Emancipation Day holiday. Nonetheless, during the 1940s, one elderly former slave undertook a campaign that ultimately resulted in a presidential proclamation creating just such a holiday. The movement to create the National Freedom Day holiday on February 1 was the brainchild of Major Richard R. Wright Sr. Born a slave in Georgia in the 1850s, Wright earned a degree at Atlanta University, attained his military rank as a quartermaster during the Spanish American War, and served as a delegate to five Republican national conventions. He was a prominent journalist and educator in Georgia, then moved to Philadelphia in 1921 and founded a very successful bank. His political, personal, and professional prominence was such that he was said to have known personally all the presidents from Hayes through Truman. Still spry and active daily at his bank office at the age of 92, Wright was preparing to depart for Liberia, where he had been invited to attend the celebration of that nation's centennial, when he died on July 2, 1947.[9]

During the second half of this long and productive life, Major Wright engaged in numerous projects relating to the celebration and commemoration of African Americans' role in shaping United States history. As early as 1906 he became one of the earliest proponents of holding a semicentennial commemoration of the Emancipation Proclamation.[10] Wright's commemorative zeal seems to have waned temporarily while he established himself and his bank in Philadelphia during the 1920s. But during the 1930s, as he entered his eighties, Wright's interest in historical memory and commemoration rejuvenated. In 1933 he was appointed to a Pennsylvania commission overseeing the creation of a monument erected in Philadelphia's Fairmount Park in memory of African Americans who had died in the service of their country.[11] In the 1930s Wright also began revitalizing emancipation celebrations in his adoptive city of Philadelphia.[12] He then successfully lobbied the postmaster general's office to issue first a 1939 stamp commemorating Booker T. Washington, and a 1940 stamp commemorating the seventy-fifth anniversary of the Thirteenth Amendment abolishing slavery.[13]

On the heels of his Thirteenth Amendment stamp project, the eighty-five year old Wright began lobbying local, state, and national government officials for the creation of a national holiday commemorating the end of American slavery. In 1948, a year after Wright's death, President Harry S. Truman designated February 1 as National Freedom Day, commemorating the date in 1865 when Abraham Lincoln signed the congressional joint resolution that would become the Thirteenth Amendment. Major Wright's National Freedom Day campaign ultimately achieved the goal of creating a national holiday commemorating the end of American slavery, and it is still observed annually, on a small scale, in Philadelphia and a few other locales, largely through the efforts of the National Freedom Day Foundation and Major Wright's descendants. But even though in the 1940s Wright gained the support of numerous national politicians, and dozens of states held National Freedom Day observances (some of them involving thousands of participants), relatively few communities outside of Philadelphia now celebrate the event, and it remains largely unknown and unobserved.[14]

In terms of current celebrations of emancipation in the United States, then, we have two rival national events—Juneteenth and National Freedom Day—as well as numerous local and regional traditions. Many of the traditions from the nineteenth century have not been practiced for many years. But others have either persisted almost continuously over the years, or, in some cases, have been rediscovered and revived by local historians digging up long lost details of African American history in their communities.

Some of these traditions have even been sanctioned through state or local legislation and executive proclamations. One example is a date that has been maintained fairly consistently by African Americans in Washington, DC, since 1862. On April 16th of that year, Congress, which has jurisdiction over the federal district, passed a law that had been sought by abolitionists for decades, formally abolishing slavery in the nation's capital city. District abolition sparked enormous, and sometimes contentious, celebrations in Washington between the 1860s and 1890s, but the celebrations were toned down considerably in the early twentieth century. Nonetheless, the tradition lived on, and early in the twenty-first century the celebration of emancipation in the District of Columbia gained new energy and has been celebrated annually since 2002. In April 2007 Congress passed legislation formally establishing April 16th as a permanent public holiday in the District. Incidentally, that is why Americans' tax returns were due on April 17th that year—the 15th was a Sunday and the 16th was a federal holiday.[15]

An example of the revitalization of a largely forgotten tradition from Tennessee, where community activists in the Knoxville area be،--- --- countering references to African Americans in that region celebrating emancipation on the Eighth of August. Oral traditions contend that August 8th was the day to celebrate because that was when then president Andrew Johnson freed his own slaves at his Greeneville, Tennessee, home in 1865. Blacks in eastern Tennessee had been celebrating on that date at least since the early 1870s. Somewhat like Juneteenth, this tradition radiated into surrounding communities in Tennessee, Kentucky, and eventually into parts of Illinois, Arkansas, and Missouri. This tradition had not been forgotten, but it had been flying under the radar across this region for quite some time. A new enthusiasm for this celebration began to emerge around 2003, when activists involved in the Community Economic Development Network of East Tennessee (CEDNET) formed an African American Task Force to investigate the historical significance of the Eighth of August celebrations. They got research assistance from a local Legal Aid organization, researched the history, held rallies and conferences, and put together a movement to work for the establishment of an official state holiday.

At their first large conference, in 2006, they gathered together historians, community activists, and, most importantly, dozens of African Americans from Tennessee and Kentucky, many of them well on in years, who shared their recollections of Eighth of August celebrations from their youth. Longtime August 8th celebrants shared their personal experiences and listened with rapt attention to scholars describing the long and varied history of other celebratory traditions. Many conference participants were genuinely surprised, as well as empowered, as they learned that people like them all over the South had been celebrating freedom all along. In 2007 Tennessee Governor Phil Bredesen signed a bill establishing the Eighth of August as "Emancipation Day" in the state of Tennessee. Perhaps even more meaningful than that formal recognition, organizers of the Eighth of August movement were very much following in the footsteps of their nineteenth-century forebears, by consciously using Emancipation Day to generate community solidarity and to mobilize people toward the political and economic empowerment of the community. These were some of the most important functions the celebrations served in the nineteenth century, and it is intriguing to see this renewal of the long dormant potential and purpose of public commemorative traditions.[16]

Other communities have, in recent years, expressed great pride in their local Emancipation Day traditions, with some vying for the honor of claiming the oldest continuously observed tradition in the nation. As mentioned earlier, the Juneteenth advocates generally make this claim for the date of June 19. But the community of Thomaston, Georgia, where African Americans have reportedly been celebrating emancipation annually since 1866, claims the status of the community with the longest continuous tradition. They traditionally celebrated on May 29, probably because that is when enslaved blacks there learned of their freedom in 1865. There was actually a military skirmish around Thomaston in late April 1865, well after Lee's surrender at Appomattox, so it might have taken another month to settle the business of liberating the slaves there. Today the organizers plan the celebration for the fourth Saturday in May. Like the Tennessee activists, the celebrations are run by an organization, the Emancipation Committee of Upson County, whose mission is to maintain the celebration of black freedom for the purpose of "raising awareness" and working for "the betterment of local communities." The Committee does not limit itself to commemorating emancipation, but also works for community causes through the celebration of Martin Luther King Day in January.[17]

A challenger for the title of longest celebrating community comes from Gallia County, Ohio, near the West Virginia border, which claims to have celebrated emancipation continuously since 1863. There they celebrate on September 22, the date in 1862 when Lincoln issued the Preliminary Emancipation Proclamation, which essentially threatened to end slavery in areas that had not surrendered by January 1, 1863. As was often the case with small-town celebrations in the North—both the August First events before U.S. emancipation, and those that came on assorted dates afterward—the actual celebration site rotated among different communities from year to year—in this case, the towns of Bidwell, Gallipolis, Vinton, and Rio Grande. This strategy shifted the burdens of travel, the responsibilities for organization, and the pride of hosting among the different communities. This pattern served a very important function for African Americans who were scattered in relatively small numbers across a region. During the nineteenth century, in places like rural Ohio or upstate New York, blacks didn't have many opportunities to gather together in large numbers in one place, and emancipation celebrations brought people in from fifty to a hundred miles away. Congregating in one place allowed them to renew acquaintances, meet potential marriage part-

ners, socialize, form business relationships, mobilize regional politic
ism, and build solidarity through the very fact of their collective int
These regional functions were especially important in the nineteenth century,
before the days of mass media and instantaneous communication. At least
some of those functions are still a part of today's celebrations. Recent Gallipolis
celebrations feature lots of food, speakers, games, historical reenactors, and
music, but for one local historian, "The Emancipation" as they call it, is "most
of all, a place for people to come together to recall their common ancestry."[18]

These modern celebrations of emancipation, on different dates and in different regions, reflect many of the same themes that surrounded celebrations
in the nineteenth century. Historian William A. Blair has recently labeled "two
distinct modes" of celebrating emancipation: the "didactic" and the "festive."
Both in the nineteenth century and today, celebration organizers generally
have some serious purpose in mind, often combining lessons in African American history, celebration of black cultural heritage and solidarity, and the pursuit of more pointed political or civil rights objectives. At the same time, many
participants are far more interested in the parades, baseball games, food,
music, beauty pageants, and other festive elements of the celebrations. And at
times one even hears objections to the very idea of celebrating emancipation
as a distracting reminder of slavery's degradation that is not relevant to the
lives and aspirations of modern Americans.[19]

The recent celebrations noted above offer examples of all these facets of
Emancipation Days. And these particular celebrations and dates by no means
constitute an exhaustive list of current celebratory dates. Rather, these various
dates and locales suggest the range and variety of local, regional, and national
commemorations of the end of American slavery. So where does this leave us
in considering emancipation celebration traditions in the early twenty-first
century? We do have an official national holiday—the February 1 National
Freedom Day—marking the end of slavery. And we also have a campaign to
create another national emancipation holiday, the Juneteenth National Freedom Day.

The growing momentum behind the movement to establish a national
emancipation holiday based on the Juneteenth tradition suggests the degree
to which the February 1 National Freedom Day has failed to garner attention
and support, even among African Americans. As William Blair has aptly put
it, "There is more publicity for Punxsutawney Phil on Groundhog Day—the
day following February 1—than for the anniversary of the legislation that

memory as community

changed the meaning of freedom in this country." There may be some fundamental reasons behind the movement for considering Juneteenth over other
dates as most appropriate for an emancipation holiday. For one thing, it is quite
possible that the organizers of the Juneteenth movement may have been unaware of National Freedom Day's existence, or of the historical traditions
celebrating other dates. But even if they were aware, the date, June 19, 1865,
serves an important symbolic function. Juneteenth calls attention to the lengthy
delay between Lincoln's 1863 Proclamation and enslaved Texans being informed of their liberation. As journalist Askia Muhammad put it in 1997, "the
lesson of Juneteenth can teach us something . . . because, by definition, Juneteenth means 'justice delayed.' "[20] This lag poignantly symbolizes the continued delays in achieving full racial equality in America, thus making Juneteenth
more fully representative of the ongoing emancipation process than some other
dates. Recall some of the early twentieth-century critics of emancipation celebrations emphasizing the emptiness of celebrating emancipation, when what
was needed was a new emancipation from social, political, and economic
injustice.

Both the January 1 date of Lincoln's Proclamation and the official February
1 National Freedom Day call attention primarily to the actions of white politicians, rather than the actions of blacks or the complexities and contestation
emancipation engendered in American history and culture. I am reminded of
the hot water Hillary Clinton got herself into during the 2008 Democratic
presidential primary campaign for implying that America's civil rights gains
in the 1960s were due more to the efforts of President Lyndon Johnson than
those of Dr. King and the thousands of black and white activists who put their
bodies on the line.[21] While one can argue that the Juneteenth date in fact
commemorates the landing of the U.S. military in Texas, rather than the actions of African Americans, one can at least see Juneteenth as a celebration
that emerged organically from black Americans themselves. Still, one could
make the same claim for the celebrations in Thomaston, Gallia County, and
Washington, DC.

What also requires explanation are the reasons National Freedom Day did
not emerge as a significant site of political activism and protest during the post-
World War II African American freedom struggle. During the nineteenth century, emancipation celebrations were important vehicles for galvanizing the
antebellum abolitionist movement and, later, for calling attention to the continuing racial injustices of the postbellum era. African Americans' celebrations

had been declining anyway during the first half of the twentieth century, and one could argue that the 1940s and 1950s offered no compelling reason for celebrating a freedom that still had limited relevance for most African Americans' day-to-day experiences of racial violence, discrimination, and second-class citizenship. Given the activist roots of the tradition, an official national holiday commemorating the end of slavery seems to have offered a potentially useful venue for attracting media attention to the plight of black Americans during the 1950s and 1960s. But then again, Philadelphia's National Freedom Day celebrations were, for the most part, conventionally celebratory and patriotic, rather than militant, though Martin Luther King Jr. did appear as a keynote speaker at one observance during the late 1950s.[22]

Despite Juneteenth's seeming preeminence, even the current Juneteenth movement has its critics. The African American linguist and cultural critic John McWhorter recently published an essay entitled, "Why Juneteenth's Not My Thing," in which he explains why "I just can't wrap my head around celebrating the fact that someone else freed my ancestors." First of all, McWhorter argues, "It puts too much focus on a time when we were so starkly in the down position." "Juneteenth seems to be about what someone else did." While African Americans were surely active in the abolitionist movement, and there is considerable evidence of slave unrest, McWhorter argues, "we cannot say that blacks in America made their freedom happen. Freedom happened partly as the result of whites making other whites see the error of their ways." McWhorter also admits that "Juneteenth has also always left me a little cold because of what happened after slaves were freed." For McWhorter, "the real day of celebration" should be July 2nd. That was the date in 1964 when the Civil Rights Act was signed into law. He goes on to say that "I am always more interested in what we did rather than what somebody did to us," implying that the Civil Rights Act—Hillary Clinton's perspective notwithstanding—was the direct result of African Americans' assertive activism over the preceding decade, and not merely the doing of a beneficent white Congress and President.[23]

McWhorter echoes the complaints of emancipation celebration opponents from earlier periods, while also corroborating some of my own ideas about why certain other dates are not celebrated. There are a number of arguments one could raise with McWhorter's logic, not least of which is his assertion that blacks had nothing to do with their own emancipation in the 1860s. Historical scholarship over the past generation has expanded our understanding of

African Americans' participation and leadership in the abolition movement, not to mention the actions of fugitives, contrabands, and of course the roughly 200,000 black men who played active roles in bringing about emancipation during the Civil War.[24]

Those arguments aside, one must wonder why and how Juneteenth—a regional emancipation celebration along the lines of Tennessee's Eighth of August, Washington's April 16, and many others—came to acquire its national constituency. The local and regional examples discussed here illustrate not only African Americans' rich and varied commemorative traditions, but also Americans' renewed interest in celebrating emancipation at the start of the twenty-first century. Yet if one date were to be selected for a single national holiday, Juneteenth has to be considered the frontrunner. In fact, it has the only organized movement to that effect. The national holiday, along with a commemorative stamp drive, is being spearheaded by the Rev. Ronald V. Myers Sr., MD, who is listed as founder and chairman of the National Juneteenth Observance Foundation, as well as a Baptist minister, jazz musician, and medical doctor. The web site juneteenth.us claims the status of "the official site for the National Juneteenth Holiday Campaign."[25]

But Juneteenth's recent return to prominence did not begin with Rev. Myers or these websites; rather, it emerged from the convergence of a number of factors, beginning with post-emancipation patterns of African American migration. Historian Steven Hahn has described how African Americans facing oppression in the rural South used physical relocation as a form of political assertion. "In the process," Hahn argues, "they would establish new sites and terrains of struggle in the dawning age of Jim Crow." As early as the 1880s, an estimated twelve thousand black Texans had abandoned the state, hoping for better prospects in Kansas and other Great Plains states and territories. Between 1910 and 1920, as the great migration of blacks out of the South accelerated nationally, some 17,000 African Americans left Texas for other states from Massachusetts to California. Tens of thousands more fled the economic devastation of the Great Depression, and even more left to seek opportunity in the U.S. military or in northern and western defense industry jobs during the 1940s. As black Texans set down new roots in other regions, they carried along both their struggles for economic and social justice and their Juneteenth traditions.[26]

The tradition reached a new national audience in 1968 when, a mere two months after the assassination of Dr. Martin Luther King Jr., Ralph Abernathy and other leaders of King's planned Poor People's March on Washington used the imagery and the date of Juneteenth to revitalize their cause. The campaign encountered numerous problems and did not come close to meeting the organizers' expectations. In late June, as tired and disappointed participants prepared to dismantle the "Resurrection City" they had built on Washington's Mall, a group of Texans reportedly suggested that they hold a Juneteenth celebration to raise everyone's spirits. William H. Wiggins, a leading historian of Juneteenth, has suggested that many of the tens of thousands of participants took this historical celebration of black liberation back to their own communities. Subsequent years saw Juneteenth celebrations emerge in Brooklyn, Buffalo, Milwaukee, Chicago, Minneapolis, and many other new locales. In 1980 the state of Texas passed legislation designating Juneteenth as an official state holiday, generating attention and observances from mainstream institutions such as the Smithsonian Institution, the Chicago Historical Society, and the Henry Ford Museum and Greenfield Village near Detroit.[27]

It was not until the mid-1990s that a group began explicitly calling for a nationally sanctioned Juneteenth holiday. In that year the National Association of Juneteenth Lineage (NAJL) urged President Bill Clinton "to issue an executive order declaring the 19th of June as Black African-American Independence Day." NAJL founder and President Lula Briggs-Galloway made it clear that "the NAJL does not celebrate President Lincoln, the Emancipation Proclamation or the 13th Amendment. Most slave owners and overseers are still prospering [from] the inheritance that was acquired from hundreds of years of slave labor." One congressional supporter of the NAJL, Rep. Barbara Rose Collins of Michigan, also emphasized the time lag between Lincoln's Proclamation and Texas slaves finally learning they were free. "The political significance of Juneteenth," Collins argued, "is that Black people were forced to live under the horrid conditions of slavery longer than necessary because someone failed to communicate the truth." A national Juneteenth independence holiday would bring that truth annually to the nation's attention. The NAJL planned a major fundraising event for August 1996 and a national conference for January 1997 in order to pursue their goals. In 1997, Senate Majority Leader Trent Lott of Mississippi and Rep. J. C. Watts of Oklahoma joined Michigan's Collins in passing a congressional resolution commemorating Juneteenth as African Americans' Independence Day. A major actor in these efforts was Dr. Ronald Myers, who was at the time the national chairman of the NAJL.[28]

While the NAJL, based in Saginaw, Michigan, is still active and still headed by Briggs-Galloway, the organization no longer advocates a national holiday. According to an Internet statement, the NAJL primarily "supports, encourages, and perpetuates cultural awareness. We also endeavor to pursue community revitalization, health education, leadership and economic development." Briggs-Galloway emphasizes that "our mission is simply to create Juneteenth chapters in every city and state so that we will never forget our heritage."[29] By 1999, however, former NAJL national chairman Ronald Myers had formed another organization to take up the national holiday campaign. Myers's Mississippi-based National Juneteenth Christian Leadership Council (NJCLC) pushed President Clinton to "appoint a National Juneteenth Commission to advise him and educate the American people on how the annual observance of Junteenth can best accomplish . . . 'reconciliation in America.'" Again, Myers urged Clinton to support the creation of a Juneteenth national holiday, while simultaneously building grassroots organizations and mirroring efforts by the NAJL and other groups to foster community and regional Juneteenth celebrations across the nation.[30]

By 2000 Myers had formed the National Juneteenth Observance Foundation (NJOF) in his own state of Mississippi, while another organization, Juneteenth America Inc. was established in Ontario, California. The first years of the twenty-first century saw an explosion of Juneteenth celebrations across the country. Thousands of petitions calling for an executive order reached the White House. Hollywood celebrities and members of Congress joined the cause to push for a holiday. Yet while Bill Clinton had made positive statements regarding the tradition, neither he nor President George W. Bush formally established a Juneteenth holiday. When Bush—a longtime Texan—failed even to acknowledge the holiday during the June 2001 Washington celebration, Juneteenth activists were outraged. Myers claimed the President had "missed a historic opportunity to bring all Americans together to celebrate freedom and encourage racial reconciliation through the acknowledgement of the end of slavery in America."[31]

The twenty-first century ramping up of Juneteenth activism resulted in state after state issuing some sort of formal recognition of Juneteenth as a sanctioned day to celebrate the end of slavery in America. Even Tennessee and the District of Columbia, each of which maintains its own homegrown emancipation tradition, have passed resolutions recognizing Juneteenth. In 2008, then Senator Barack Obama of Illinois was one of seventeen senators to co-sponsor a bill which "recognizes the historical significance of Juneteenth Independence Day to the Nation; . . . supports the continued celebration of Juneteenth Independence Day to provide an opportunity for the people of the United States to learn more about the past and to understand better the experiences that have shaped the Nation; and . . . encourages the people of the United States to observe Juneteenth Independence Day with appropriate ceremonies, activities, and programs." While this measure fell short of calling for a national holiday, advocates believed that Obama's election to the presidency boded well for their long sought presidential proclamation officially establishing the Juneteenth Independence Day holiday.[32]

Juneteenth in 2009 offered even greater cause for celebration because of the unprecedented concurrent resolution passed in Congress on June 18, which "apologizes to African-Americans on behalf of the people of the United States, for the wrongs committed against them and their ancestors who suffered under slavery and Jim Crow laws." In a public statement acknowledging Juneteenth, President Obama noted that "the occasion carries even more significance" because of the congressional apology. Nonetheless, Obama has yet to indicate any intention to issue the desired proclamation. In fact, after Obama's rather tepid 2010 Juneteenth statement, Myers chastised the president for holding "receptions, celebrations and ceremonies" for "other significant ethnic days" like St. Patrick's Day, Cinco de Mayo, and Jewish Holocaust Remembrance Day, while failing to do likewise for Juneteenth. "Since becoming the first African American president of the United States," Myers wrote in his public response, "President Obama and his administration continues [sic] to distant [sic] themselves from our movement." Myers regarded "President Obama's *'impersonal'* Juneteenth statement [as] an *'insult'* to the *'Modern Juneteenth Movement'* and our ancestors."[33]

Despite the continuing wait for official national sanction, Juneteenth activists can only be encouraged by the increasing name recognition their movement has garnered over the past decade. One popular vehicle for spreading the word about Juneteenth has been through a dramatic expansion of books targeting juvenile audiences. Paralleling the state holidays, relatively few children's books about Juneteenth appeared prior to 2000. Valerie Wesley's thirty-two-page 1997 picture book, *Freedom's Gifts: A Juneteenth Story,* used a story surrounding one Texas family's 1943 Juneteenth celebration to introduce the holiday to elementary readers. Two years later, Muriel Miller Branch's *June-teenth: Freedom Day* provided a similar age group with a nonfiction introduction to the holiday, including both historical background and first-person accounts of contemporary celebrations. A handful of other twentieth-century titles were joined after 2000 by dozens of books directed at reading audiences from preschool through young adult. Charles A. Taylor's *Juneteenth: A Celebration of Freedom* (2002) is noteworthy for being actively promoted on several Juneteenth websites; Rev. Ronald Myers was photographed presenting a copy to then Alaska Governor Sarah Palin at the second annual Alaska Juneteenth Conference in Anchorage in 2009, where the governor spoke about "the significance of Juneteenth in Alaska." Other representative titles include June Preszler's *Juneteenth: Jubilee for Freedom* (2006), Angela Leeper's *Juneteenth: A Day to Celebrate Freedom from Slavery* (2004), and Carole Boston Weatherford's *Juneteenth Jamboree* (2007), which also appeared in a Spanish-language edition title *Celebremos Juneteenth*. It should be no surprise that in Laura Krauss Melmed's 2009 *Heart of Texas: A Lone Star ABC*, the letter J is for "Juneteenth Festival."[34]

The world of adult literature was not left out. In 1999, as the Juneteenth movement gained momentum, the late novelist and essayist Ralph Ellison's long-awaited second novel was published posthumously. Its title, selected by Ellison's literary executor John F. Callahan, was *Juneteenth*. Ellison, best known for his National Book Award–winning 1952 novel, *Invisible Man*, was born in Oklahoma in 1914 and apparently was quite familiar with the region's Juneteenth tradition. The novel's title was also the title of a short story Ellison published in 1965, a version of which serves as a pivotal chapter in the 1999 book. The story and chapter recount the events of a stirring Juneteenth celebration in a southern black church sometime in the early twentieth century. Ellison's powerful prose and trenchant insights into America's history and racial heritage bring into sharp relief the meaning of Juneteenth and the broader power of collective memory in shaping black Americans' sense of their own history and identity.[35]

The Juneteenth sermon at the heart of Ellison's novel, like many actual Emancipation Day speeches from the past, recounted the glories of African civilizations, the brutality of the slave trade, the dehumanizing centuries of slavery, the power of Providence and perseverance through which blacks survived the ordeal, the glorious day of deliverance, and finally that story's relevance for the present. Through call-and-response sermonizing between the prototypical black preacher, Rev. Alonzo "Daddy" Hickman, and his mixed-race child protégé Rev. Bliss, Ellison delivers a transformational jazz-influenced symphony of black identity to the five thousand people in attendance. Juneteenth, says Rev. Hickman, is the "God-given day" when African Americans "come together to praise god and celebrate our oneness, our slipping off of chains"; it presents the ideal opportunity to "[take] a look at the ledger" and "tell ourselves our story," especially for the benefit of "the younger generation" whose connection with the past must be maintained. As the middle-aged Bliss—now a race-baiting southern senator who has built his life passing for white—reconstructs the event in flashback, he thinks of it as "the celebration of a gaudy illusion." But when he asks Hickman whether blacks still celebrate Juneteenth, the senior preacher "looked at him with widened eyes" and assured him: "Why, I should say we do. . . . Because we haven't forgot what it means."[36]

African American celebrations of emancipation have always contained multiple layers of meaning. Most fundamental has been the idea of black collective identity and solidarity. The coming together of black Americans to celebrate a historical milestone signified struggle, perseverance, and strength in numbers. As in Daddy Hickman's sermon, blacks have used emancipation celebrations to tell their own story as a reminder of what has been overcome and what remains to be accomplished. Especially important is the responsibility to inform and empower the younger generation with knowledge of the race's history and heritage, and tools to confront present and future struggles. Emancipation celebrations continue to raise both money and awareness to strengthen local community organizations, while also providing a festive occasion on which to congregate in large numbers, cut loose, and have fun.

Those meanings remain very much a part of the current Juneteenth national holiday movement and other regional emancipation festivals. And as we mark the sesquicentennial anniversary of America's Civil War, the larger meaning of that national trauma must also engage our thoughts. With the possible exception of determining whether one nation or two would occupy the middle latitudes of North America, the Civil War's most powerful impact was liberation of nearly four million enslaved Americans and the abolition of slavery. It seems perfectly consistent with America's national ethos that we have a national observance celebrating the end of slavery. Until 1865 the nation was living a lie. Legally condemning and forbidding human bondage finally put the nation's laws in alignment with its founding principles. John McWhorter and others surely have a point that ending slavery did not end racial discrimination. And a holiday in itself, of course, cannot create social, political, and economic justice. But an official day of national observance can serve as a reminder that there are ideals toward which we still need to strive, in our communities, in our nation, and in the world.

As to the question of the most appropriate date for such a celebration, it is clear that regardless of the date selected, some people would be dissatisfied. Generations of celebrants in Georgia, Washington, Texas, Tennessee, Ohio, and elsewhere have maintained strong attachments to dates that are historically significant for them. Is it appropriate for a national holiday to displace such persistent and meaningful local traditions? Might it be better not to impose a national holiday, and instead encourage communities to develop their own traditions?

But if there were to be a single date for a national holiday, which would it be? Should Juneteenth trump all the other local and regional traditions? The Juneteenth movement, in a sense, is quite provincial, and seems to ignore or distort the complex and varied history of African American emancipation celebration traditions. The February 1 National Freedom Day has several things to recommend it. First, it is already on the national calendar. It also makes a nice kickoff for Black History Month.[37] Coincidentally, February 1 is also the date in 1960 when four African American college students sat down at a white-only Woolworth's lunch counter in Greensboro, North Carolina, ushering in a new and important tactical approach to the postwar black freedom struggle. That calendrical convergence would seem to satisfy some of the concerns of Juneteenth critics like John McWhorter. But given the practicalities of how Americans like to celebrate—with parades, cookouts, ball games, and the like—February 1 may well be the worst possible date for much of the nation. June 19th certainly has the advantage in terms of the weather.

Regardless of how the issue of the date is resolved, the bottom line is that Americans—black, white, and otherwise—can benefit from raising their awareness of the longstanding and ongoing struggle for the nation to live up to the ideals of liberty, equality, and justice that were articulated in its founding documents. In 2008 Barack Obama's historic run for the presidency brought race squarely into the national spotlight. Obama's victory has allowed some to suggest that the nation had entered a "post-racial" era; yet after Obama's inauguration, events continue to illustrate race's persistent significance.[38] In light of race's ongoing place in the nation's public discourse, it would seem that some sort of annual reminder of America's commitment to the ideals of equality and justice seems both appropriate and useful, as long as it does not imply a "mission accomplished," but rather reminds us of a goal toward which we must always continue to strive. *ha!*

CHAPTER FOUR

The Civil War and Contemporary Southern Literature

Robert H. Brinkmeyer Jr.

In his account of contemporary manifestations of the Civil War, Tony Horwitz notes that despite their general amnesia about the past, Americans remain obsessed with the war, its remembrance invoking issues, including those of race, sovereignty, and heritage, still central in the ongoing evolution of American identity and society.[1] The fascination with the Civil War is most intense in the South, where the war's presence still haunts the social and political landscape. In *Still Fighting the Civil War*, David Goldfield writes that the war "is like a ghost that has not yet made its peace and roams the land seeking solace, retribution, or vindication. It continues to exist, an event without temporal boundaries, an interminable struggle that has generated perhaps as many casualties since its alleged end in 1865 as during the four preceding years when armies clashed on the battlefield."[2] And Rick Bass, in his short story "Government Bears," goes so far as to suggest that the southern countryside itself remains deeply scarred by the war: "I don't care if it was a hundred and twenty years ago, these things still last and that is really no time at all, not for a real war like that one, with screaming and pain. The trees absorb the echoes of the screams and cries and humiliations. Their bark is only an inch thick between the time then and now: the distance between your thumb and forefinger. The sun beating down on us now saw the flames and troops' campfires then, and in fact the warmth from those flames is still not entirely through traveling to the sun. The fear of women: you can still feel it, in places where it was strong."[3]

Judging from the subject matter of most of their works, which rarely deal overtly with the Civil War and its legacy in Southern culture, most contemporary southern writers would probably downplay the observations by Horwitz, Goldfield, and Bass. Most recent southern literature focuses on the here and now, not only of the South but also of America and indeed of the world. Unlike the literature of previous generations of southern writers, most of which was set in the South and typically gelled around several key issues concerning the dynamics of southern identity and culture, literature of the postmodern South ranges far and wide, geographically and otherwise. A quick glance at recent work by southern writers finds fiction set in all regions of the United States and beyond—in Haiti, France, Vietnam, Congo, Japan, Mexico, and South America, among other places. In browsing new southern fiction on Amazon .com, one is almost as likely to find novels dealing with civil war on foreign soil as with the American Civil War. One might easily conclude that in contemporary southern literature the Civil War has become the forgotten war.

With a closer look, however, it is clear that the Civil War has in fact not only not disappeared from the southern literary landscape but that in some crucial ways it still profoundly shapes the southern imagination. A steady, if somewhat diminished, stream of historical fiction and verse about the war still flows, its imaginative histories coded and configured in ways that speak tellingly to contemporary issues. Many of these works imaginatively engage with America's more recent wars, particularly the Vietnam and Iraq Wars (and what the government has deemed the War on Terror), superimposing the newer war onto the older, each conflict bleeding into the other.[4] In literature depicting the contemporary South the legacy of the Civil War is often hard to find (characters in these works typically struggle with their own recent personal history rather than their region's more distant past), but significant works that invoke the ghostly presence of the Civil War still regularly appear. The discovery that occurs in these works, that a slaveholding and/or Confederate past remains deeply embedded in the present-day South, as in the example of Rick Bass's southern forests, suggests that for a number of southern writers the Civil War has an ongoing relevance to the region and nation.

Examining the ways that recent southern writers invoke and configure Civil War history and its significance to the contemporary South is precisely what I want to do in this broad survey.

I want to begin by noting the fundamental difference in focus between white and black southern writers when they turn back to what Allen Tate once termed the South's "immoderate past."[5] Broadly speaking, white and black writers stand as mirror images in their writing about the Civil War: white writers typically focus on the war itself, largely avoiding the problematic ethical issues of chattel slavery; black writers for the most part ignore the war, focusing instead on the complex dimensions of the slave experience.

For contemporary black writers, the slogan often bandied about by white southerners, "never forget," means something quite different from celebrating the Lost Cause and the Confederacy. What's never to be forgotten for southern blacks is the history of the slave experience, not only because that experience haunts the identities of all black Americans but because it also casts a long shadow on southern history and American history in general. The comment by one of the characters in Alice Randall's *The Wind Done Gone*, concerning her struggles to survive as a slave, also speaks to the contemporary black response to white remembrance of the war: "I fought my war before the war."[6] So, too do the words of a black basket maker, as reported by Tony Horwitz, to those whites who continue to celebrate the Confederacy: "They can remember that war all they want. So long's they remember they lost."[7]

From the African American perspective (and of course one doesn't have to be black to adopt this perspective), slavery, strikingly characterized by Edward P. Jones as "the world of human property,"[8] is the central issue of American history, still vitally relevant for understanding contemporary African American identity and contemporary America. Jones emphasizes the ethical problems and complexities of slavery in his byzantine novel, *The Known World* (2003), about a black slaveholding family and their slaves in pre-Civil War Virginia. For Jones, it's not merely the experience of slavery that still shapes African American identity: it's the experience of being enmeshed in what the system of slavery really was at its barest—the pursuit of money and power at the expense of others. Slavery for Jones, in other words, is raw capitalism, a soul-damaging system in which blacks have suffered both as the workers and the bosses—and still do.

More typical of the black depiction of the slave experience and its continued haunting of black identity are Octavia Butler's *Kindred* (1979) and Toni Morrison's *Beloved* (1992). Both use innovative narrative techniques to conjoin antebellum and contemporary history, the very structure of their novels embodying the authors' perspectives on the long reach of history. For Butler, in *Kindred*, that technique is time travel. *Kindred* involves a black woman, Dana, who in 1976 repeatedly travels back in time to the slaveholding South, where, as a slave, she must help keep safe a white boy who is destined to grow up and father a line of Dana's family. The stakes are high, because if Dana cannot save the boy, she, along with the rest of her family line, will never exist. That's one part of the story. The other part is how Dana uses what she learns from her enslavement to understand her life in 1976, particularly the dynamics of her interracial marriage. While Dana disturbingly discovers that she easily acclimatizes herself in the nineteenth century to her life as a slave, she finds herself growing progressively alienated as a contemporary woman, her bondage on the plantation, she comes to see, mirroring her bondage in marriage. On her final trip back from the nineteenth century, Dana finds herself caught in a wall and survives only by pulling her arm off (her version of battlefield surgery, inextricably linked to the carnage of the Civil War). Butler's point seems clear: Dana's physical disfigurement literalizes the ongoing damage wrought by slavery on black Americans. As *Kindred* shows, the slave past is not forgotten but is, through its psychological scarring, still being lived.

Toni Morrison's *Beloved* likewise foregrounds the trauma of slavery, collapsing conventional notions of time in a startling ghost story. The story focuses on a former slave, Sethe, who is haunted by the ghost of a daughter, Beloved, whom Sethe had killed years before to keep her from a life of slavery. Whether Beloved is a "real" ghost or merely Sethe's manifestation of her traumatic past is finally not all that important; whatever she is, Beloved calls forth the dark past of slavery that haunts both Sethe and the American landscape. That landscape, as Sethe tells her other daughter, Denver, is awash with what she calls "rememories." "Someday," she says, "you be walking down the road and you hear something or see something going on. So clear. And you think it's you thinking it up. A thought picture. But no. It's when you bump into a rememory that belongs to somebody else. Where I was before I came here, that place is real. It's never going away. Even if the whole farm—every tree and grass blade of it dies. The picture is still there and what's more, if you go there—you who never was there—if you go there and stand in the place where it was, it will happen again; it will be there for you, waiting for you. So, Denver, you can't never go there. Never. Because even though it's all over—over and done with—it's going to always be there waiting for you."[9] How best to navigate this world of black trauma is, finally, the subject of *Beloved*. In giving witness to this trauma, Morrison challenges African Americans to confront their own traumatic world of rememories, at the same that she challenges whites to pay more attention to the rememories of southern slavery rather than to those of southern battlefields.

Two other African American writers, Ishmael Reed and Alice Randall, present a different, but related, challenge—to rethink the notions of slavery and the Old South as they have appeared in the popular American imagination. In *Flight to Canada* (1976), Reed rewrites the traditional slave narrative, using an aesthetic he calls "Neo-HooDoo," mixing together events and characters from various time periods to create a narrative that, pushing into the bizarre and fantastic, challenges the reader to reconceptualize the "authorized" versions of the slave experience. For Reed, history is always under production, always being made and remade by various hands, always a gumbo of fact and belief. With *Flight to Canada*, Reed underscores that his history follows a recipe that uses traditional ingredients—events available to all, including those described in Harriet Beecher Stowe's *Uncle Tom's Cabin*—to make something entirely new. "Why do I call it the 'The Neo-HooDoo Aesthetic'?" he writes elsewhere. "*The proportions of ingredients depend upon the cook!*"[10] *Flight to Canada*'s reconstituted history emphasizes that whatever its rhetoric of equality, America has been and still is a nation grounded in racial oppression. Reed drives home this perspective in his harsh depiction of Lincoln as a master gamesman who espouses national unity and the abolition of slavery while envisioning a nation firmly established in whiteness.

If Reed remixes commonly configured conceptions of slavery and nation, including those deriving from *Uncle Tom's Cabin*, Alice Randall in *The Wind Done Gone* (2001) reconfigures another key document in those conceptions, Margaret Mitchell's *Gone with the Wind*. In writing what she said was "an antidote to a text that has hurt generations of African-Americans,"[11] Randall retells the events of *Gone with the Wind* through the diary of a mulatto slave, Cynara, who is half-sister to Scarlett (who is called "Other" in the novel). Cynara describes a plantation South in which slaves are neither loyal nor passive and in which white masters sexually prey on black women. As in *Beloved*, the focus ultimately is on the trauma of the slave experience and how to confront one's

memories. While enslaved, Cynara comes to see that survival demands forgetting, since the pains inflicted, particularly in the separation of families, are
too intense to bear if one cannot dispose of them. Invoking the image of battlefield surgery (as Butler does in *Kindred*), Cynara describes the self-mutilation
that allowed her to survive: "My shield against pain was my own seamless,
bloodless, battlefield surgery performed without ether or alcohol. . . . I amputated and cauterized with searing thoughts, thoughts so disgusting I not only
never thought them again, I recollect distinctly I have never thought again in
the particular place that spawned the particular thought. And with the bleeding parts cut away, the necessary places cauterized, I survived, as fortunate
soldiers do" (174–75). Once free and no longer living in fear, Cynara moves on
with her life, her diary itself suggesting that forgetting must give way to something else for her to reach fulfillment. That something else, Cynara comes to
see, is forgiveness, expressed in a beautiful line from her diary: "Forgetting is
to forgiving as glass is to a diamond" (31).

While black writers are fairly consistent in their perspective on the slave
experience—that its scars are still with us and the maiming should not, and
cannot, be forgotten—it's harder to find similar consistency of perspective when
we turn to Civil War fiction by contemporary white southern writers. Recent
representations of the war by white writers contrast sharply with those of southern writers from the early twentieth century, most of whose historical fiction
manifested the clash of civilizations, with the imminent destruction of the
South's cultured way of life by the aggressive North looming tragically from
the first page to the last.[12] No doubt somebody, somewhere, is still writing
fiction in this straightforward tragic mode, celebrating the glorious lost cause
of the Confederacy, but this is not the way most white southerners typically
now write about the war. For these later southerners, as I have already suggested, other more recent wars and crises have affected how they conceive
and represent the Civil War. Once the South's *Iliad*, the Civil War has become
its *Odyssey*—the story of individuals who, having been scarred and trauma-
tized by a devastating conflict, must now search for themselves, their homes,
and their families in a world no longer clearly mapped.

The *Iliad* approach to the Civil War now seems largely confined to the writers of alternative history. The appeal of alternative histories comes in their
challenge to imagine a newly configured present, evolved from a profoundly

different past. Alternative histories, thus, are almost always deeply grounded in and pointed commentaries on contemporary affairs. Harry Turtledove's *The Guns of the South* (1992), for instance, in which time-traveling Afrikaners deliver AK-47 assault rifles to the Confederate Army, allowing the Confederacy to defeat the North and establish its own nation, ends up suggesting that when compared to South African apartheid and Nazi persecution of the Jews, southern slavery (and by suggestion, its later practice of segregation) was relatively beneficent. Even more pointedly, at least in terms of current affairs, is Newt Gingrich and William Forstchen's trilogy Confederate victory at Gettysburg and the ensuing battlefield and political crises (the North still wins the war, though it takes Grant's and Lincoln's heroics to seal victory). Published between 2003 and 2005, Gingrich and Forstchen's trilogy (comprised of *Gettysburg* [2003], *Grant Comes East* [2004], and *Never Call Retreat* [2005]) is ultimately a right-wing call to arms in the wake of 9/11. In the introduction to the final volume, the authors single out Lee and Lincoln as the works' heroes, writing that they were "two men of courage who shared as well a deep sense of Christian compassion, and [who] at the end of the war set the example for a tragically divided nation that did indeed bind up its wounds and made us one again." "We are humbled by their example," Gingrich and Forstchen continue, equating America's war on terrorism with the heroism (and Christian faith) of Lee and Lincoln, "and we hope that in some small way our work pays tribute to them and pays tribute as well to all our veterans, right up to today and those who tonight stand the long watch for freedom on distant fronts. We believe firmly in that declaration by Abraham Lincoln that America is, indeed, 'the last best hope of mankind.' "[13]

Such sweeping conclusions, however, are rare in the Civil War novels by other less politically motivated contemporary white writers, who characteristically focus narrowly on individual sufferings of everyday folk lost in the chaos of the war, on both the battlefield and the home front. There's very little Confederate horn tooting in these works; in fact, there is often just the opposite, with partisan sympathies replaced by bitter disenchantment. And notably it is not only the common soldiers but often their leaders who decry the killing fields and their participation in the slaughter. In Charles Frazier's *Thirteen Moons* (2006), for instance, the Confederate colonel Will Cooper (based on the figure of William Holland Thomas, longtime defender of the Cherokees), reaches this simple conclusion when he hears of Lee's surrender: "Four fucking years down a hole."[14] Years later, assessing his wartime experiences,

Will says, "I now believe that leading the Indians into the War was the greatest of my failures, or at least prominent among many. The War was no business of the Indians. They ought to have stayed home. For that matter, we all should have stayed home" (359). "I have little to say about my role in the War," he comments elsewhere. "As a subject, the entire period bores me senseless. My tolerance for stupidity is at low ebb, especially when the stupidity's my own" (351).

Even more striking, in terms of portraying a southern military leader (and others) ultimately questioning the war and the Confederate cause, is Madison Smartt Bell's novel about Nathan Bedford Forrest, *Devil's Dream* (2009). Bell certainly gives Forrest his heroic due in depicting his tactical verve, but he also suggests that in both wartime and peacetime pursuits Forrest is driven by passions that he rarely can control. Forrest's daring on the battlefield, the novel suggests, has less to do with patriotism or valor than with wanton abandon, a point driven home when during a raid in Memphis Forrest sneaks away to have sex with one of his slaves, Catharine, the only woman who satisfies his lusts. When, years before, he had first pursued Catharine, Forrest had for a moment wondered why, with a wife and family, he was putting all at risk, why, when he knew better, he was allowing himself "to be no longer master of anyone, and least of all himself."[15] But that moment of awareness does not stop Forrest then with Catharine or later in any other passionate pursuit, because he is addicted to the thrill of putting everything on the line, of living recklessly as a slave-trader, gambler, lover, and general. Only rarely does Forrest question himself, as he does when he addresses his battle-weary men in the concluding words of the novel, "Hit's sometimes I wonder, what in the Hell are we doen this for?" (307). Forrest's non-partisan comment here returns us back to one of *Devil's Dream*'s epigraphs, George Garrett's observation that "Soldiers do not fight any better because of a good cause or a bad one" (n.p.).

If contemporary white writers typically downplay wartime partisanship, they also typically pay scant attention to the great issues that swept the South into war, including slavery. When these writers do deal with slavery, the issues foregrounded are almost always economic and political rather than moral; and when moral issues are raised, they characteristically become lost in the swirl of more pressing matters for the characters, such as surviving the war's carnage. *Devil's Dream* is an exception to this, because the myriad issues bound up in race and slavery—from the morality of owning a person to the complex economic system undergirding the slave enterprise, from the passionate entanglements of masters and slaves to the Haitian revolution and John Brown's actions at Harpers Ferry, from the physical abuse of slaves to the psychological degradation of masters, all this and much more—end up touching upon just about everything that happens in the novel. Indeed, the novel's title ends up referring as much to the slave system as to Forrest's exploits. Crucial to the novel's rendering of the devil's dream (and a clear look back to Faulkner's *Absalom, Absalom!*) is the subplot following the relationship between Forrest and his two sons serving with him during the war, one white (William), the other black (Matthew). Matthew repeatedly demands recognition from Forrest, asking him to own up to being his father. But as did Sutpen in his relationship with Bon, Forrest remains oblivious to his responsibilities as a father and to the depth of Matthew's feelings. At one point, Forrest goes so far as to dismiss Matthew's calls for "owning up to" with a discussion of property and ownership. "I'll tell ye one thing," he says. "All that ye really can own is yore actions. . . . Because that's the only thing that's truly in yore hand" (237).

Issues of slavery, of course, do circulate through other Civil War novels by white writers, but generally these issues are of secondary concern. Both Allan Gurganus's *Oldest Living Confederate Widow Tells All* (1989) and Kaye Gibbons's *On the Occasion of My Last Afternoon* (1998) illustrate a pattern of raising the moral issues of slavery only to turn away from them. Throughout much of Gurganus's sweeping novel the abusive slave system is ambitiously detailed, from the seizing of slaves in Africa to their placement on southern plantations, including a harrowing story of the Middle Passage told by the slave Castalia. And yet the cruelties of slavery—and how those cruelties have degraded not only blacks but also whites—are not the focus of the novel. Indeed, Castalia's story is all but lost in the white narrator Lucille's ceaseless stories about her attempts and those of her husband to triumph over their sufferings. This downplaying of the slave perspective can be seen in the transmission of Castalia's story; not only is the veracity of her tale widely questioned, but her voice is filtered through Lucille's. "Ain't a secret, child," Lucille says at one point: "storytelling is one kind of revenge. Maybe losers get better at it than the winning side. Honey, us losers have to be."[16] In *Oldest Living Confederate Widow Tells All* it's ultimately only the white losers—that is, the southern whites—who get their revenge through storytelling. Or put another way: "The deeds and sufferings of light make colors" (274), Lucille notes from Goethe, an observation that speaks both to her storytelling and Gurganus's novel, narratives primarily about the deeds and sufferings emanating from white—rather than black—light.

Gibbons's *On the Occasion of My Last Afternoon* is likewise narrated by an elderly white woman, Emma, looking back on her life, with the novel moving toward, but finally backing away from, fully delineating the human damage inflicted by the South's slave system. Most of Emma's story safely displaces the evils of slavery onto her cruel father (who is certainly deserving of scorn); what Emma does not reveal, until late in the novel, is that throughout the war she has kept her family slaves enslaved despite their manumission. While she easily rationalizes her actions ("With the War, if I had freed them, they would have been in great danger, such was the animosity against uncontracted Ne-groes"[17]), in her heart she knows better, as do the slaves who, when she finally admits what she has done, stare her down in disbelief. What might have been the central issues of the novel—the caustic effects of slavery on Emma, together with the ethical quandary of slave ownership—are finally all but forgotten by the end of her story. "I feel my life closing—memories, pain, anger, frustration all now reconciled," Emma says on her deathbed, adding, "I feel no sorrow, feel no regret, for I have done what [her husband] told me to do: *Face it all dry-eyed*" (273). We are back, as we were with Gurganus, to the issue of en-durance, to keeping the world intact amid the chaos of the home front, with deeds and sufferings making for a colorful, if not always clearly illu-minated, life.

Thus, despite its title, Gurganus's *Oldest Living Confederate Widow Tells All*, together with Gibbons's *On the Occasion of My Last Afternoon*, shows a white storyteller failing to "tell all," leaving out a good deal about the fraught in-terior lives of slave owners. While both narrators clearly sympathize with the sufferings of slaves and know well the injustices of the slave system, they ignore these issues, focusing instead on their own struggles to survive amid the chaos of the war and its aftermath. Driven by self-interest, both materi-ally and psychologically, they repress the guilt-laden knowledge that they are responsible for much human suffering and that they benefit from that suffering. Both authors suggest that what most haunts white slaveholders are their own sufferings from wartime terror and deprivation. Similar suf-ferings, by non-slaveholding whites, can also be seen in a number of other historical novels by contemporary southerners that focus on the wartime experiences of soldiers and common folk adrift on the battlefield and the home front.

In the most highly regarded Civil War novel of the past two decades, Charles Frazier's *Cold Mountain* (1997), the protagonist, Inman, turns his back on the war not because he fears for his life but because he fears that the war has already taken his life—that is, that the war has shattered his belief that one can live with meaning and purpose. At one point, Inman thinks about what he has lost: "His spirit, he feared, had been blasted away so that he had become lonesome and estranged from all around him as a sad old heron standing pointless watch in the mudflats of a pond lacking frogs. It seemed a poor swap to find that the only way one might keep from fearing death was to act numb and set apart as if dead already, with nothing much left of yourself but a hut of bones."[18] Inman concludes "that every man that died in that war on either side might just as soon have put a pistol against the soft of his palate and blown out the back of his head for all the meaning it had" (240). He will not go back to such a world, and instead, like many other Americans before and after him, he heads west, guided by the "the idea of another world, a better place" (17)—Cold Mountain.

If *Cold Mountain* depicts the crushing psychological trauma inflicted on those on the battlefield, resulting in a powerful reshaping of southern white identity, Josephine Humphrey's *Nowhere Else on Earth* (2000) portrays a transformative trauma suffered by those on the home front. "It was a lawless, savage time," says Rhoda Strong, the novel's protagonist, describing life in Robeson County, North Carolina, late in the war.[19] As Rhoda's comment suggests, it's not the Yankees who are terrorizing the southerners—it's the southerners who are terrorizing themselves. The social order is in such disarray, with the home guard preying upon rather than protecting people and with roving bands of deserters and scalawags putting their hands on anything they can, that for Rhoda the real war is in the local countryside—where there are no organized troops—rather than on the battlefield. "It was a sneaking, no-rules war now," she says. "Uniforms meant nothing, except if you saw a gray or butternut you guessed Union, and if blue then Reb, for the soldiers slinking around were ones who didn't want to be identified—beats and skulkers, malingerers, bummers, deserters, escapees" (128). "When there's no food and no law," says another character, "war don't stay where it's meant to stay but spreads wilder and meaner out on the fringes. Nobody in command, and everybody scrambling for advantage" (187). So bad have the times become that Rhoda wishes that a large battle would take place nearby, since she believes that it would bring clarity, with men in lines wearing identifiable uniforms and following recognizable flags.

Judging from the novels of probably the best contemporary writer of south-ern soldiers at war, Howard Bahr, Rhoda's vision of battlefield clarity is prob-ably a chimera. Bahr's Civil War novels, *The Black Flower* (1997), *The Year of Jubilo* (2000), and *The Judas Field* (2006), portray men whose loyalties rarely extend beyond the few buddies at their shoulders and whose concerns rarely reach beyond basic needs. There is generally not much difference between what we find in the fiction of the Vietnam War (in which Bahr served) and what we find in Bahr's Civil War novels: soldiers gripped by cynicism, fear, and despair; soldiers venting their frustrations on innocent civilians, through plunder and worse; soldiers immobilized by what we would now call post-traumatic stress. "In a battle," says the protagonist of *The Judas Field*, "everything is wrong, nothing you ever learned is true anymore. And when you come out—if you do—you can't remember. You have to put it back together by the rules you know, and you end up with a lie. That's the best you can do, and when you tell it, it'll still be a lie."[20] Bahr's great theme is precisely this: how one lives with the lie, not only as a soldier, but even more importantly, after the war, as a family member and citizen.

Living with lies is also the point of David Madden's *Sharpshooter* (1996), a novel that is mostly about a veteran's struggles to adapt after the war. As in Bahr's novels, there's little concern here for the larger issues of the war, as the protagonist blindly falls into soldiering, easily switching sides when circum-stances call for it. He enters the war because he is bored, tagging along with a group of men out to burn a Confederate-controlled bridge. "I went right on with them," he says of his decision, "—to burn the bridge, wherever that is, do something in the Civil War, whatever that is, do something for the Union, whatever that is, I didn't know, but I thought it was a good idea, it would be something *different*."[21] After the war, having served as a battle-hardened sharpshooter for the Confederates and then a guard at Andersonville, he re-mains fascinated by other veterans who talk endlessly about the war. For them, fighting in the war seems like something immensely important, whereas for him it was just something he did—or so he would like to think. It slowly be-comes clear that the protagonist's downplaying of the war involves his delib-erate attempt to forget deeds he has done as a soldier. He describes his struggle to hold his memories of the war in check: "You would think that once it was over, certainly a decade gone, the thing would be still, so a body could look at it, but after all these years, it is like a nest of cottonmouths" (56). Only much later, after he has admitted killing a prisoner who had trusted him, is the protagonist ready to put the war—and its terrifying hauntings—behind him and to move forward.

※

Contemporary white southern writers who do not write historical novels appear at first to have accomplished a similar moving forward, as the Civil War's significance in the cultural landscape of their works seems largely diminished. For earlier white writers coming to terms with the Civil War was a touchstone event in the formation of white southern identity, even if those feelings were tangled and confused (one thinks in this regard of Allen Tate's "Ode to the Confederate Dead," in which the poet stands outside a Confederate graveyard, trying to figure out how and why, as a southerner living in 1927, he should connect with the soldiers and the history they represent). That touchstone is harder to locate in contemporary works. The connection with the Old South/Civil War/Reconstruction past is often so mediated by postmodern skepticism that it seems more the stuff of immature escapism, a wish to withdraw from a fast-changing world into a fictionalized never land. And that's only when there is a connection. More often than not, characters in contemporary southern fiction rarely mention the Civil War, let alone look back to it for grounding and meaning. Typically, these characters know next to nothing about the Civil War, so that when constructing their identities as southerners and Americans, they are characteristically pondering the significance of—and the trauma inflicted by—more recent cultural crises, such as the Vietnam War or 9/11, crises that appear to have pushed the Civil War and its central issues if not into the dustbin of history then at least into the curio shop. And yet the Civil War does emerge as a usable past in a number of noteworthy works, its significance interrogated through the lenses of more recent events.

The Civil War's waning significance in the contemporary white southern imagination is perhaps best illustrated in the fiction of Bobbie Ann Mason, particularly her short story "Shiloh" (1982) and her novel *In Country* (1985). "Shiloh" is about a young couple whose marriage is coming undone, with Leroy's and Norma Jean's lives heading in different directions: Leroy is a truck driver who is disabled and living at home and learning needlepoint; Norma Jean, besides working her regular job, is going to night school, learning to play rock and roll, and taking a body-building class. Norma Jean's mother, a member of the United Daughters of the Confederacy, suggests the couple visit Shiloh; it is

where she went on her honeymoon and for her it is hallowed ground. Visiting
Shiloh, Mabel believes, will re-consecrate Leroy and Norma Jean's marriage in
the church of southern history. (I'm reminded here of a comment from another
United Daughter of the Confederacy, as reported by Tony Horwitz in *Confederates in the Attic*, on her marriage: "We were raised Methodists. But we converted
to the Confederacy. There wasn't time for both" [33].) But Leroy and Norma
Jean, when they visit Shiloh, feel no connection to the battlefield and its history. Norma Jean drives aimlessly about, lost in her private thoughts; Leroy
cannot envision the landscape as a battlefield. "It is not what he expected," the
narrator reports him thinking. "He thought it would look like a golf course."[22]
A bit later, trying to imagine the battle itself, he realizes that he can "only think
of that war as a board game with plastic soldiers" (15). Shiloh's emptied history
ends up mirroring Leroy and Norma Jean's emptied marriage.

Mason's *In Country* also suggests the seeming irrelevance of Civil War history to many contemporary white southerners. Here a young woman, Saman-
tha (or Sam, as she goes by), has graduated from high school and is trying to
plan a direction for her life. Because the Vietnam War has touched her so
deeply (her father was killed in the war and her uncle, with whom she lives,
came back from the war psychologically scarred), she comes to believe that
understanding the war is the means for her to understand herself and, more
generally, the role of women in a male-dominated society. As she seeks this
understanding, by studying the history of the war and reading her father's
diary, talking with her uncle and other Vietnam veterans, together with her
mother and grandparents, Sam's views harden and darken; she comes to see
herself and other young women as facing their own version of Vietnam, beset
by men and threatened with the penetrating wound of unwanted pregnancy.
She begins withdrawing into cynicism, her own version of post-traumatic
stress. It is only when Sam visits the Vietnam War memorial in Washington,
DC (rather than a Confederate graveyard), that she achieves a more generous
and forgiving vision that allows her to re-integrate herself into her community of family and loved ones, most of whom she had earlier spurned. The Civil
War is mentioned only once in the novel, in a comment on the backwardness
of the town in which Sam lives.

Both "Shiloh" and *In Country* suggest that the Civil War has little relevance
for understanding the problems and concerns of modern-day white southerners, particularly those coming of age. Other writers, such as Barry Hannah,
invoke Civil War history more overtly to make a similar point, underscoring

the fictionality of southern history and legend, often through wicked parody. In Hannah's novel *Ray*, for instance, the title character, a doctor from Birmingham, repeatedly thinks back to the past, fluctuating between his memories as a fighter pilot in Vietnam and his imagined exploits as an officer in Jeb Stuart's cavalry. It is a wild ride. "Oh, help me!" he says at one point. "I am losing myself in two centuries and two wars."[23] Ray turns to the past because, as he says, he is looking for his "best mind" (5), by which he means the martial ideals by which he would like to live but which have no place in his humdrum present. As does Hannah, Ray knows these ideals are largely cultural myths rather than universal truths; and so when he invokes Civil War glory, he simultaneously celebrates the ideal and reveals its fictionality (underscored because none of Ray's reported Civil War exploits ever happened). An example of this doubled dynamic comes in Ray's brief description of one of his cavalry charges: "Then sabers up and we knock the fuck out of everybody. With the cherished dream of Christ in our hearts. Basically, the message is: Leave me the hell alone or give me a beer" (69–70). Ray here and elsewhere is both southern hero and Bubba, a madcap time traveler who repeatedly connects with the past and then happily explodes that connection, as gleeful as a little boy setting off fireworks. Hannah's fiction is nothing if not pyrotechnic.

Central to Hannah's fiction is the recognition of the danger looming in hero worship and the unthinking celebration of southern idealism. This point is also made in M. A. Harper's *For the Love of Robert E. Lee* (1992) and Amanda C. Gable's *The Confederate General Rides North* (2009), two novels that in their straightforward narratives are quite different from Hannah's mind-bending work. At first glance the two novels actually appear to endorse the type of uncritical hero worship Hannah warns against, with both depicting two young southern women who turn to heroes of the Civil War to help guide them through their turbulent lives (and in this they also initially appear as partisan rewritings of Mason's *In Country*). But both novels complicate the invocation of the Civil War past, suggesting that for its legendary heroes to be useful models of conduct, their lives (rather than their legends) must be understood in all their complexity and contextualized in the entire scope of the nation's difficult history rather than merely in that of the Confederate nation.

As the title of Harper's novel suggests, studying the life of Robert E. Lee eventually brings the novel's protagonist, Garnet, to fall head over heels in love with her vision of him (she equates her feelings to her friends' infatuation with rock stars). But it is not Lee as the "Marble Model" (as he was known at West Point), the military leader faultless in honor and dignity, that attracts Garnet, but the man disguised by and standing behind the myth: the sad and lonely Robert E. Lee, the man who was locked in an unhappy marriage and felt unworthy of love, the Robert E. Lee who, often wishing to do otherwise, denied himself personally to give himself professionally to causes he sometimes questioned, including that of the Confederacy. It is her empathic connection with Lee's disappointments in love and fulfillment—rather than with his military greatness—that provides Garnet with the means to work through her feelings of unworthiness and her conflicted loyalties as a southerner. In the end, as does Sam in *In Country*, Garnet visits Washington, DC, but unlike for Sam, it is the Lee home that helps her achieve the vision that guides her back to her place within her family and her community. She returns to the southern fold, however, not as an unthinking backward-looking patriot but as an enlightened modern woman, aware of the good and the bad of her southern heritage, ready to embrace that heritage in order to revitalize it with a more humane and caring vision.

It is significant that *For the Love of Robert E. Lee* takes place in the early 1960s, beginning on the day of Kennedy's assassination and closing in 1966, one year after American combat troops were deployed to Vietnam and two years after the passage of the Civil Rights Act of 1964. These were days of cultural ferment and debate, particularly in the South; and amid this cultural turmoil, the Civil War centenary was also being celebrated. Many white southerners during this period, as does Garnet in the novel, had one eye on the past and the other on the present and beyond to the future.

Gable's *The Confederate General Rides North* also takes place in the 1960s, specifically 1968, a year of extreme social and political turmoil and of the assassinations of Martin Luther King Jr. and Robert Kennedy, which serve as the novel's backdrop. The novel follows the growth in strength and character of its eleven-year-old protagonist, Katherine, as she reluctantly accompanies her mother as she flees her marriage. Beginning in Georgia, the two drive north, toward Maine and a new beginning. Along the way, Katherine convinces her mother to stop off at various battlefields (largely under the influence of one of her aunts, Katherine has become engrossed with all things Civil War), with the two ending up in Gettysburg for a fateful few days. Katherine copes with her mother's instability and her own confusions by imagining herself as a Confederate general facing a myriad of strategic problems. Through dealing with these problems, Katherine matures, drawing from the examples of the generals on which she models herself and from the people she meets who help her put the Civil War into a larger context of the nation's history ("the lost cause that needed to be lost"[24]), including the recent unrest resulting from the Vietnam War and the assassinations of King and Kennedy. Just as importantly, she comes to see her mother's flight (which has carried her into deep depression and attempted suicide) as a lost cause that she herself must now bring to a close, for the sake of all her loved ones. "I am honorable and brave, and I am in retreat; the battle is over," she declares as she takes charge, drawing inspiration from the defeated at Gettysburg. "It is time to gather the wounded and get them to safety" (270).

Could *For the Love of Robert E. Lee* and *The Confederate General Rides North* have just as appropriately been set in the contemporary South, when Harper and Gable wrote their novels? Perhaps, but I don't think they would have rung true. Unlike during the 1960s, with the centenary looming large, most contemporary southern youth do not find the Civil War so compelling and relevant. Both Harper's and Gable's novels suggest this very point, as both intimate that while Garnet's and Katherine's Civil War fantasies are crucial in their growth into young adults, their fascination with the war can carry them forward only so far, that at some point they will have to set aside their Civil War imaginings in order to face the complex pressures of adulthood and citizenship. In this regard, both novels look forward (though written later) to the fictional world of Bobbie Ann Mason, where only the elderly and collectors seem to care about the Civil War, with more recent wars and crises dominating the cultural landscape and the lives of the young.

But *For the Love of Robert E. Lee* and *The Confederate General Rides North* also complicate the fictional world of Mason by suggesting that Civil War history, when viewed with the right eyes, helps us understand our own identities and those of the nation, uncovering the long road of history leading to more recent events, including the Vietnam War. The keys are vision and context, bringing a critical consciousness to interrogate the interplay and interconnections of the past and present. Ron Rash's novel *The World Made Straight* (2006) and Judy Budnitz's story "The Kindest Cut" (2005) suggest the significance of such a vision, with both contextualizing traumatic events from the Civil War with equally traumatic events from European history. Understanding one history, these works tell us, demands understanding the other, not separately but together.

Rash's *The World Made Straight* centers on the struggles of two men, Leonard and Travis, to understand the significance to their friendship and more generally to their lives of a Civil War massacre in which their ancestors participated, one family with the perpetrators, the other with the victims. In pondering the massacre (now known as the Shelton Laurel Massacre, in which Confederate soldiers killed a group of Union sympathizers in the North Carolina mountains), both men focus less on the political issues that divided the two sides than on the forces at work—social and psychological—that compelled soldiers to slaughter civilians, some of whom they probably knew as neighbors. To comprehend his ancestor's participation in the massacre, Leonard turns to Simone Weil's observations on war and violence in her famous essay, "The *Iliad* or the Poem of Force." Weil's observations on the dehumanizing power of war circulate freely throughout the novel, and at one point Leonard reads to Travis a central passage from her essay: "Force is as pitiless to the man who possesses it, or thinks he does, as it is to its victims; the second it crushes, the first it intoxicates. Those who use it and those who endure it are turned to stone . . . a soul which has entered the province of force will not escape this except by a miracle."[25] Written early in World War II, Weil's essay is less about Homer's poem than it is about Hitler's threat to Europe and the destructive power of war; and similarly Rash's novel about the Shelton Laurel Massacre is as much about how the onslaught of World War II (together with the events leading up to it, particularly the rise of the totalitarian state and its mass purging of citizens), help us to understand the violent events shaping Leonard's and Travis's destinies. "You got any books about what Hitler and Stalin done?" Travis asks Leonard (94), immediately following one of their discussions of the local massacre, his question all but announcing the novel's sobering conflation of the killing fields of the Civil War with both those of modern Europe and those of the drug wars in which Travis and Leonard are currently enmeshed.

A similar conflation of violent histories occurs in Judy Budnitz's "The Kindest Cut" (2005), a story that follows a present-day man reading the journal of his ancestor, a Jewish immigrant and battlefield surgeon for the Union army. The journal depicts the surgeon's descent into madness, his job of dismembering wounded soldiers eventually pushing him to believe his work is not to save the wounded but to save their limbs, which he imagines not only as still living but as "innocent bystanders, abused beasts of burden,"[26] victimized by their cruel, irresponsible bodies. He begins tending to a crop of severed arms that he has planted upright in a field. Like *The World Made Straight*, Budnitz's story depicts the Civil War in the context of massacre, looking both backward to European pogroms (the surgeon, we learn from his diary, survived a pogrom that took his family) and forward to the Holocaust. In the story's final scene, apparently imagined by the narrator as he himself slides into madness, the field of arms is now fenced with barbed wire, with hands furiously waving, perhaps for recognition, perhaps for help, perhaps for vengeance. The surgeon, caught among the arms, sinks into the earth, his body breaking apart and disappearing into the soil. As does Rash's novel, Budnitz's story suggests that the unchecked power of force destroys both its victims and its perpetrators. In its contextualizing the Civil War within the violent history of anti-Semitism in Europe, the story underscores humanity's startling capacity for cruelty, "carnage and devastation so great," in words from the journal regarding the pogrom from which the surgeon had escaped, "that afterward witnesses swore that even the farm animals wept to see what man had done to man" (237).

꽃

A remarkable meditation on the Civil War, Natasha Trethewey's *Native Guard* (2006) is a collection of poems that in some ways represents a stitching together of all the responses to the war I have discussed here by contemporary southern writers, connecting the war to slavery, battlefield and home front suffering, regional and national history, and personal identity in the contemporary South. Crucial to both the collection's structure and meaning is the title poem, "Native Guard," which appears almost exactly mid-way in the text. The poem's speaker is a member of the 2nd Louisiana Native Guard Volunteers, a black regiment that fought with the Union Army on the Gulf Coast (after initially mustering in support of the Confederacy, the militia reformed after the fall of New Orleans to support Union forces). A member of a military unit betwixt and between, fighting against the Confederacy but suffering from unalloyed racism from many in the Union army, the speaker keeps a journal on pages of a plantation diary he has recovered, his script crosshatched over the original writer's script, "On every page, / his story intersecting with my own."[27] The image of the two diaries, the black writer's written over the white's, exemplifies the strategy of the entire collection.[28] With *Native Guard*, Trethewey writes her own story—and the stories of other black southerners—

over and against the old, monolithic stories of white southern culture, creating, in words from another poem in the collection, a "tangle of / understory—a dialectic of dark / and light" (45); and it is with this dialectic that Trethewey works to recenter the truisms of southern traditionalism—family, place, and history, including that of the Civil War.

"What matters is context," Trethewey writes in "What the Body Can Say," and this is perhaps the key point in the collection: that the landmarks, truisms, and history of the South mean one thing to whites, another to blacks; and that the two perspectives, while working against each other, can be brought together in dynamic play. In "Pilgrimage," Trethewey describes white tourists marveling at the fine old homes in Vicksburg, reliving their version of the Old South and the Civil War, while for her these same homes call forth a dream in which "the ghost of history lies down beside me, / rolls over, pins me beneath a heavy arm" (20). Both here and elsewhere in the collection, Trethewey struggles to lift up that heavy arm of history—the monumental white history of the South—to free other histories to be told and thus not forgotten.

Trethewey's collection thus simultaneously affirms an observation by Robert Penn Warren that "the Civil War is, for the American imagination, the great single event of our history,"[29] while writing over it, recasting it among a number of other stories that complicate and enrich our understanding of the Civil War and its relevance to present and future America.[30] In this redrafting, *Native Guard* raises a warning flag against the diminishment of the Civil War in both the contemporary South and the southern literary imagination. That both black and white southerners, in the face of more recent cultural crises, now often downplay the significance of the Civil War is both understandable and most often entirely appropriate. And yet as Trethewey's collection suggests, deciding on the right path forward often means knowing the origins of the path we are on. The epigraph of *Native Guard*'s title poem, words from Frederick Douglass, points to the importance of never forgetting the path that leads back to the Civil War: "If this war is to be forgotten, I ask in the name of all things sacred what shall men remember?" (25). A timely question, Trethewey suggests, in Douglass's time and now, and a question that *Native Guard* challenges us to answer.

CHAPTER FIVE

Lincoln and the Civil War in Twenty-First-Century Photography

Elizabeth Young

The histories of the Civil War and photography have long been intertwined. Invented in 1839, photography was transformed as a mode of documentary representation by the Civil War. Photographs of battlefield sites by Mathew Brady, Alexander Gardner, Timothy O'Sullivan, and others helped to establish a new standard in the depiction of war; their graphic images of landscapes strewn with corpses have remained among the best known of all war photographs and a foundation of contemporary photojournalism. So too did portrait photography and the most famous figure of the Civil War era, Abraham Lincoln, mature together. Photographic portraiture existed before Lincoln, and he was represented in many other media besides photographs, including cartoons, paintings, statuary, and prints. But Lincoln was the first president to be photographed extensively—more than a hundred photographs of him exist—and these images were widely acclaimed; they helped to legitimate the new medium of photography as well as the new president. Photography shaped both the figure of the wartime president and the ground of the Civil War battlefield, and photographs of Lincoln and the battlefield, in turn, became among the war's most famous figure and ground.[1]

Contemporary photographers are radically transforming this legacy. Consider, for example, two photographs by Greta Pratt, an artist who often photographs people involved in historical pageants, commemorations, and reenactments. In numerous images, Pratt has photographed members of the Association of Lincoln Presenters, or Lincoln reenactors. In one photograph from this set, *Nine Lincolns, Hodgenville, Kentucky*, nine reenactors pose together near Lincoln's birthplace. In another, *Lincoln and Log Cabin RV, Hodgenville, Kentucky*, a single reenactor poses next to a recreational vehicle painted to resemble a log cabin.[2]

These two Pratt photographs depict what we might be tempted to call a postmodern Lincoln, who seems in stark contrast with his photographic foundations. Nineteenth-century Lincoln photographs were famous for their verisimilitude, depth, and gravitas, as in Alexander Gardner's portrait of a somber,

Greta Pratt, *Nine Lincolns, Hodgenville, Kentucky*, 2000. Used with permission of Greta Pratt

Greta Pratt, *Lincoln and Log Cabin RV, Hodgenville, Kentucky*, 2000. Used with permission of Greta Pratt

mid-war Lincoln. By contrast, Greta Pratt's photographs emphasize the post-modern hallmarks of inauthenticity, surface, and humor. Her images begin with the anachronistic, made-up Lincoln of the reenactor. In *Nine Lincolns*, the singularity of Lincoln further gives way to nine copies; the whole comprises a kind of family portrait, or perhaps, in its grouping of nine men, a baseball team or Supreme Court. With its focus on the reproduction of copies rather than originals, the image presents a repeating Lincoln not unlike a figure in an Andy Warhol photographic silkscreen, as in Warhol's serialized Jackies and Marilyns.[3] In *Lincoln and Log Cabin RV*, Lincoln is so far removed from his nineteenth-century foundations that his log cabin is painted, literally, with a veneer of the past. Below the log cabin, at the bottom of the vehicle, is a swath of painted prairie; this is trompe l'oeil grass, abutting a made-up cabin. As the photograph's title indicates, the vehicle is as important as the figure it carries;

Alexander Gardner, *Abraham Lincoln*, 1863. Library of
Congress

indeed, the vehicle provides the defining metaphor for that figure. Both of
these images present Lincoln as himself an "RV"—a recreational vehicle for the
construction of photographs and the reconstruction of history.

If Pratt's photographs are anchored to postmodernity, however, they also
point back to the past. Photographs of Lincoln were highly constructed in
their original nineteenth-century moment as well. For example, Lincoln photographs were altered, in proto-Photoshop ways. Beards were added to photographs of a beardless Lincoln; images that originally depicted another person
were reproduced with Lincoln's head.[4] Lincoln's photographed body might be
kept whole, but transported to new visual environments. Photographs of him
were often used, with his active participation, as the basis for paintings and

Franklin Courter, *A. Lincoln Showing Sojourner Truth
the Bible Presented by Colored People of Baltimore,
Executive Mansion, Washington, D.C., Oct. 29, 1864,*
1893. Library of Congress

sculptures, in a process of exchange that Harold Holzer terms "iconographi-
cal interdependence."[5] This interdependence could be between icons as well as
media: in the 1890s, for example, Franklin Courter recreated the 1864 meeting
between Lincoln and Sojourner Truth in a painting he based on a photograph
of Truth, to which he added an image of Lincoln; the painting was destroyed
in a fire, but a photograph of it survived.[6] This image honored not one but two
public figures keenly interested in their photographic representation, as Truth
had sold her photographic cartes-de-visite to support her abolitionism. In the
1893 painting, photography was both the foundation and outcome for a project that retroactively validated the power of Truth through her visual proximity to a president whose face was the ultimate calling card of authority.[7]

Nineteenth-century Lincoln photographs, then, were already multiply constructed, mutable, hybridized, and socially contingent images; from the first moment that he was photographed, Lincoln became a recreational vehicle for the cultural imagination of nineteenth-century America. This essay explores contemporary photography of Lincoln and the Civil War, with a focus on battlefield photographs by John Huddleston and photographically inspired Lincoln portraiture by Ron English. I argue that these new images unground and refigure their subjects, while transforming the relation between figure and ground. Such transformations are less a break with a stable photographic past than an extension of the instabilities already present in nineteenth-century visual culture. Throughout, I interpret this mutable relation between past and present with a focus on racial representation. As the Sojourner Truth painting suggests, the visual history of Lincoln is inseparable from the racial questions of the Civil War era, and I explore this inseparability through analysis of both nineteenth- and twenty-first century images that "blacken" the president. Race, often muted in the nineteenth-century battlefield photograph, is overtly represented in contemporary images in several ways: through explicit racial markers, through implicit metaphors, and, especially, through provocative juxtapositions that shift the locus of battle from field to body and from white bodies to black ones.

This essay aims to bring attention to new photographic work, showing how contemporary artists—including Sally Mann, William Earle Williams, and Sonya Clark, in addition to Greta Pratt, John Huddleston, and Ron English—provide important commentary on Lincoln and the Civil War. In discussing this commentary, I hope both to illuminate the cultural politics of the present moment and to refocus analysis on the nineteenth-century visual archive. Despite the wealth of existing scholarship on Civil War battlefields and on Lincoln, there remains insufficient close reading and interpretation of nineteenth-century photographs on these themes. It is important to expand both the range of images under study and the analytic tools applied to them. There is much more to see in the photographic archives of Lincoln and Civil War, as well as new ways of seeing.

❦

From the moment they appeared, Civil War photographs claimed the ground of authenticity as well as battle. Oliver Wendell Holmes, for example, traveled to Antietam, viewed Mathew Brady's photographs of the battlefield, and gave

Alexander Gardner and Timothy O'Sullivan, *A Harvest of Death*, 1863/1866. Library of Congress

them his highest praise: "Let him who wishes to know what the war is look at this series of illustrations."[8] Photographs by Brady, Gardner, and O'Sullivan became known as the representations of "what the war is," both in the circulation of individual images and in volumes like Gardner's *Photographic Sketch Book* (1866). As shown in perhaps the most famous single image from this era, Gardner and O'Sullivan's *A Harvest of Death*, the emblematic illustration of war was a black-and-white photograph of corpses, stretched in death, strewn in clumps on a field.[9]

Yet there are numerous absences and paradoxes in the acclaimed authenticity of these photographs. Representations of the aftermath of battle, these images were distanced from war by their belatedness. As Timothy Sweet has argued, the most famous battlefield images delimit horror by showing whole bodies, rather than dismembered ones, and by positioning them in a framework of pastoral regeneration.[10] More fundamentally, Gardner meticulously staged some of these photographs, with significant alterations to their subjects. For *Home of a Rebel Sharpshooter*, for example, Gardner dragged a corpse forty yards from where it originally lay and propped a rifle next to him; in the caption for *A Harvest of Death*, Gardner claimed that the image represented Confederates, but in another photograph, he termed the same bodies, correctly, Union soldiers.[11] Documentary images of the Civil War landscape were thus not only intrinsically belated, but also staged and misdescribed. At its moment of foundational authenticity, the battlefield photograph was already a form of reenactment.

manipulation of reality

These paradoxical legacies have been embraced in different ways by contemporary photographers. In *What Remains* (2003), for example, Sally Mann revisits the battlefield of Antietam—site of some of Gardner's most well-known images—in a series of large, unpopulated, visually dark black-and-white landscape photographs.[12] Mann's *Antietam* series reenacts Gardner less in content than in form: she uses the same wet-plate collodion process as he and her images are deliberately marked by the blotches, jagged edges, and other imperfections of this process, building questions of death and decay into the surface of the image itself.[13] William Earle Williams also represents unpopulated Civil War landscapes in black-and-white images, but he takes the battlefield photograph in more overtly political directions. *Unsung Heroes: African American Soldiers in the Civil War* (2007) depicts sites where African American soldiers trained, fought, and died in the war.[14] These photographs—several dozen small silver prints—address a major historical absence: the lack of commemoration for the more than a hundred and eighty thousand black soldiers who served in the war. The erasure of black service was underway as soon as the war ended, and by the early twentieth century, histories of the war constructed it as a conflict among white men who eventually reconciled; those few monuments that did note African American experience offered a hierarchical iconography of what Kirk Savage characterizes as "standing soldiers, kneeling slaves."[15] Williams also addresses a specifically photographic erasure: black soldiers appear infrequently in the photographs of Brady, Gardner, and O'Sullivan, and their images seldom represent struggle over slavery directly. Williams's photographs thus constitute a recovery project of both uncommemorated physical ground and unseen photographic figures.

Williams's project generates its own paradoxes. Other recovery projects have brought black soldiers directly into view, as in exhibitions of photographic

William Earle Williams, *Jamestown Island, Virginia*, 1996. Used
with permission of William Earle Williams

portraits of black soldiers, celebrations of Augustus Saint-Gaudens' sculpture
honoring Colonel Robert Gould Shaw and the 54th Massachusetts Regiment,
and cinematic representations of black Civil War experience like *Glory*.[16] By
contrast, Williams depicts no people; his images represent not the heroes suggested in his title, but rather their "unsungness," and in so doing they both
displace and heighten the challenges of representing black heroism. *Jamestown
Island, Virginia* (1996), for example, shows an unpopulated landscape of flat
ground, bisected by a leafy tree, with water and a landmass beyond; the image
is framed by trees and shadows at the top and bottom of the foreground. Williams explicates the image, which is reproduced on the cover of the exhibition
catalogue, as follows: "This is near the place where the first African indentured
laborers landed in the English North American Colonies in 1619. Later this site
became a Civil War fort built by enslaved Africans for the defense of the Confederate States."[17] The caption provides an origin story—a literal point of
disembarkation—for Africans in America, but that story stands historically at

several removes from that of black Civil War soldiers, the vast majority of whom fought for the Union; instead, it references enslaved black labor in the Confederacy, on a site, Jamestown, far better known for its seventeenth-century history. Visually, the image is even more oblique: depicting no people or any markers of a built environment, Williams challenges the ground to provide its absent figures. "Landscape," notes W. J. T. Mitchell, is "both a frame and what a frame contains . . . both a package and the commodity inside the package."[18] In this case, the tree functions, internally, as a frame for the black bodies marching beneath it, both as indentured seventeenth-century laborers and as enslaved Confederates. As the opening image in the catalogue, the photograph also frames what is to come: images of sites where African Americans openly rejected their commodification by fighting for freedom in the Union Army.

John Huddleston reframes the Civil War landscape in complementary but different ways, in *Killing Ground: Photographs of the Civil War and the Changing American Landscape* (2002). In this volume, he pairs nineteenth-century black-and-white Civil War images with his own color photographs of battlefield sites as they look today; sixty-three of these pairings appear on facing pages, with eight additional single images.[19] This project can be situated in the context of "rephotography," in which artists return to previously photographed sites, simulating the vantage point, lighting, and composition of the original image as much as possible. In the "Rephotographic Survey Project" led by Mark Klett, for example, new photographs reprise the precise coordinates of images of the American West taken for nineteenth-century government surveys.[20] *Killing Ground* has affinities with rephotography, as signaled on the volume's cover, which pairs *A Harvest of Death* with a photograph of a site that was part of the battle of Gettysburg but is now a well-kept athletic field.[21] But the cultural work of *Killing Ground* extends far beyond rephotography's organizing reliance on latter-day fidelity to a stable original. In his choices of nineteenth-century images, his own photographs, his juxtapositions between them, and his verbal commentaries, Huddleston ungrounds the Civil War landscape from its photographic past. Moreover, his pairings refigure the earlier landscape into body parts and link it to African American people and sites. While these transformations do not occur in every pairing in the volume, I here analyze six pairs, roughly in order as they appear, to identify a trajectory from ungrounding to refiguration that characterizes the volume as a whole.[22]

Even in the most rephotographic of his pairings, Huddleston juxtaposes nineteenth-century battlefield photographs with contemporary photographs that work to disrupt the original. As the cover pairing of *A Harvest of Death* with the athletic field suggests, Huddleston's photographs emphasize the lack of commemoration in the present. This contrast is particularly severe in *Petersburg, Virginia*, a Civil War landscape by Gardner and O'Sullivan that Huddleston juxtaposes with a contemporary photograph of a Kmart near the same site (38–39). The visual contrast ungrounds the battlefield site by showing the erasure of its history in the present. In so doing, Huddleston effects a plea to preserve sites of battle. This plea is made explicit in one of his appendices to the volume, in which he lists the many battlefield sites that are now private property and argues that "The major battlefields are a living, physical embodiment of critical change and must be preserved" (175).[23] This plea for preservation is reinforced by the caption under the right-hand image, which gives casualty figures for the battle—in this case, 70,000—and thereby enumerates just how many deaths are not being commemorated. In the contemporary image, moreover, the Kmart is empty; the lights are on and the store looks open—as confirmed by the flowers, a commercialized version of pastoralism, for sale in the front—but no people are visible. If the small interior spaces of Fort Sedgwick exist for matters of life and death, the big-box Kmart offers only an empty monument to American low-budget commerce. Notably, in contrast to most of the pairings in the volume, here the twenty-first century image is printed on the left. In another kind of ungrounding, the rephotograph becomes "pre-photograph," sullying the foundation for the Civil War image to come.[24]

While this pairing alters the ground of the Civil War battlefield in its harsh juxtaposition with the present, it nonetheless uses a nineteenth-century image recognizable as a landscape. Elsewhere, however, Huddleston changes the definition of the Civil War landscape, using on the left-hand side nineteenth-century photographs of soldiers' bodies, particularly those of amputees.[25] In *Chantilly, Virginia*, the nineteenth-century photograph is that of a man in a domestic interior, fully dressed except for his amputated leg, whose stump is prominently displayed; the caption identifies him as "Wounded at Chantilly: Lorenzo E. Dickey, of Maine, Age 21" (36–37). On the right is a commercial building under construction; at the image's center is a landscaped traffic island featuring a sign with the phrase "Have a Nice Day." If, in Huddleston's words, the battlefield site is a "living, physical embodiment," then the image

15 June 1864–2 April 1865
PETERSBURG, VIRGINIA

Site of Fort Sedgwick

70,000 American Casualties
PETERSBURG, VIRGINIA

Bombproof Quarters of Fort Sedgwick, a Key
Position on the Eastern Union Siege Line

John Huddleston, *Petersburg, Virginia*, 2002. Used with permission of John Huddleston on the left redefines that embodiment; the battlefield becomes the wounded body of the soldier, here healed enough that he could be photographed in civilian dress; the contemporary photograph fails to honor either that injury or his recovery. This photograph recalls that of the Kmart, in its focus on commercialism and its contained display of flowers. But its contrast with the battlefield is even more brutal, particularly in the injury inflicted by its injunction, "Have a nice day," in the presence of the scarred body on the left. The name of the street sign in the contemporary photograph, "Monument Drive," not only ironizes the lack of historical monuments within this photograph, but also provides a gloss on the nineteenth-century image. In Huddleston's refiguring of landscape, the truest commemorative drive through the Civil War becomes the journey along the injured soldier's body—the ultimate Civil War monument.

The Civil War landscape is even more severely altered in *Amputated Feet* (110–11). This nineteenth-century image is also drawn from wartime medical archives, but it contrasts sharply with the fully dressed and named body of Lorenzo Dickey; here, Huddleston has chosen two separate photographs showing only amputated feet, images characteristic of their photographer, Civil War surgeon Reed Bontecou.[26] On the right-hand side, the photograph is of a battlefield at Richmond, Kentucky, as a field of bright green grass. This contemporary image seems almost deliberately bland, offering only the ground in which figures would appear, or perhaps the grass on which bare feet would walk. By contrast, the left-hand image is shocking, so dislocated and dislocating that it lacks the locational title that Huddleston gives the other images; this is simply called "Amputated Feet." The disturbance created by these photographs is not that they show body parts, since it is customary to see images of another body part: the head. But these are parts at the wrong end of the body, a dissonance enhanced by the oval frames around them, which would normally surround facial portraiture. These are, moreover, body parts from different bodies; they seem to be two left feet, and cannot, together, build a functioning body. In a different register of symbolism, the amputated feet also suggest a radically dismembered body politic, one disarticulated by civil fracture. If Lincoln is the symbolic head of the Civil War body politic, this is, conversely, a body politic so unheaded as to be disembodied—a wartime nation made radically "footloose."

The motor for this national dismemberment, *Killing Ground* suggests, is race. At different moments in the volume, Huddleston foregrounds the roles

1 September 1862
CHANTILLY, VIRGINIA

Wounded at Chantilly: Lorenzo E.
Dickey of Maine, Age 21

2,100 American Casualties
CHANTILLY, VIRGINIA

The Confederate center received the first
Union charge here.

John Huddleston, *Chantilly, Virginia*, 2002. Used with permission of John Huddleston

29–30 August, 1862
6,050 American Casualties

Center of the First Engagement Near Mt. Zion Church
RICHMOND, KENTUCKY

Amputated Feet

John Huddleston, *Amputated Feet*, 2002. Used with permission of John Huddleston

of slavery, racial violence, and black experience in the photographic representation of the Civil War. The project is complementary with, but different from, William Earle Williams's *Unsung Heroes,* not only in the rephotographic structure of the paired images but also in the visible presence of African Americans in the volume. In *Cold Harbor, Virginia* (78–79), Huddleston uses as his nineteenth-century image a Gardner photograph, *A Burial Party, Cold Harbor, Va.,* which depicts four African American men collecting body parts on a battlefield and a fifth sitting alongside a cart of skeletons; in front of the cart is an amputated foot in a shoe. One of the few photographs in Gardner's *Photographic Sketch Book* depicting African Americans, the image shows black men in the Union army assigned burial detail, assembling remains and digging trenches for graves. In Gardner's framing of this labor, the seated man, who is facing the camera, provides an implicit challenge to the racial hierarchies of the battlefield labor represented in the photograph. His direct gaze bears witness to the grueling labor he and the other men perform, and, more generally, to the potential power of black spectatorship.[27] The photograph on the right shows the Cold Harbor landscape as an empty field dominated by high brown grass. It echoes Gardner's landscape, with its clouds and line of trees, but in contrast to other pairings in the volume, the rephotographic elements imply a tribute rather than a rebuke to the original; here, Huddleston suggests that Gardner's *Burial Party* already does at least some work in bringing race in the war into view. With its prominent foot, *Burial Party* may also be paired with *Amputated Feet*. Gardner's photograph restores a larger visual field—literally and symbolically—to the dismembered feet in the medical photographs. It gives body to the people whose feet appear in *Amputated Feet,* while also supplying for them a context—both defining figure and underlying ground—of African American labor.

A different landscape of racial conflict organizes *New York, New York* (100–101). The left-hand image in this pairing shows a lynching during the New York City Draft Riots; as Huddleston explains at volume's end, "The selection of the first draftees for the new army conscription act set off three days of rioting by mobs estimated at 50,000 to 100,000 people. A number of blacks were beaten and lynched" (171). His inclusion of this event connects episodes of civilian violence with the war's declared battlefields, while emphasizing the intensity of racism in the Civil War North. This image is not a photograph but an illustration from *Harper's Weekly,* showing a black man lynched in a tree, with a fire burning beneath him; at least two men fan the flames with *why are these pictures?*

torches, while another seems to applaud, and a fourth, perched on a wagon at the right, looks on. The horror of this scene is literally hard to see, in the image's grainy, low-quality reproduction, even as its own composition emphasizes the centrality of spectatorship to the act of lynching. Lynching, which became a central instrument of anti-black terror in the post-war period, was inseparable from voyeurism, as commodified, for example, in turn-of-the-century lynching postcards.[28] Huddleston works against the violations of voyeurism in his own caption for this scene. Whereas the original illustration in *Harper's* was captioned "Hanging a Negro Clarkson Street," Huddleston restores a name and syntactic agency to the victim: "William Jones, a black man, is lynched and burned on Clarkson Street on the first day of the draft riot."[29]

The photograph on the right shows an urban intersection in present-day New York, not the same locale but linked to it, as the caption notes, by the history of lynching: "Abraham Franklin, a twenty-three-year-old black man, was lynched here at 7th Avenue and 27th Street on the last day of the riot." As the two captions verbally connect lynching on the first and last days of the Draft Riots, the photograph on the right visually parallels that on the left in its composition. A stoplight hanging from a metal pole, for example, echoes the hanging figure in the *Harper's* illustration, while a blurred figure occupies the same space as the applauding spectator in the left. At the same time, the photograph on the right introduces a new context for racist violence. In the foreground is a mailbox pasted with political posters headed "Fight Back!" and "No More!" The protest is against an infamous episode of anti-black police violence and its aftermath: the beating of an African American man, Rodney King, by white policemen in Los Angeles in 1991. The top illustration on the poster is a still from the widely circulated amateur video of the beating of King; the bottom illustration is a photograph of the uprising that followed upon the acquittal of the police by an all-white jury in the subsequent trial.[30] In conjunction with the illustration on the left, the photographs within these posters signal the continuity between nineteenth- and twentieth-century acts of racism, while their exhortation to "Fight Back!" foregrounds political resistance to this tradition as a whole.

In a pairing near the end of the volume, the African American soldier's body comes directly into view, as Huddleston juxtaposes a photograph of an African American soldier with a landscape of Fort Pillow, Tennessee (156–57). As with *Amputated Feet*, the body, rather than a place name, gives the title to the left-hand image: "Unidentified Black Soldier." In what looks like a studio setting, a soldier poses against an obviously fake backdrop, off to fight in battles that might include the one commemorated on the right: Fort Pillow, known not only for the bravery of the African American troops who fought there but also for their massacre by Confederates after capture. The armed black soldier, finally shown in full, provides an image of embodied resistance to populate the battleground signaled on the right. This climactic pairing—an implicit realization of William Earle Williams's goal to honor "unsung heroes"—does not, however, settle the project of commemoration. The photograph of Fort Pillow is a forest scene featuring tree trunks, fallen branches, and green and brown leaves. It gives no sign of the national park now on this site: unlike the Kmart pictured in *Petersburg*, this is not an uncommemorated site, and Huddleston could presumably have chosen to photograph a commemorative element in the park. That he chooses the unpopulated forest instead leaves the commemorative work of the site unfinished. The legacies of Fort Pillow—massacre as well as heroism—linger.

The trees in this photograph may also evoke another kind of racial violence. Images of swaying trees appearing frequently in *Killing Ground*; its last image, for example, is a stand-alone color photograph of leafy green tree-tops and sky at an artillery site in West Virginia (163). Huddleston suggests that the trees in his photographs "signify a return of peace to the killing ground, but they also remove the signs of violence against which we value that peace" (16). This description finds in trees an ambivalent pastoralism, which smoothes over a legacy of violence. Perhaps we could also see Huddleston's trees as, themselves, possible sites of violence, as in the illustration of the New York City Draft Riots, in which the tree that anchors the rope attached to William Jones is part of a landscape of lynching. Visual representations of lynching more commonly included bodies and ropes, but images of trees alone may also bear traces of this history. In his photographic series entitled *Searching for California's Hang Trees*, for example, Ken Gonzales-Day chooses to represents the history of lynching in California through images of trees alone. For Gonzales-Day, in the absence of public preservation of this history, trees function as "the last living witnesses" to lynching.[31]

So too may William Earle Williams's *Jamestown Island* evoke this violent history. "Unsung heroes" is taken from a poem by Paul Laurence Dunbar, turn-of-the-century African American writer, about the heroism of slaves, but a more famous poem by Dunbar, "The Haunted Oak," provides a different gloss on this photograph's tree. A poem about a lynching, "The Haunted Oak" makes the leafless bough of a tree a scar of racist violence, and the shade of the tree a terrifying reminder, to the poem's first-person speaker, of histories of violence: "[W]hy, when I go through the shade you throw, / Runs a shudder over me?"[32] Like Dunbar's poem, William Earle Williams's photograph may offer an apostrophe to a tree to speak a history of violence politically and photographically kept in shadow. The trees of Williams, like those of Huddleston, may evoke the "haunted oaks" of lynching sites and—to turn to a twentieth-century image—the "strange fruit" such trees might bear.

These evocations might extend, at their fullest reach, to Civil War photography in its better-known iterations. Although the war's most famous battlefield photographs feature white bodies, they prefigure the images of corpses that will follow in the era of lynching. The fields of corpses are both a "prephotographic" metaphor for the violence to come and a metonymic extension of that violence; the landscape of the "harvest of death" includes the "hang tree" of lynching.[33] The photographs taken by Huddleston and Williams—who are, respectively, white and African American—begin to restore this wider view of landscape through their ungrounding of the battlefield landscape from its usual visual coordinates and their refiguration of landscape in the bodies of the dead, both white and African American. Their images suggest that it is only by finding ways to restore the photographic importance of slavery, racism, and black resistance that the dismembered body politic of the wartime nation can be fully reconstructed. In this reconstruction, the dismembered body of the Civil War landscape may be rearticulated, and amputated feet may find bodies—black and white—with which to stand.

And where is the head of that Civil War body politic? Lincoln does not appear in *Killing Ground*, but contemporary artists have refigured his photographic legacy in racially transformative ways. In *Afro-Abe II* (2007), for example, Sonya Clark takes a five-dollar bill and embroiders the hair of Lincoln on its face, extending the embroidery beyond the top edge of the bill to create the appearance of an Afro. The artist, who is African American, often works with craft traditions and with the cultural meanings of African American hair. Here her canvas is money, the most reproduced and circulated of forms. Through the medium of embroidery, Clark transforms the image of Lincoln on the five-dollar bill—taken from a Brady photograph of the 1860s and standardized as currency in the 1920s—into a singular, crafted artwork of 2007. The esthetic transformation of Lincoln is also a political one, as Clark notes in her Artist's Statement for a 2008 exhibition: "Lincoln . . . is given a new hairdo. In a sense he is crowned with the hair of those he helped to Emancipate."[34] The iconography of a black Lincoln appears elsewhere in contemporary African American culture: for example, two plays by Suzan-Lori Parks, *The America Play* (1994) and *Topdog/Underdog* (2001), feature black Abraham Lincoln impersonators, implicitly joining the world of Lincoln presenters in Greta Pratt's photographs to questions of African American identity.[35] Like Parks, Clark plays with the iconography of a black Lincoln, but her *Afro-Abe II* appears in a specific moment, the 2008 presidential campaign, when representing a black president in the past might presage a black president in the imminent future. "Stay tuned," she writes, "for the upcoming elections."[36]

The visual convergence of Presidents Obama and Lincoln is made explicit in *Abraham Obama*, an installation made by Ron English, a white artist who specializes in political provocations he calls "popaganda." This piece was commissioned by a Boston gallery, Gallery XIV, for a group show on political art. English first generated a small black-and-white portrait, then enlarged and reproduced it eleven times, saturating these images with bright pastel colors, to create a large "digitized print mural." *Abraham Obama* was first installed on a wall in Boston in summer 2008, where it received substantial media attention; it moved to venues on the West Coast, and was exhibited at an art exhibition at the Democratic National Convention in Denver in August 2008; it has had a robust life on the Internet and in other media. Along with Shepard Fairey's portrait of Obama entitled *Hope*, it was the best-known of the artworks that were a prominent feature of the 2008 presidential campaign. It is also central to a rich and ever-growing archive of materials, verbal and visual, that combine Abraham Lincoln and Barack Obama—an archive shaped, in no small part, by Obama himself.[37]

With its use of what English calls "Warholian pop style" and its pastiche of icons, *Abraham Obama* announces itself as a "postmodern visual statement," but it is important to understand its multiple connections to nineteenth-century visual culture.[38] It is based on nineteenth-century Lincoln photographs; specifically, English combined the Gardner photograph of Lincoln I have already discussed with a photographic image of then-candidate Obama from the cover of *Time* magazine.[39] English is an avid Obama supporter, and here, in contrast to his customary approach of satirizing icons, he uses photographic sources to create a pro-Obama campaign poster.[40] *Abraham Obama* idealizes Obama with

Ron English, *Abraham Obama*, Boston, 2008. Photograph by Elizabeth Young

the visual currency of Lincoln, himself already an object of literal currency. Lincoln operates as the gold standard for the new presidential candidate, or to put it in religious rather than monetary terms, the iconography of Lincoln sanctifies that of Obama—as, in the nineteenth century, the iconography of George Washington had sanctified that of Lincoln. Lincoln actively forged visual connections between himself and Washington, a connection that accelerated after his death, when artists frequently apotheosized them together. In one composite image called *Apotheosis*, for example, the two men embrace as they ascend to Heaven; in another, *National Picture*, Washington flanks Lincoln and both are touched by the rays of Providence, while the caption reads "Washington Made and Lincoln Saved Our Country."[41] *Abraham Obama* adds another leg to this relay of sanctifications, whereby Washington made, Lincoln saved, and Obama remade—or promises to remake—America.[42]

The push forward Lincoln gives to Obama is also a push backward Obama gives to Lincoln. As Alexandre Borrell shows in his analysis of *Abraham Obama*, there is a kind of double "grafting" at work in the image, whereby Lincoln visually absorbs the traits of Obama even as he transplants his political legitimacy onto his successor.[43] Such double grafting has particular force in relation to Lincoln's iconic image as Great Emancipator. This iconography took shape in visual as well as political form with the Emancipation Proclamation. In an 1865 lithograph, for example, the words of the Proclamation are used to outline Lincoln's face and body; based on a Brady photograph, this calligraphic portrait also included scenes of slaves being whipped and freed.[44] The heroic imagery of Lincoln as Great Emancipator has been contested at least since the 1960s, with such well-known critiques as the 1968 essay by Lerone Bennett Jr. entitled "Was Abe Lincoln a White Supremacist?"[45] *Abraham Obama* restabilizes Lincoln's emancipatory role, presenting Lincoln as a foundational figure in the story of black freedom that culminates in Obama. As with the earlier calligraphic portrait, Lincoln's identity as icon of emancipation can be both seen on his face and taken at face value.

English's image also comments implicitly on a highly negative strand of nineteenth-century visual culture, in which political caricaturists attacked Lincoln for his alleged proximity to and affinity with blackness. For example, in a Currier & Ives lithograph from the presidential campaign of 1860, entitled *"The Nigger" in the Woodpile*, a prospective voter talks to Horace Greeley, the abolitionist editor, while Lincoln crouches atop a "Republican Platform" concealing a black man; the voter declares "You can't pull that wool over my eyes, for I can see 'the Nigger' peeping through the rails." This image combines the populist iconography of Lincoln as a humble "rail-splitter" with the ideas, usually left metaphorical, of a political platform and a hidden agenda. It makes both dependent on the African American man, who is vilified with the racist slur "nigger." As rail-splitter and platform-maker, Lincoln both relies upon and conceals the African American man directly beneath him.[46]

Elsewhere, Lincoln was portrayed as visually dark-skinned, as in an anonymous caricature from 1864, *Behind the Scenes*, which depicted him as Othello. Lincoln is at the center of this image, costumed as Othello, Shakespeare's Moor; two men stand behind him, one commenting, "Not quite appropriately costumed, is he?" and the other replying, "Costumed, my dear Sir? Never was such enthusiasm for art: —Blacked himself all over to play the part, Sir!"[47] This image casts Lincoln's blackness as external theatrical make-up, his "Moorishness" akin to minstrelsy, but Lincoln's blackness was also seen as internal, in the persistent rumor that he had African ancestry. For example, the cover of *Abraham Africanus*, an 1864 pamphlet attacking Lincoln as the "African

Abraham," portrayed his face as dark-skinned, with exaggerated African features, and wearing a crown.[48] Adalbert Volck, the best-known Confederate caricaturist, attacked Lincoln in one image by giving him exaggerated African features and costuming him in orientalist dress, under a veil.[49] These "blackenings" of Lincoln were inseparable from fears of interracial sexuality; the term "miscegenation" was invented in the presidential campaign of 1864, in a hoax pamphlet that claimed to be Lincoln's political views. Numerous cartoons portrayed Lincoln as a participant in and advocate of interracial sexuality, combining the spectre of Lincoln with black women with that of white women with black men.[50] Lincoln's perceived visual blackness thus traveled from blackface makeup to veiled blackness, and from admirer of abolition to advocate of racial mixture.

In the context of these racist caricatures, the image of a "black Lincoln" in *Abraham Obama* is a reappropriation, perhaps inadvertent, of an existing visual vocabulary. Intentionally or not, English revalues the blackening of Lincoln, offering an inversion of an inversion. This double inversion is implicit in Clark's artwork as well. In both *Afro-Abe II* and *Abraham Obama*, the image of a black president—a cultural fear of the nineteenth-century—becomes a twenty-first century cultural fantasy. The fantasy is also that of a mixed-race president. Obama's face has frequently served as the site for visual commentaries on his race.[51] With its overt incorporation of Lincoln, the face of *Abraham Obama* signals racial hybridity; bifacial echoes biracial. The president's face, in turn, is synecdoche for a multi-colored body politic, a Rainbow Coalition that goes far beyond black-and-white.[52]

The idealized iconographies of *Abraham Obama* are not, however, unambiguous. The blackened Lincoln in this artwork is also a whitened Obama. The pastel variations of the mural lighten the face of Obama, visually assimilating him into a world of white leaders. The Warhol palette adds color, but it does not point toward race, either denotatively or in the stylistic nod to Warhol, whose portraiture is not known for providing racial or other overtly political commentary.[53] Moreover, the image has generated its own hostile responses. The street-level installation was vulnerable to public defacement, which it suffered almost immediately. In Boston, alterations made anonymously to individual panels included tearing it vertically and ripping holes in it; particular attention was paid to changing the figure's eyes, by adding eyeglasses or an eye patch or scratching the eyes out.[54] These alterations may have been playful in intent, but their effect was ominous: in the scratched-out panel, *Abraham Obama* is not

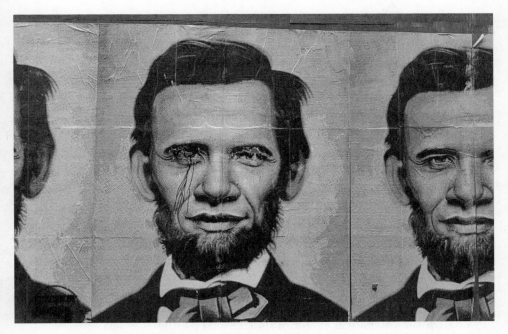

Ron English, *Abraham Obama*, Boston, 2008, detail. Photograph by Elizabeth Young

only scarred but blinded. Analyzing iconoclasm in art, David Freedberg notes the frequency with which eyes in paintings are defaced: "[The eyes] are the clearest and most obvious indications of the vitality of the represented figure. . . . Take away the eyes and remove the signs of life."[55] In the case of *Abraham Obama*, the scarring of eyes implicitly looks backward to the signs of life removed from Lincoln as well as forward toward Obama. The iconoclastic destruction of their merged image may hint at the most frightening of possible similarities between the two men: that both might be the victims of violence.

The defacement of *Abraham Obama* is, however, only one of many alterations to its meanings, a process that began as soon as it was installed. Even interpreted in its most adulatory mode, the visual analogy between Lincoln and Obama has shifted in the period since this piece was first installed in July 2008. Since then, Obama accepted his party's nomination, won the general election, was inaugurated, and began his presidency; accordingly, the piece has moved from an exhortation to a celebration to a ratification of the Obama presidency. The meaning of *Abraham Obama* continues to shift, depending on how

President Obama's actions in the present are assessed, and it is certain to shift further, in ways not yet known, during his presidency. Even and especially in an artwork devoted to repetition, there will no longer be—and has never been—any single "Abraham Obama."

The shifting meanings of a repeating Lincoln bring us back to Greta Pratt's *Nine Lincolns*. In Pratt's photograph, distinct individuals pose as an identical, if repeating, Lincoln; in the English installation, a single repeated image becomes a set of distinct individual panels. The installation fulfills the Warholian seriality implicit in *Nine Lincolns*, as well as providing another angle on its Lincoln presenters: like the men whom Pratt photographs, Obama, in English's image, seems another Lincoln "reenactor." To return to Pratt's *Lincoln and Log Cabin RV*, we could also see *Abraham Obama* as a "recreational vehicle" for English's own reenactment of Lincoln. In the images of both artists, the representation of Lincoln, photographic and reenacted, escapes fixity—an escape, I have argued, that was already underway in the visual archive of the 1860s.

In these many Lincolns, as in John Huddleston's photographic pairings about battlefields, we see a war whose photographic legacy, like its political one, constantly changes. In one of Huddleston's pairings, *Carnifix Ferry, Western Virginia*, the twenty-first century photograph features a wooden sign, presumably for tourists, bearing the words "THIS IS AN AUTHENTIC REPRODUCTION" (29). The sign locates this image squarely in the domain of the postmodern, with its oxymoronic idea of "authentic reproduction." But the nineteenth-century image here is a map, not a photograph, of the 1861 battlefield; since the map only reproduces the contours of a landscape, this image is also an "authentic reproduction." As this pairing of map and sign suggests, the ungrounding of the wartime landscape works both ways, toward the nineteenth as well as the twenty-first century. On battlegrounds, including the battlefield of racism, and in portraits of figures, including the president, the photographs of the Civil War continue to reshape the past as well as the present, and to illuminate both photography and war anew.

CHAPTER SIX

Reenactment and Relic

The Civil War in Contemporary Art

Gerard Brown

American visual artists have recently shown considerable interest in historical themes. Exhibitions like *Ahistoric Occasion: Artists Making History*, organized by the Massachusetts Museum of Contemporary Art in 2006, and *The Old, Weird America: Folk Themes in Contemporary Art*, which opened at the Contemporary Arts Museum Houston in 2008, have featured new interpretations of many aspects of the American experience. The Civil War has commanded a significant proportion of this artistic effort. Of the seventeen artists involved in *The Old, Weird America*, for example, no fewer than five produced substantial sets of work reflecting on the war. On the whole, the first ten years of the twenty-first century have yielded a more important body of Civil War art than any decade since the 1930s and perhaps since the nineteenth century.[1]

This work differs sharply from the image of the Civil War in contemporary art offered by the movie *Junebug* (2005), in which a sophisticated Chicago gallery owner pursues a reclusive, illiterate southern outsider artist who spews out apocalyptic visions of Confederate soldiers and slaves. The Civil War may remain a lively theme in that genre, but a leading conceptual artist interested in the war offers a useful counterweight by reporting that "the closest I get to the romantic idea of the artist in the studio splattering the canvas with paint is when I'm researching. There can be moments when I have twenty books laid out on the floor, spread out like a giant Pollock painting, and I somehow see the connections."[2] The crucial books for such artists have not been the encyclopedias of military uniforms and accoutrements that inform the market for reverential Civil War prints recently surveyed by Gary Gallagher. More intellectually ambitious artists have explored the living political meanings of the Civil War while in many cases invoking nineteenth-century precedents as insistently as illustrators Mort Künstler, Don Troiani, and John Paul Strain claim the mantle of printmakers Louis Prang and Currier & Ives.[3]

Current artistic interest in the Civil War comes from several different directions. The importance of the war to the history of photography has encouraged further exploration of the war in that medium. Thematically, re-examination of the legacy of slavery has been a primary source of fresh attention to the Civil War era, especially from African American artists; prominent examples include Kara Walker, Leo Twiggs, Whitfield Lovell, Glenn Ligon, Stephen Marc, and Radcliffe Bailey.[4] In the years since the attacks of September 11, 2001, and the American invasion of Iraq in February 2003, the renewed centrality of war in contemporary American life has nourished another strand of interest. Barnaby Furnas, one of the participants in *The Old, Weird America,* started to reconsider the Civil War in this vein shortly before September 11 and has since developed the theme further. A former graffiti artist, Furnas has made sensationally violent paintings of Civil War scenes in watercolor or urethane dye that have prompted comparisons with video games, action films, and rock concerts. His frenzied compositions, angular figures, and electric colors suggest that the aggressive restlessness of American culture long predates the diagnosis of attention deficit disorder.[5]

This essay focuses on two artists who participated in both *Ahistoric Occasion* and *The Old, Weird America,* Allison Smith and Dario Robleto. Like Furnas, they treat the Civil War as the template for a culture marked by its military heritage. Modeled on practices through which Americans began to remember the Civil War in its immediate aftermath, Smith's adaptations of Civil War reenactment and Robleto's manipulations of Civil War relics testify to the continued influence of nineteenth-century precedents at the same time that Smith and Robleto situate their performances and assemblages firmly in the recreational pastimes and consumer commodities of twenty-first-century popular culture. The artists' appropriations of the reenactment and the relic complicate the quest for authenticity that some commentators have identified as the chief appeal of Civil War memory in America today. If hobbyists maintain that a nation of farbs should adopt the values of the hard-core, a term borrowed from pornography with implied endorsement of the gender relations promoted by that industry, Smith and Robleto propose an alternative Civil War strategy for combating the hollowness and deceit that militarism has fostered.[6] Though differing in details, their independent formulations of this argument both center on martial ideals of manhood and womanhood. Their work points to the Civil War for validation of gender traditions exemplified by the flamboyant homosexuality of Walt Whitman and the sentimental feminism of Victorian mourning.

❧

Born in 1972, Allison Smith grew up in what she has called "a hyper-suburban historic facade" in Manassas, Virginia. Her hometown was a remarkable junction of Civil War battlefields and the consuming sprawl of a postmodern edge city. The collision of these two local identities drew national attention in the early 1990s when the Walt Disney Company proposed to build a historical theme park to be called "Disney's America" in nearby Haymarket, Virginia. Protesters led by the National Trust for Historic Preservation objected that the simulated historical sites, slated to include a replica Civil War battlefield, would destroy preserved historical sites, most notably the grounds of the first and second battles of Manassas. Prominent scholars divided on the merits of proposal. C. Vann Woodward called the Disney project "an appalling commercialization and vulgarization of the scene of our most tragic history." James Oliver Horton retorted, "If we want to educate people . . . then we have to use a little imagination to make [history] engaging."[7]

In this environment Smith took an early interest in artifacts and images of the Civil War, along with a respect for crochet, cross-stitch, needlepoint, quilting, stencil painting, and other forms of domestic creativity widely popular in suburbs. "My mom is an early-American crafts enthusiast, and my dad designed spy gadgets for the CIA, so they're both eccentric craftspeople in their own ways," Smith has recalled, adding that she found the parallel "humorously gendered."[8]

Smith has focused on the Civil War in several major projects. Her installation *Victory Hall*, originally presented at Bellwether Gallery in spring 2005, included more than one hundred Civil War-styled wooden rifles, pistols, and knives arranged on a wall "in decorative patterns, in the spirit of an arms ex-position hall." In the same show she presented five life-size ceramic dolls made in her image and dressed in hand-sewn Civil War "Zouave" uniforms; she exhibited these dolls again in *The Old, Weird America*. She designed a series of hand-woven coverlets between 2006 and 2008 using the traditional pattern called "Lee's Surrender." She has displayed these blankets in various ways, in-cluding an installation at the Wave Hill estate in the Bronx, where failed Confederate soldier Mark Twain once lived. For *Hobby Horse* (2006), at Art-pace, San Antonio, she sculpted a monumental rocking horse from wood. She mounted the horse while dressed in a modified period uniform and sang an original song that she set to the tune of the Civil War standard "When Johnny Comes Marching Home." Her purpose, she wrote, was to ask "when or if sol-diers ever can 'come home,' rocking in place as a way of gesturing toward a contemporary state of cultural impasse."[9]

Smith's most important Civil War initiative has been *The Muster*, a public participatory performance staged on Governors Island, New York, on May 14, 2005. This project developed through several stages. In an early version Smith organized a mock campout at which her friends from the art world attended in such roles as "General Mayhem" and "The Ghost of Abraham Lincoln." For the Governors Island event, sponsored by the Public Art Fund, Smith sought to mobilize a much larger group of volunteers, which eventually numbered more than one hundred presenters and more than two thousand spectators. Her plan incorporated an elaborate process of recruitment into the artwork. She delivered a public address in New York in February 2005 to stimulate enlistment. A month later she played on the original location of the New York Armory Show art fair by setting up a recruiting booth stocked with an armory of more than one hundred muskets, rifles, and swords patterned on Civil War weapons but painted in a bright array of colors. She required collectors of these pieces to sign a limited edition printed certificate attesting that they had "voluntarily armed themselves with art" and would " 'muster into action' when called to duty on future occasions." Smith held sessions for the making of uniforms and banners at her studio, which she denominated "regimental head-quarters," and she organized regular meetings for "Muster Cocktails" at Fraun-ces Tavern, where George Washington had bidden farewell to the officers of the Continental Army. She also published several broadsides, designed by Jorge Colombo in nineteenth-century format and written in a self-consciously archaic style, that advertised the structure of the "creative encampment" and

Allison Smith, *Hobby Horse*, 2006. Wood, paint,
horsehair, leather, brass, glass; 98×112×36 inches.
Commissioned by and performed at Artpace, San
Antonio, Texas. Courtesy of the artist and Saatchi
Gallery, London. Photograph by Todd Johnson

sought to rally volunteers around the query, "What are you fighting for?"
Smith invited participants to fashion uniforms, build campsite installations,
and reenact or perform "whatever activities you deem necessary to engage
spectators in your Cause." The culmination of the event was to be a formal
roll call in which each participant declared his or her cause from a platform
built for the occasion.[10]

   As one inflection of the motto "what are you fighting for?" indicates, *The
Muster* aimed in part to expose the pointlessness of an ongoing conflict. By the
time of the gathering on Governors Island, more than two years had passed
since the United States had invaded Iraq, and the continuing war had already

use of history to bring
insight to current events

claimed the lives of 1,620 Americans and many more citizens of other countries. Though "engaging in a collective spirit that aims to Proclaim rather than Protest," in the words of Smith's call to arms, *The Muster* did not lack for direct criticism of the military policies of the Bush administration. In the "Tour of the Encampment" that Smith wrote for the documentary record of the event, she noted that participant Mary Purcell's commitment to the broad cause of "Questioning" was particularly apt in light of the disturbing revelations about American torture practices in the interrogation of alleged terrorists. Eugene Jarecki's cinematic investigation of the military-industrial complex, *Why We Fight* (2005), applied Purcell's principle and echoed the motto of *The Muster*, Smith observed, in borrowing the title of Frank Capra's famous World War II propaganda film series. Gary Graham, "taking his cue from the state of current affairs around the world," stood up for "the right to be scared." Espousing the cause of "Inner Peace in a Warring Nation," Michael Cluer, Marc Mayer, and Tavia Nyong'o dressed as male orderlies and read from the poetry of Civil War wound-dresser Walt Whitman in a hospital tent "lined with hand-drawn murals depicting graphic scenes taken directly from the American news media." Another visual artist and two musicians "recalled the powerful fusion of youth culture and radical politics of the Vietnam era" in an installation that featured an original folk ballad protesting the war in Iraq.[11]

The Muster offered a particularly direct alternative to the infringements on civil liberties effected by the USA PATRIOT Act of 2001 and, more broadly, the tensions between genuine personal freedom and a military mobilization officially designated in part "Operation Enduring Freedom." Smith underscored the contrast in her catalogue description of the installation devoted to "the freedom to express your inner self, a.k.a. wigs and disco," which Smith quipped might adopt as its rallying cry "support our dance troupes!"[12] The assembly of an army of artists, each free to choose his or her own cause, presented itself as the opposite of the process that had placed American troops in Iraq and Afghanistan. Where Smith had enlisted volunteers to act on their independent ideals, the Bush administration had invented a cause of war and relied on propaganda to impose mobilization on the country.

The location of *The Muster* deepened its relationship to what Bush liked to characterize as a "War on Terror." A crew as local in its origins and outlook as many Civil War regiments comprised of northern or southern neighbors, the participants who gathered at Governors Island in May 2005 looked directly across New York harbor to the Manhattan skyline still dominated by the absence of the World Trade Center towers destroyed in the attacks of September 11, 2001. Governors Island, where fortifications from the Revolutionary War and Civil War remain standing, was an ideal site for reimagining the military presence in American culture. At the same time, the largest undeveloped tract of land in the metropolitan area also offered a prime location for reimagining New York City as debate swirled around the future of Ground Zero. Exempt from some regulatory restrictions applicable to city parks, the island fittingly offered more freedom for the staging of *The Muster* than any other site in the city.

If the so-called War on Terror provided immediate context for *The Muster*, the event also explored the American culture of war more broadly by appropriating the form of a Civil War reenactment. "Using the American Civil War battle reenactment as our aesthetic palette and point of departure," Smith wrote in her call to arms, "we will participate in the cultural practice of Living History, founded on the belief that historic events gain meaning and relevance when performed live in an open-air, interactive setting."[13] The medium was an ironic choice, as Civil War reenactments typically glorify the militarism that *The Muster* disdained. The performance transcended simple parody, however, because it identified intersections between the ostensibly distant worlds of contemporary American art and Civil War reenactment.

Klara Hobza's performance at *The Muster* illustrated this achievement. At the 2004 gathering in Pennsylvania, Hobza transmitted live reports by Morse code from the protests outside the ongoing Republican National Convention. For the event on Governors Island, she highlighted the dangerous convergence of corporate-controlled technology and warfare by noting that Samuel F. B. Morse had tried to avoid capitalist exploitation of the telegraph and had hoped that his invention would avert the Civil War but had lived to see his revolution in communications facilitate unprecedented military destruction. For her cause in *The Muster*, Hobza accordingly championed "the improvement of communication," which Smith noted "many would consider the primary role of the artist," by creating her own methods for sending and encoding messages rather than relying on corporate or military standards. She adopted the suitably archaic Civil War technology of semaphore flags, a performance vehicle for many parodies but also the visual source of the iconic peace symbol.[14]

The disruption of gender convention was at the heart of Smith's success in turning the genre of Civil War reenactment into a contemporary antiwar happening. Several installations stressed the disturbing logical implications

YES

of war as a system for the definition of manhood and womanhood. Jocelyn
Davis celebrated two traditional forms of "women's work" during wartime, sewing and prostitution, by preparing a cot with thematically appropriate hand-
sewn bedding and "a banner-like clothesline of lacy unmentionables." An
army of fifteen women headed by Rhode Island School of Design professor Liz
Collins under the name Knitting Nation pointed out that "during every his-
yep toric American war there has been a knitting craze." The drill-like work of
the women impressed one observer as a "pointed militant absurdism, marrying the frenetic urgency of a battlefield hospital with the fevered righteousness
of a Ladies Home Auxiliary." To the accompaniment of Union needlework
ballads ("While they the rebels in battle meet / Be yours to fashion with fin-
gers fleet / the nice warm socks for the weary feet / Knit! Knit! Knit!"), the
women of Knitting Nation made a forty-foot-long American flag, "an emblem
of a time of war when orgies of home front needlecraft became sublimated
metaphors for stitching the divided country back together again."[15] The Civil
War had not preserved but instead collapsed distinctions between sexes and
had confused sexual morality. _Footnote ???_ .

This emphasis made homosexuality crucial to *The Muster*. The title of the
event evoked Paul Monette's essay "Mustering," which reflected on the author's
participation in the March on Washington for Gay and Lesbian, Bisexual,
Transgender, and Transsexual Rights in April 1993. Written amid controversies
over Clinton administration policies on AIDS and the service of gays and les-
bians in the armed forces while Monette was "fighting a pitched battle against
the predations of the virus," the composition repeatedly claimed and challenged martial imagery. Monette concluded that Lincoln, "warrior and wise
man," surely would have espoused the cause of gay and lesbian rights. The keynote to the essay was the opening passage of a poem by Sappho:

> Some say a cavalry corps
> some infantry, some, again
> will maintain that the swift oars
>
> of our fleet are the finest
> sight on dark earth; but I say
> that whatever one loves, is.[16]

Herself openly lesbian, Smith was keenly alert in planning *The Muster* to
parallels between the culture of Civil War reenactment and the culture of gay

[handwritten: This sounds something like Judith Butler would have word]

flamboyance. She acknowledged that her models for the camp, in both senses of that word, included not only reenacted bivouacs but also gay pride parades and the Wigstock drag pageant held annually in Greenwich Village. Her published call to arms included as parallel sub-headings "Enlist!" and "Let Every Person Come Out!" She exhorted possible recruits to

> Enact your own costume drama. Wear your war on your sleeve. Show off your revolutionary style. Assume a historical personage. Dress up in soldier drag. Go into total role-playing. Take your shirt off. Form alliances. Form companies. Raise a border regiment. Marshal a Middlesex infantry.[17]

[handwritten: this remixing of the civil war is particularly unique]

Smith discussed the political concerns of her "middlesex" army most directly and fully in her February 2005 recruiting address, which centered on crisis of the Union as a metaphor for "the ambivalence between mainstream and countercultural values in the art world, feminist and queer communities, and the nation at large." Observing that George W. Bush had mustered fear around the issue of same-sex marriage and civil unions in the 2004 elections, she called on her audience to respond with a mustering in the tradition of the Stonewall riots of 1969, the formation of Queer Nation, and the spread of the rainbow flag that she has often invoked in banners, compass roses, and other settings.[18] The similarity between Civil War reenactment and gay flamboyance was similarly important to the installations for which Smith has made life-sized dolls based on Zouave soldiers. Her *Victory Hall* exhibition included framed Civil War ballads that celebrated how "Gayly the bold Zouaves / Dash o'er the plain."[19]

Smith's recruits did not disappoint her plan to foreground "soldier drag" in *The Muster*. One of the most striking volunteers, William Bryan Purcell, announced as his cause "the Power of Pink." Dressed in a meticulously "authentic" but entirely pink Confederate infantry uniform that nicely comple- *[handwritten: HA!]* mented the mutton-chop sideburns he grew for the occasion, Purcell set up an all-pink tent marked with a pink flag and decorated with pink ribbons and pillows on a pink shag carpet. Activities at his installation included "hair brushing and braiding, putting on makeup and nail polish, and talking about feelings and relationships." Purcell also brandished a set of pink muskets and pistols. Another installation featured "a tribe of nine queer, genderqueer, and transfeminist artist-activists" who "combined traditional community hand-sewing with theoretical discussions about the intersections of queer community and contemporary art." Walt Whitman was the patron saint of *The Muster* and figured in several installations. Daphne Fitzpatrick, who had recently walked the full length of Broadway wearing a Whitman T-shirt, costumed herself as a "squirrel dandy" and pasted her tent with copies of Whitman's wartime dispatches. Smith's recruiting broadside reproduced "First O Songs for a Prelude," a celebration of Manhattan on the march and male sexual attraction to other men. The Community HIV/AIDS Mobilization Project sponsored one of the few completely non-satirical installations.[20]

The gay presence in *The Muster* called attention to the homosocial bonding that so many Civil War reenactors enjoy, including physical elements like the practice of "spooning" at chilly encampments. "The Last Love in Iraq," performed by Malik Gaines and Alex Segade of the performance ensemble My Barbarian, made clear that such a homosocial military environment is not a thing of the past. The song focused on a married man involved in a gay sexual relationship with a fellow soldier while serving on the front lines: "Brush away the sand / Put your gear aside / Strip off standard issue / Tonight if they won't ask we won't tell."[21] The ballad brought together the current political and long-term cultural dimensions of the antiwar theme of *The Muster*.

For Smith, the Civil War is a vital artistic resource insofar as it remains a touchstone of nostalgia, like the needlecrafts, crockery, and mom-and-pop stores that her work also examines. *The Muster* embraced the ideal of a national tradition but challenged the militant heterosexuality that has often claimed ownership of patriotic identity. Smith's army represents a national culture in which the expression of sexuality is the epitome of freedom and as fully American as the Civil War.

❦

Dario Robleto was born the same year as Allison Smith in San Antonio, Texas, and has spent almost all of his life in his hometown. The economically robust, politically volatile tourism industry of San Antonio offered Robleto an introduction to history as spectacle comparable to the early environment that influenced Smith's imagination, but Robleto did not follow the local path into fascination with the past. He has expressed no particularly strong ties to Latino culture, to which his familial link is the Nicaraguan heritage of a father with whom Robleto never lived.[22] His deep interest in the history of American wars rarely touches on the conflict that has made the Alamo one of the most ideologically charged tourism sites in the country. Robleto's work came to focus on war, and often specifically on the Civil War, in the aftermath of September

11, 2001, but his exploration of the theme carries forward many of the auto-
biographically inspired approaches to history that have shaped his art from
the outset.

Robleto's sculptures are assemblages of found objects that he has altered
in ways that comment on the history of the materials. His early work involved
the modification of mass-distributed consumer commodities, which critics
since Karl Marx have identified with suppression of the underlying relations
of production. For example, Robleto purchased a ten-pack of Big Red chewing gum, chewed each stick until it was sugarless, reshaped the gum into its
original form, and returned the packaging to what appeared to be its original
form. Some of these projects included subversive distribution of his work, as
when he unwound a roll of fax paper, turned it inside out, placed it back in
the package, and "restored" it to the shelves from which he had purchased it.
(He did not do the same with the chewing gum.) He quickly identified himself, however, less as a consumer than as a collector interested in objects with
densely freighted pasts. He shredded his love letters from seventh through
ninth grades, inserted the fragments in pill capsules, and created a package
that promised "fast pain relief." He unraveled his first baby blanket, spliced
lengths of its thread into thread purchased from fabric stores and thrift stores,
respooled the newly combined thread, and placed the spools back on the
shelves from which he had purchased them.[23]

In his passion for popular music Robleto found a rich vocabulary for the
reconstruction of memory-imbued objects, specifically vinyl records. Few if
any non-musical artists have so thoroughly and thoughtfully identified themselves with the creative methods of DJ culture, in which the juxtaposition of
provocatively mixed fragments of musical recordings becomes an independent art form. He reports that he "did dabble in the DJ stuff" and "thought that
was my opening to be a musician, but soon I realized I could explore these
topics in a better way through art and specifically through materials."[24] He
specifically invokes visual and tactile parallels to the remix process in a series
of works that incorporate melted or otherwise manipulated vinyl records and
magnetic tapes of specific songs. His artistic practice also adopts many distribution conventions of popular music. He has described his exhibitions as
his "albums" and also as "concerts." He has paired works in the manner of
two-sided singles, such as his *I Wish the Ocean Sounded More Like Patsy Cline b/w
The Words to All the Love Songs Start Making Sense When You've Gone Away* (1998).
The elaborate printed descriptions of his assemblages are "liner notes."[25]

A consumption-based technique that characteristically pays tribute to recognizable musicians, sampling enables the DJ to become a creative artist but also marks that DJ as a fan. Robleto treats the emotional bond between musician and fan as a complement to the intimate relationships that are the subject of the overwhelming bulk of pop songs. As the B-side of his Patsy Cline homage indicates, he embraces the promise of pop music to provide a meaningful repository for unrequited love. For *There's an Old Flame Burning in Your Eyes, or, Why Honky Tonk Love Is the Saddest Kind of Love* (1998), he coated matches with ground and melted records by Patsy Cline, Hank Williams, Tammy Wynette, and Conway Twitty before "boxes of these altered matches were laid on bars in several honky tonks around town, waiting for their chance to go out in flames." *Girl Singing in the Wreckage* (2000), a simulated black-box flight recorder made from melted Dusty Springfield records, indulges a metaphor that even sympathetic friends of the broken-hearted might consider overwrought. Punning on the visual and collectible similarities of records and buttons, Robleto describes love of music as the basis for a coherent and resilient social identity in *Sometimes Billie Is All That Holds Me Together* (1998–1999), for which he made colorful buttons from melted Billie Holiday records to replace missing buttons on discarded shirts and then returned the mended shirts to the locations in which he found them. He made a similar point in *If We Do Ever Get Any Closer at Cloning Ourselves Please Tell My Scientist-Doctor to Use Motown Records as My Connecting Parts* (1999–2000).[26]

Robleto emphasizes that fans not only find solace in popular music but also play important roles in the lives of the stars. A series of trophies cast with melted vinyl records, including *I Wish I Could Give Aretha All the R. E. S. P. E. C. T. She Will Ever Need* (1999), expresses the fan's yearning to register his or her admiration effectively. The fan succeeds most fully in helping the recording star survive the passage of time. This peril entails not only the vicissitudes of popularity but also the specter of death. Works like *We Miss Sid!* (1998), in memory of Sid Vicious, illustrate a focus on dead celebrities that Robleto explores most extensively in *Mourning and Redemption (At the Gates of the Dance Floor)* (1999) and *I Miss Everyone Who Has Ever Gone Away (The Suite)* (2000), which honor artists ranging from Karen Carpenter and Freddie Mercury to Jimi Hendrix and Edith Piaf. *It Sounds Like They Still Love Each Other to Me* (1999), a set of matching ear plugs made from melted records by the bands of Kurt Cobain and Courtney Love, suggests that musicians achieve immortal bliss in the imagination of the fan. Like Robleto's return to the theme of disappointed love, his declarations of loyalty to unfashionable or deceased musicians bathe his work in sentimental nostalgia, or as he put it in the title of one work, a belief that *The Past Is Made of Gold, The Future Is Made of Coal* (1999). He commented wryly on this tendency in *Some Memories Are So Vivid I'm Suspicious of Them* (2000–2001), a miniature reproduction of his mother's bedroom as a teenager in which Robleto placed a miniature record made from a melted recording of an original song he wrote for her, "I Thought I Knew Negation Until You Said Goodbye."[27]

Robleto's interest in the awareness of loss prompted him to turn to more fantastic materials than ground and melted vinyl records or magnetic tapes. *The Sad Punk (Named Extinction)* (1998) was a set of singles aptly made from hand-ground dust of the Ammonite fossil known as *discoscaphites gulosus*. Robleto began to incorporate bone fragments of extinct animals by the time he made *It Was Your Age, It's Our Rage* (1999), a fragment of a prehistoric bison filled with a melted vinyl record of Bob Dylan's "The Times They Are A-Changin.'" Other works included dust or fragments from bones of dinosaurs, mammoths, whales, and cave bears. Robleto also alluded to the extinction of the dinosaurs in *We'll Dance Ourselves Out of the Tomb* (2000–2001), a work made from "impact glass" formed when the heat of a meteorite strike melts sand. A more complicated variation was *I Won't Let You Say Goodbye This Time* (2001–2003), a suite of photographs recording the blooming of tomato seeds that NASA sent into space in 1984 on a probe from the shuttle *Challenger,* which exploded two years later at the outset of a mission slated to include retrieval of the seeds, and brought back to earth in 1990 aboard the equally ill-fated *Columbia.* Robleto reported that the porcelain cups in which he planted the tomato seeds incorporated dust from fragments of the ceramic heat shields of space shuttles.[28]

Robleto's use of exotic but thematically appropriate materials perhaps made it inevitable that he would turn to the human body as basis for art. He summarized the central theme of popular music since Elvis Presley in *Our Sin Was in Our Hips* (2001–2002), which combines dust from male and female pelvic bones with hand-ground, powderized, and melted vinyl rock-and-roll records owned by Robleto's father and mother. More thematically original was *Men Are the New Women* (2002), which Elizabeth Dunbar has rightly described as "Robleto's philosopher's stone." A female ribcage bone ground to dust and then recast and carved as a male ribcage bone, this "sampling" of the Book of Genesis suggests the divine power exercised in the art of transmutation. The reversal of the origin myth celebrates a fluidity of gender identity that Robleto had previously evoked in *I've Kissed Your Mother Twice and Now I'm Working on Your Dad* (1998), a cast of an antique lipstick holder made from melted records by the androgynous David Bowie, the New York Dolls, and the Sex Pistols.[29] The feminized image of manhood endorses a gender ideal aligned with the sentimental conventions that Robleto's work on pop music has embraced.

In the wake of September 11 and the invasion of Iraq, Robleto began to apply his established principles and working methods to the subject of war. His written descriptions of his assemblages, still integral to each piece, frequently stress the generality of his interest. For example, *At War with the Entropy of Nature/Ghosts Don't Always Want to Come Back* (2002) is a battered cassette made in part from carved bone and bone dust from every bone in the human body and from trinitite glass produced during the first test of the atomic bomb. The cassette holds an unwound and damaged audiotape that according to Robleto contains an original composition of military marches, sounds of weapon fire, and "soldiers' voices from battlefields of various wars" preserved through electronic voice phenomena recordings of "voices and sounds of the dead or past, detected through magnetic audiotape." He similarly underscored the breadth of his interest in war by mounting a series of exhibitions centered on a fictional soldier who travels through time across all of American wars.[30] Despite this attention to war as a long-term or even timeless social process, Robleto has noted that recognition of his selective historical specificity is important to understanding his work.[31] His "liner notes" mention the Civil War more often than any other conflict. This repetition has little to do with the political issues that precipitated the war, the geographical sites at which the war was fought, or any ideal images of national division and regeneration. Robleto has singled out the Civil War in part for its distinctive patterns of physical suffering but especially for its distinctive patterns of emotional suffering and sympathy. His assemblages alluding to the war explore Victorian mourning and gender conventions as a historical analogue to the sentimentality he has endorsed in his work on pop music.

Several of Robleto's works recall dramatic forms of soldiers' suffering characteristic of the Civil War. Not surprisingly, he has taken interest in the restoration of amputated limbs, a defining image of the Civil War that figures the human body as an assemblage and offers opportunities for extending Robleto's work with bodily materials.[32] *A Defeated Soldier Wishes to Walk His Daughter Down the Wedding Aisle* (2004) features a cast, made from femur bone dust and melted vinyl recordings of the Shirelles' "Soldier Boy," of a hand-carved wooden and iron leg that a Civil War amputee made for himself. Robleto inserted the cast prosthesis in a pair of World War I cavalry boots and placed the boots atop "dirt from various battlefields," suggesting the continued relevance of the Civil War icon well after military amputations became less common. Robleto makes a similar point in *The Creative Potential of Disease* (2004), which began with a self-portrait doll fashioned by a hospitalized Union soldier who had lost a leg. Robleto repaired the doll with new surgical thread, inserted a cast leg made from femur bone, melted bullets, and other materials, and added to the pant legs new material from a modern soldier's uniform.[33] "Pain bullets," into which Civil War soldiers bit during surgery conducted without anesthesia, are another period artifact of suffering that Robleto has extended to subsequent soldiers in *An Atheist as Described by a Surgeon* (2004), for which the artist made a cast of a Civil War original from "re-melted bullet lead salvaged from battlefields of every American war."[34] Horrific as this image is, however, Robleto does not limit it to a military context. He applies it to the anguish of pop music fans in *Not All Dead Rather Be Living* (2001–2002), for which he made the casts of Civil War "pain bullets" from melted vinyl records of musicians killed or seriously wounded by gunfire, including Marvin Gaye, Sam Cooke, and John Lennon.[35]

A respect for sympathetic suffering beyond the battlefield is the main link between Robleto's early work and his interest in the Civil War. He has repeatedly highlighted the material culture of mid-nineteenth-century women's mourning by making the woven hair of a Civil War soldier the only period-specific element in assemblages that otherwise conflate a variety of wars. An autumnal basket that combines Civil War hair flowers with preserved bridal bouquets, dried chrysanthemums, and fragments from a mourning dress, *No One Has a Monopoly over Sorrow* (2005) is an especially haunting remix of Victorian bereavement crafts that incorporates men's ring-finger bones, coated in melted bullet lead from various American wars and decorated with wedding bands excavated from American battlefields. Robleto made his own simulated Civil War hair braids with stretched and curled audiotape recordings of survivors' voices for *The Pause Became Permanence* (2005–2006) and *Daughters of Wounds and Relics* (2006), which also included flowers woven from hair. An overlapping cluster of works, including *A Century of November* (2005) and *Obsequies in Albany* (2006), honors women's Victorian mourning needlework, including dresses, quilts, and dolls.[36] Robleto foregrounds not only the female material culture of mourning but also the Civil War voluntary societies founded and led by women in such works as *Greenville Sanitary Fair* (2005) and *When Pincushions Are Political* (2005). The latter assemblage lists a curriculum sponsored by the Woman's Central Association of Relief that includes a course entitled "Sewing is a Form of Memory."[37] Like the scholarship of Alice Fahs and Judith Ann Giesberg, such work highlights the feminist potential in the Woman's Central Association and other alternatives to the male-led U.S. Sanitary Commission, which devoted its Civil War relief efforts to strengthening the combat readiness of the army and the bureaucratic institutions of the nation.[38] Robleto encourages attention to the individual lives shattered by war rather than any supposed collective justification for inflicting such pain.

Drew Gilpin Faust has provided a framework for understanding Robleto's historically specific vision by comparing mourning conventions of the Civil War with Sigmund Freud's famous analysis of "Mourning and Melancholia" in World War I. Freud described mourning as a process of grief designed to transfer emotional attachment away from the lost object of love. He characterized melancholia, in contrast, as a pathological wallowing in sorrow. Americans in the Civil War era, Faust suggests, often did not share this value system. They frequently believed not only in an eventual reunion with the dead in an afterlife but also in the possibility of communicating with the departed in séances and other spiritualist practices, a faith that Robleto treats respectfully in works that incorporate electronic voice phenomena recordings, an antique Ouija board, and "spirit photographs" that purport to detect ghosts on film.[39] Victorians feared excessive forgetting more than the excessive remembering that Freud warned against, and they surrounded themselves with the loving domestic tributes to the dead that Robleto has updated. Significantly, his work very rarely alludes to the element of military material culture through which Americans since the Civil War have most intently sought transference of love for lost soldiers, the flag. This exclusion is particularly striking in the context of the intensification of reverence for the American flag since September 11. But the diffusion of love for an individual person into an ideological abstraction would contradict Robleto's insistence on the primacy of private rather than public life. His assemblages might also be considered the antithesis of the war memorial, another key artifact of the military commemorative tradition that took its modern form in the Civil War. As Daniel Sherman has shown in a study of such *monuments aux morts* in France after

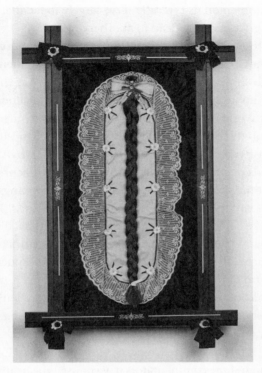

Dario Robleto, *Daughters of Wounds and Relics*, ⊘ᴡ
2006. Hair braid made of stretched and curled
audiotape recordings of the last known Union
Civil War soldier's voice and the last known
Confederate Civil War widow's voice, home-
made paper (pulp made from sweetheart letters
written by soldiers who did not return from
various wars, sepia, bone dust from every bone
in the body), lace and fabric from mourning
dresses, hair flower braided by a Civil War
widow, colored paper, silk, milk paint,
ink-stained ash, glass, typeset; 30×19×3 5/16
inches. Blanton Museum of Art, The University
of Texas at Austin, Promised gift of Jeanne and
Michael Klein, 2007. Courtesy of the artist

World War I, war memorials typically serve largely to facilitate and mask the transference of grief from the dead to another object.[40]

In addition to endorsing the Victorian sentimental culture that Americans took into the Civil War rather than the flags and monuments they brought out of it, Robleto shows a specific affinity for the Civil War through the contrast his works invite with the antiwar assemblages fashioned by Dadaists during and after World War I. Like Marcel Duchamp's ready-mades, these works often centered on the assertion of aesthetic significance in the arbitrary rearrangement of everyday commodities. Kurt Schwitters's *Merzbau* was an especially elaborate reconstruction of the shards of twentieth-century commercial and intellectual life, including scraps of packaging, clippings from newspapers, and a wide variety of other miscellaneous fragments.[41] Robleto's use of precious relics like bone dust or soldiers' letters constitutes a diametrically opposite approach in which war, and its representation by artifact, is not an uncontrollable expression of random modernity but the idiosyncratic and sometimes unique form of individuals' lives.

Robleto's insertion of Civil War motifs into a comprehensive interpretation of the American military experience extends the thematic purposes of his earlier work on popular music as well as the DJ methods that authorize such remixing. His art has shifted logically from unrequited love to unending mourning. Though some commentators have praised the healing power of his work, his aim is less to promote recuperation than to redefine health and reconnect with death. Toward that end he has defended the sentimental culture of the nineteenth as well as the twentieth century. His assemblages consistently propose a reformation of gender ideals that combines normatively masculine tendencies toward science and tinkering with normatively feminine tendencies toward emotion and handicraft.

The selection of *Alloy of Love* (2005) as the "title track" for Robleto's major retrospective epitomizes the important place of the Civil War in this vision.[42] This assemblage is one of several in which a Civil War soldier's woven hair is singled out for mention among materials that also include fabric from soldiers' uniforms of various wars; blanket wool from various wars; military buttons, melted excavated bullet lead and shrapnel; an excavated locket and chain; and paper that Robleto made out of pulp from letters between soldiers and the home front in various wars. The piece also refers specifically to Victorian mourning conventions by simulating a nineteenth-century needlework "sampler," punning on Robleto's own "sampling" methods. At the center of

Alloy of Love, which sounds much like "a law of love," is a sampler-within-the-sampler offering the reminder that "you will outlive the one you are used to loving." The universality of loss, a dominant motif of Robleto's work on pop music, finds its historical precedent in the pervasive suffering of the Civil War.

"The ideals of the past for men have been drawn from war, as those for women have been drawn from motherhood," declared Civil War veteran Oliver Wendell Holmes Jr. in a famous Memorial Day address.[43] Allison Smith and Dario Robleto have engaged Holmes's observation by advancing reinterpretations of sexuality and gender in artworks that draw on the legacy of the Civil War. Sharing a common starting point in the aftermath of September 11 and the Iraq War, they proceed in separate but similar directions. Both suggest with incisive wit that the Civil War offers valuable alternatives to Holmes's narrow ideal of militarized masculinity. Smith's adaptation of the reenactors' encampment opens a bridge between Civil War commemoration and homosexuality. Robleto's assemblages of relics update Civil War sentimentality for the postfeminist era. Their thoughtful work demonstrates that the Civil War remains a useful resource for visual artists in the twenty-first century.

CHAPTER SEVEN

African American Artists Interpret the Civil War in a Post-Soul Age

W. Fitzhugh Brundage

In almost every regard Willie Levi Casey is indistinguishable from thousands of other Confederate reenactors. He traces his Confederate heritage to his great-grandfather's brother, a Confederate enlisted man who died on the battlefield in 1862. Like his fellow Confederate reenactors, he dresses in gray and salutes the Confederate battle flag. Yet, in one conspicuous regard, Casey is unlike most other Confederate reenactors: he is African American. His Confederate ancestor was a white man who fathered six children out of wedlock with Casey's black and Indian great-grandmother.[1]

That Casey has claimed his Confederate heritage is more than a curiosity. It is suggestive of the ways in which contemporary African Americans are recasting our understanding of the Civil War in unexpected and sometimes jarring ways. Against the backdrop of increasingly nuanced scholarship on the causes and impact of the war, and in the context of contemporary frustration with lingering racial inequality, African Americans have produced some of the most provocative recent reinterpretations of the war. Alice Randall, for instance, has retold Margaret Mitchell's plantation romance, *Gone With the Wind*, from the perspective of Scarlett O'Hara's mulatto half-sister Cynara.

Kara Walker, by reviving the lost art of silhouettes and recycling images from the nineteenth century, has inverted mythic images of the war. The gaping holes in and complexities of our national memory of the Civil War inspired poet Natasha Trethewey in her collection *Native Guard*. For Suzan-Lori Parks, the searing legacy of Lincoln's assassination provides the grist for *The America Play*, a postmodern ironic drama about the weight of the past. DJ Spooky's subversive remix of D. W. Griffith's notorious film classic, *Birth of a Nation*, has transformed a familiar icon of early cinematography into a meditation on racial imagery and popular culture. And Kevin Willmott's caustic mockumentary *C.S.A.* seems to take Faulkner's oft-repeated observation—"The past is never dead. It's not even past"—literally when it depicts a present-day Confederate dystopia, complete with slavery, brought about by Confederate victory a century ago.[2] As these examples suggest, the Civil War is now as potent a catalyst for African American creativity as at any time since the war itself. Yet these works also indicate that African American artists either cannot or elect not to escape the constraints of long-established myths and clichés about the Civil War. For all of their creative inversion, subversion, and revision of received images and myths about the Civil War, these artists nevertheless remain tethered to them.

This renascence of Civil War art and letters is led by African Americans who, like reenactor Willie Lee Casey, were born during the late 1950s and 1960s. (Paul Miller is a youthful outlier in the group; he was born in 1970.) Still young children when the modern civil rights movement was cresting, these artists were educated and came of age during the 1970s in a post-segregated United States. They grew up in a liminal moment when the nation's long established racial hierarchy was rapidly collapsing, but American culture remained cluttered with enduring Civil War icons, totems, and shibboleths that continued to confound even the most creative interpreters of the conflict.

One illustration of the cultural landscape that prevailed during the formative years of these African American artists was Edmund Wilson's *Patriotic Gore: Studies in the Literature of the Civil War*, published in 1962. Wilson, the preeminent literary critic of his generation, presented a compendium of authors who had addressed the Civil War. His most striking claim, at least to present-day ears, is that the Civil War was a war of northern aggression, a northern power grab cloaked in meaningless, "rabble-rousing," and "pseudo-moral" anti-slavery

slogans. Wilson openly admired Alexander Stephens, a tireless defender of secession and the vice president of the Confederacy. Stephens' notorious benedic-
tion of slavery as the cornerstone of the Confederacy in the early days of the
slaveholders' republic elicited not even a wince from Wilson. Instead, Wilson
dwelled on what he interpreted as Stephens' prescient fears of a leviathan state.
Wilson even proposed that, in an age of apparent bureaucratic tyranny, "the
cause of the South is the cause of us all." When Wilson considered the nation's
predicament in 1962, he urged his contemporaries to turn to the vice president
of the Confederacy for wisdom.[3]

Wilson's prejudices—political and aesthetic—may strike us as idiosyncratic
and contrarian now. Yet many of them were consonant with the conventional
wisdom of the nation, circa the Civil War centennial. During the century after
Appomattox, white Americans reached a durable national consensus that many
chronic disputes—states' rights versus national consolidation, industrial capitalism versus agrarianism—had boiled over in the Civil War. Slavery, however, was seldom stressed as the war's precipitating cause. The providential
restoration of the Union, and not the eradication of the blight of slavery, was,
in the eyes of most commentators, the war's most important outcome. Thus,
Wilson's blindness to the central importance of blacks to both the sundering
and reuniting of the nation was unexceptional.[4]

The consequences of this amnesia were broad and profound. During the
late nineteenth century, at precisely the moment when white supremacists
mounted their assault on post-war black rights, the nation's cultural arbiters
and historians erased almost all historical traces of black participation in the
nation's past. Blacks were reduced to objects of patronizing sentimentality or
violent rage, but not respect or empathy. The consequences for American
thought and artistic expression were equally far-reaching, as historians David
Blight, Kirk Savage, and others have explained.[5] A decade after the publication of Wilson's critique of Civil War literature, Daniel Aaron reached different conclusions in *The Unwritten War*. Why, Aaron queried, was the Civil War
"the unwritten war"? He conceded that library shelves groaned under the
weight of the novels, plays, and poetry inspired by the war. But, he lamented,
fiction about the war was marred by evasions, silences, and clichés. His scholarly labors left him convinced that "the War was not so much unfelt as un-
faced" in American arts. The explanation for this creative blockage, he rea-
soned, was the reluctance of whites to acknowledge the salience of slavery and
race to the nation's history, and the Civil War especially. "Without the Negro,

there would have been no Civil War," Aaron insisted. Because whites refused to accept this fact they rendered blacks peripheral in the literature about the nation's greatest trauma. By being complicit in the erasure of race and blacks from the war, Aaron charged, the nation's writers forsook their appropriate, even crucial, role as critics, moralists, and prophets.[6]

If white writers and artists skirted the vexing questions of the Civil War, their black peers did not. Even during the late nineteenth and early twentieth centuries when the literature of sectional reconciliation threatened to suffocate dissenting interpretations, Frederick Douglass, W. E. B. Du Bois, Jacob Lawrence, and other African American nonconformists jousted with the ascendant interpretations of the war as the Brothers' War and the Lost Cause. Their voices of protest, however, elicited little response from white commentators. As late as 1962 most commentators found Edmund Wilson's canon of Civil War literature impressively capacious, even though it failed to include Douglass, Frances Ellen Watkins Harper, or any other African American voices. This void was the result of white deafness, not black silence.

When Alice Randall, Kara Walker, Natasha Trethewey, and their peers turned their attention to the Civil War, they were not answering Aaron's call for writers and artists to reconsider the Civil War so much as they were responding to the accelerating revision of the historical understanding of slavery, the Civil War, and the African American experience already underway. The mid-twentieth century conventional wisdom that informed Edmund Wilson's *Patriotic Gore* was being turned on its head. By the 1980s, if not earlier, more and more scholars were agreeing that slavery was at the root of sectional conflict and that blacks, both enslaved and free, were historical actors who took the lead in transforming the Civil War into a war for emancipation. The extraordinarily successful television miniseries based on Alex Haley's *Roots* made this new historical scholarship and the long ignored black counter-memory of slavery accessible to vast audiences.[7]

Simultaneously, Randall and her generation of African American artists embraced a "post-soul aesthetics" that gave them a new orientation toward the nation's troubled past.[8] In particular, they moved away from the underlying assumptions of the black nationalist arts movement of the 1960s and instead promoted a self-conscious repudiation of any essential notion of blackness or black experience. Playwright Suzan-Lori Parks has summarized one of the fundamental tenets of the post-soul aesthetics, observing that "there is no single 'Black Experience,' [so] there is no one way to write or think or feel or *sounds postmodern*

dream or interpret or be interpreted."[9] This post-soul generation viewed with suspicion the traditional separation of elite art and mass culture. In a commencement speech to graduates of Mount Holyoke College, Parks urged her audience to balance the sublime and the quotidian: "For every 30 min of TV you watch, READ one poem out loud. For every work of literature you read, spend at least 30 min in the mall, or in a mall equivalent, such as Wal-Mart. This is cross-fertilization—a new-age form of crop rotation—a way to cross train your spirit and keep interested in everything and not get too stuck in your ways."[10] Having been immersed in mass consumer culture and media in their youth, Parks and the other black artists who came of age in the 1970s were predisposed to use popular culture parody, pastiche, and reversal to undermine negative racial stereotypes and symbols. In order for African American subjects and concerns to win a place in the nation's collective memory, the thinking went, black artists had to challenge, subvert, or revise iconic myths that already littered it, ranging from the idealized Old South plantations of *Gone With the Wind* to the martyred emancipator, Abraham Lincoln. There was no shortage of subjects awaiting reinterpretation in the 1970s. Black artists had to do more than add to the national memory of the Civil War. First they had to renovate it.

❦

To confront this challenge, Randall, Walker, Willmott, and other black artists adapted to their circumstances the African American tradition of "signifying."[11] Appropriating purportedly American ideals or symbols and turning them back on white oppressors were essential components of black expression well before the Civil War. Signifying enabled African Americans to use a rhetorical strategy of inversion, repetition, and parody to contest conventional wisdom about race and identity. The inversion of tropes and symbols, the manipulation of popular genres, and the splicing of narratives were time-honored devices in African American signifying before they were elevated to cultural theory by twentieth-century intellectuals, and the long history of this mode of dissent appealed to recent black artists. To employ it was to make cause with black activists stretching back to the dawn of the American republic.

Randall's 2001 novel, *The Wind Done Gone*, illustrates how signifying makes it possible for African Americans to both lay claim to and revise a Civil War icon such as *Gone With the Wind*.[12] Randall's novel is simultaneously faithful to and subversive of Margaret Mitchell's enormously popular and influential novel. The cast of characters that populated Mitchell's saga is present in Randall's parody, but they are identified by revealing nicknames assigned by their slaves. Scarlett is "Other"; Rhett Butler becomes "R" and later "Debt Chauffeur." Ashley Wilkes is "Dreamy Gentleman," and his wife Melanie is "Mealy Mouth." Mr. O'Hara, who bears the name "Planter" and is married to "Lady," presides over the "Cotton Farm" plantation. Pork, a slave on the O'Hara's plantation, looms large in the story, but bears the name of "Garlic."

Only Cynara, the novel's narrator, is wholly Randall's creation. The mulatta daughter of Planter and Mammy, she is Scarlett's half sister. Inheriting the status of her slave mother, Cynara was sold away from Tara (called "Tata" in Randall's book) in her youth. While working at Belle Watling's whorehouse, Cynara came under the protection of Rhett Butler, who, like a southern Henry Higgins, encouraged her to acquire literacy, master etiquette, and accumulate the accouterments of ladyhood. Randall's conceit of an interracial relationship between Cynara and Rhett is only the first of her subversions of the plantation romance genre, of which *Gone With the Wind* is arguably the archetype.

In an even more subversive twist, Randall gives new significance to a minor plot development in *Gone With the Wind*. In Mitchell's narrative, Scarlett's mother had been deeply disappointed in a childhood romance with a cousin. In *The Wind Done Gone* we learn that young Mrs. O'Hara had been forbidden from marrying her cousin because they shared a great-great grandmother who was black, and any children their marriage produced might reveal their mixed race ancestry. Because Mrs. O'Hara is black, so too is Scarlett. Thus, Cynara and Scarlett have far more in common than their status would suggest; they are half-sisters, both black, and rivals in a love triangle with Rhett Butler.

These reimagined genealogies of the protagonists in *Gone With the Wind*, however convoluted and implausible they may appear, enable Randall to explore the fraught topic of love and desire in a slave society. While *Gone With the Wind* revolves around a classic love story, Mitchell displayed no interest in love beyond the ranks of white aristocrats. In Randall's telling, love and desire torment virtually every relationship in the novel. Ashley Wilkes, for example, is a homosexual who pines for Cynara's brother. As in *Gone With the Wind* Scarlett pursues Ashley but, as a result of Cynara's machinations, she enters a stormy relationship with Rhett Butler instead. Even more tortured are the relationships between the half-sisters and their mothers. From an early age, Scarlett (mistakenly) believes Mammy to be a source of selfless, unquestioning love. Young Cynara misinterprets Mammy's attentions to Scarlett as maternal love, rather than the coerced ministrations of a slave. Cynara turns for comfort to Mrs. O'Hara, who herself yearns for the love of her daughter Scarlett, which Scarlett directs toward Mammy.

This knot of unrequited loves may result, in part, from the author's admitted penchant for the clichés of overwrought historical romances and southern gothic fiction. But through these relationships Randall reveals the distortions that slavery and racial identity imposed on every expression of love and desire in the nineteenth-century South. After "Other" (Scarlett) dies, freeing Cynara of the compulsion to compete with her half-sister, Cynara renounces Rhett. Only then is Randall's protagonist able to experience uncorrupted love, in the arms of an African American politico. And only then does she come to understand that her mother's apparent devotion to Scarlett was a display of pragmatic duplicity. Randall aspires, then, to do more than fill in the gaps in Mitchell's plantation romance by giving agency to Tara's slaves. She also explores the intricate relationships that bound slave and master, mother and child, kith and kin in the Old South—relationships that until recently received little attention in scholarship or in art.

Like Randall's parody of *Gone With the Wind*, artist Kara Walker's oeuvre exemplifies the playful subversion of genres and the self-conscious intertextuality that characterizes recent African American meditations on the Civil War.[13] Just as Randall borrows from the tradition of low-brow historical romances, so too Kara Walker ignores the conventions of high art, embracing instead an outmoded art form and fashioning many of her works from simple materials. Her work includes index cards bearing cryptic typed messages, drawings, watercolors, and, most famously, silhouettes. If contemporary art spectators are familiar with silhouettes they probably recall them as a quaint, bygone form of portraiture fashionable during the neoclassical revival of the late eighteenth and early nineteenth centuries. Mimicking the images that adorned ancient Greek and Roman vases, silhouette artists cut profiles of American gentry from black card and mounted them against white backgrounds. As the cheapest method to record a person's appearance, both silhouettes of family members as well as mass-produced profiles of the nation's great and good adorned the walls of American homes until the advent of photography.[14]

These historical antecedents do little to prepare the viewer for Walker's radical adaptation of the lost art of silhouettes, which she uses to depict scenes of servitude, rape, pedophilia, murder, and other horrors. Walker accentuates the stark, recurring duality of white and black in her silhouettes, achieving images that are at once elegant and vulgar, transparent and obscure, grim and funny. She portrays a world full of mischief, humor, and violence, where desire and contempt, sex and torture, play and brutality intermingle. Her humor evokes the comedy of the minstrel show while her imagery invokes the sentimentality of rustic Americana. The massive size and positioning of Walker's silhouettes also depart from the conventions of nineteenth-century silhouettes. Instead of small human faces in profile, Walker creates life-sized silhouettes of entire bodies positioned on large unadorned walls to create complex scenes with implied narratives.

The conceit of the silhouette is to portray the essence of an object by winnowing out extraneous detail. Scrupulously faithful to the details of the profile while effacing all other attributes of the represented object, the silhouette forces the viewer to concentrate on the defining outline of a subject. This quality made silhouettes useful for purposes of description, identification, and classification even after they fell out of favor as a form of portraiture. Thus authorities during World War II distributed silhouettes of enemy aircraft to civil defense volunteers, and nature guidebooks used silhouettes to facilitate the identification and classification of fauna.

Interpreting these and other silhouettes, however, is not as simple a task as it may seem. Silhouettes acquire meaning because viewers' minds are unsatisfied by the sparse information the images convey. Viewers tap into inherited storehouses of visual cues and tropes to fill in the missing information. Every silhouette is at once a citation of a real object and an invention of the viewer's imagination.

Coaxing viewers to plumb their storehouses of stereotypes is at the center of Walker's art. The visual vocabulary of Walker's fantasy slave plantation world includes stereotypical images from black memorabilia, folklore, historical novels, movies, cartoons, old advertisements, Harlequin romances, nineteenth-century slave autobiographies, and pornography. Walker's most obvious subjects are the racial stereotypes that have long populated American culture, and especially mass culture during the past century. Each figure epitomizes and conforms to some generally legible and familiar formula of black identity. Because we recognize the visual cues in Walker's silhouettes that distinguish a white plantation mistress and a slaveholder from a black mammy or slave child, we ignore that every figure in Walker's silhouettes is black. Her art is a dramatic subversion of the old one-drop rule that categorized as black anyone who had any African ancestry, including those who were generations removed from a dark-skinned progenitor. For Walker, "blackness" is unmistakably rendered visible against a white background. Even her white characters take on the blackness of the silhouette form so that both white and black racial identities acquire their visibility in relation to blackness.[15]

In many instances, Walker's images represent exaggerated, scripted identities that previously surfaced in Hollywood movies and on vaudeville stages. Walker explains, "The silhouette says a lot with very little information, but that's also what the stereotype does. So I saw the silhouette and stereotype as linked."[16] Silhouettes allow her to represent literally the figurative flatness of stereotypes. In the obvious sense, her images lack depth. But so too do the subjects of her images. Her images suggest that real empathy, knowledge, and memory of slavery are beyond our grasp. Instead we are limited to interpreting artifacts and reflecting on our own prejudices, fears, and desires.

Although Walker's images of the Civil War exploit stereotypes, they present the conflict in strikingly unfamiliar ways. Violence and suffering suffuse Walker's war images, but battlefield combat and conventional war scenes are almost entirely absent. In her "Battle of Atlanta" silhouettes Walker transforms the battle that had previously been immortalized in a massive cylindrical painting known as the Atlanta Cyclorama.[17] Unlike the heroic late nineteenth-century painting, which depicts fierce and close combat between Confederate and Union troops, Walker's silhouettes locate the battlefield—depicted by firing artillery—in the remote background. Uninterested in the conventional heroic narrative of the war, Walker depicts the real battlefield of the Civil War as the home front, where the mundane and systemic violence of desire and domination unfolded. Repeatedly in the "Battle of Atlanta" silhouettes she combines military and death imagery with depictions of fervid sexual desire. In one silhouette a black women clasps the limp body of a soldier on the battlefield (the dead body of her lover, a family member?). Another image depicts a black woman licking the rifle barrel of a sleeping soldier (whether he is a Union or Confederate soldier is unclear).

Walker has also crafted simple collages that mix modern advertising images with illustrations from *Harper's Pictorial History of the Civil War.*[18] Here Walker seems intent on connecting white mastery of black bodies with masculine posturing in the halls of power and on the battlefield. Whereas Edmund Wilson depicted Alexander Stephens and his ilk as principled opponents of the leviathan state, Walker suggests that libido, at least as much as principle, motivated

Kara Walker, *The Battle of Atlanta: Being the Narrative of a Negress in the Flames of Desire—A Reconstruction* (detail), 1995. Cut paper on wall; 13×30 feet. Private collection. Courtesy of Sikkema Jenkins & Co.

the Confederate cause. In one collage, Walker has almost covered a *Harper's* image of an exploding naval vessel with a modern photograph of a naked black woman, legs spread wide and aloft. The woman appears to be gagged by a Civil War–era illustration of a dying soldier; the outline of the woman's legs and crotch is covered by a cutting from a Civil War–era print that depicts African American troops assaulting a Confederate fort. Another collage depicts the Alabama delegation to Congress on the eve of secession. The delegation members' portraits are garnished with contemporary personal ads that appear, in the fashion of word bubbles above comic strip characters, as solicitations for "diaper lovers," "very healthy, thick, shapely women," bisexuals, "slave boys" interested in sadomasochism, spanking enthusiasts, and sexual partners with other exotic predilections. Like thick graffiti eyebrows and a mustache scrawled on the portrait of a dictator, Walker's collage is a subversive prank intended to humble arrogance. The juxtaposition of portraits of somber white slaveholding patriarchs and their apparent private fetishes also highlights the theme of mastery and power in the slave South; her subjects are masters of both the halls of power and bedroom, men whose appetites for power and gratification are inseparable. But are they only "masters" when it comes to these sexual predilections, or are they perhaps also "enslaved" by their desires?

Walker's subversion of the conventional imagery of the Civil War extends to icons of African American memory as well. In 1996 Walker completed a large gouache painting (a method of painting using opaque pigments ground in water and thickened with a glue-like substance) of abolitionist firebrand John Brown. His leadership of an ill-fated 1859 attack on the federal armory in Harpers Ferry, Virginia, turned Brown into one of the most divisive figures in American history.[19] For white southerners on the threshold of the Civil War, Brown's militant abolitionism was anathema. For many white northerners, he assumed a heroic, even Christ-like role, especially during the time between his capture and eventual execution. That Brown was willing to sacrifice his life, and those of his two sons who accompanied him on the raid, was interpreted as an extraordinarily selfless act. He further burnished his reputation when, on the march to his hanging, he purportedly paused to publicly kiss a black infant in the arms of its mother. At that moment, according to a widely reprinted contemporary newspaper account, he exhibited "the tenderness of one whose love is as broad as the brotherhood of man" and inspired generations of poets, writers, and artists. Within weeks poet John Greenleaf Whittier had enshrined Brown's gesture in an elegy to the martyred abolitionist; within a year painter Louis Ransom had rendered it in *John Brown on His Way to Execution*. Three years later lithographers Currier & Ives popularized Ransom's image. Additional renderings would appear in 1867, when painter Thomas Satterwhite Noble completed *John Brown's Blessing*, and in 1884, when Thomas Hovenden finished perhaps the best-known nineteenth-century painting of Brown's now famous gesture, *The Last Moments of John Brown*.[20]

African Americans were equally quick to enshrine Brown in their pantheon of American heroes. Frederick Douglass, W. E. B. Du Bois, and other black activists stressed Brown's prescience in recognizing that slavery could be vanquished only with sacrifice and bloodshed. Likewise, they contrasted Brown's singular passion for and commitment to racial equality with the cautious gradualism advocated by most subsequent white reformers. Brown's life aroused renewed interest among leading black artists during the 1940s. In 1941 Jacob Lawrence completed his twenty-two panel series of goauche paintings devoted to Brown's martyrdom. Characterized by dramatic color contrasts, stark geometric design, and conspicuous Christian symbols, especially crosses and crucifixes, Lawrence's paintings render Brown a prophetic figure whose life was an expression of piety and sacrifice. Likewise, in Horace Pippin's trilogy of Brown paintings, the abolitionist appears as a Moses figure, literally leading blacks out of their bondage and into the promised land. William H. Johnson, in his 1945 oil painting, *John Brown Legend*, returned to the tradition of capturing Brown's celebrated kiss of the black infant while bound for the gallows. The recurring image of Brown was of a saintly patriarch who was at once a savior of African Americans and a redeemer of the nation. (A notable exception to the saintly renderings of Brown was John Steuart Curry's *Tragic Prelude*, a mural in the Kansas state capitol that depicted the abolitionist with blood-soaked hands, grasping a rifle and Bible and towering over every other figure in the painting. Curry's work highlighted Brown's messianic and violent methods, but it accentuated, literally and figuratively, the abolitionist's heroic stature.)[21]

Kara Walker's 1996 painting of John Brown should be viewed against the backdrop of this rich history of depictions of the abolitionist, and especially of the iconic moments in Brown's life. Whereas Walker's silhouettes often depict the forgotten or suppressed past, her painting of John Brown is a radical revision of a familiar figure and an iconic event. Instead of Pippin's Moses-like figure, or Hovenden's saintly martyr, or even Currey's ferocious prophet, Walker renders Brown as a bearded, diminutive old man who is naked from the waist up. Opposite and near him stands a black woman adorned with a kerchief, a naked child pressed against her body. The mother ignores Brown and instead looks down at her child, whose teeth pull at the nipple of one of Brown's sagging breasts. Grimacing in pain, Brown turns away from the child. The scene is prosaic; it is bereft of spectators or background detail.[22]

The contrast with earlier depictions of Brown could hardly be starker. Walker's John Brown is enfeebled and stripped of majesty. He can provide no succor to the young black child suckling his barren breast. Nor does Walker's painting indicate that Brown has any philanthropic intentions toward mother or child. Nothing in his face or posture conveys moral urgency or commitment. Walker's painting suggests that the heroic John Brown of myth cannot nourish contemporary African Americans. As art historian Gwendolyn DuBois Shaw explains: "In Walker's critique of the pantheon of African American art and

Kara Walker, *John Brown*, 1996. Gouache on paper;
165×131 centimeters. Courtesy of the Dakis Joannou
Collection

history, Brown has been exposed as a hollow icon, a failed patriarch, and an impotent mater familias."[23]

Walker's collages, paintings, and silhouettes accentuate the absurdity and incongruity of the mythic images of slavery and the Civil War. At the same time she seems to dismiss any suggestion that there is an authentic historical memory of slavery or the Civil War uncontaminated by racism and stereotype. The memory of slavery and war, as presented by Walker, is an accumulation of inherited cultural artifacts—advertisements, minstrel show skits, Hollywood movies, plantation romances, and pornography. If there is another, richer memory of either slavery or the war she has elected to ignore it.

Playwright Suzan-Lori Parks shares many of Walker's concerns, and her disturbing and deeply ironic meditation about the inheritance and performance of identity in *The America Play* suggests a similar pessimism about the restorative capacity of memory. Parks's life story has almost certainly contributed to her acute interest in the subjectivity of racial identity. She was born in Kentucky but spent her childhood moving from military base to base with her family. During formative years in Germany, where she attended a German high school, she found herself being judged by race, not nationality. After attending Mount Holyoke she began writing plays and screenplays, including *The America Play* and her 2001 Pulitzer Prize–winning *Topdog/Underdog*.[24]

Parks's early plays, including *The America Play*, have been referred to as "the history plays" in which the playwright reconstructs historical events to fill a void or "hole" in history caused by the exclusion of African Americans. These nonrealistic, experimental plays feature characters that are alienated from the history they feel compelled to resurrect, revisit, and reconstruct. Parks explains, "Through each line of text I'm rewriting the Time Line—creating history where it is and always was but has not yet been divined."[25] But creating history, Parks suggests, is not the same thing as coming to terms with all that we inherit from the past. Getting right with the past is an unending, repetitive, and inevitably incomplete quest.

The America Play provides no simple or clear answers. Instead, Parks forces us to contemplate the motivations and circumstances of the "Lesser Known," a black man who has been told since birth that he is a "dead ringer" for Abraham Lincoln and who earns his living reenacting Lincoln's assassination. At a theme park, "The Great Hole of Historicities," tourists pay a (Lincoln) penny, select a pistol, enter a darkened booth, and "Shoot Mr. Lincoln," who is, in fact, The Lesser Known in a stovepipe hat and false beard. Like Lincoln's real-life murderer, the reenactors shout catchphrases as "The Lesser Known" slumps dramatically after each shot. What would prompt, Parks seems to ask, a black Lincoln impersonator to accept the assignment of being murdered again and again and again? And what would motivate tourists to reenact Booth's treachery and to derive pleasure and release from it?

Despite the predictable and repetitive quality of the reenacted assassinations, *The America Play* reveals Parks's suspicion of teleological or linear narratives. Each recreated assassination ends with the Lesser Known slumped in mock death, but the ersatz assassins shout unique slogans and epithets and, in one instance, even pay to shoot Lincoln twice. It is as though the meaning of Lincoln's assassination is assigned anew each time a latter-day John Wilkes Booth pulls the trigger. Only through reenacting the assassination does this pivotal event in American history acquire particular meanings for the participants. But as quickly as they are generated, these meanings dissolve.

In the second act of *The America Play* the Lesser Known's son Brazil makes his living as a professional mourner. Over and over at funerals, Brazil performs a repertoire of grieving histrionics, learned from his now deceased father. But preserving his father's craft is insufficient to satisfy Brazil's longing for some connection with his father. Joined by his mother Lucy, Brazil searches for the Lesser Known's remains. Excavating the "Great Hole of Historicities," Brazil recovers traces of his patrimony. Among the relics uncovered are a bust of Lincoln, Washington's wooden teeth, bills of sale, peace pacts, and medals for "faking." The meanings of these objects remain obscure, not only to the audience but also to the characters. Queried as to their significance, Lucy repeatedly mutters, "Can't say, can't say."[26] With this simple, cryptic retort, which confirms the indeterminable, ambiguous nature of the past, Park underscores her deep mistrust of inflated historical narratives.

Heroic narratives of the Civil War era, particularly the romance for white Americans of the Ku Klux Klan, are at the center of the multimedia historical criticism of Paul Miller (also known as DJ Spooky That Subliminal Kid). Like Parks, Miller bridles at contemporary complacency with respect to inherited historical wisdom. Like Walker, he is wary of the continuing and corrosive power of cultural icons inherited from the origins of American mass culture. Miller deplores the "culture of amnesia" that prevails in the United States. A Washington, DC-born turntablist, producer, and electronic/hip hop musician, Miller exploits the possibilities of DJing techniques of sampling and recombination, but extends them to aural, visual, and textual sources. In 2004 Miller received a commission from several international arts festivals to remix *Birth of a Nation*. He performed the remix, his first large-scale multimedia performance piece, more than fifty times around the world, and in 2008 a DVD version was released. That Miller would turn his attention to film pioneer D. W. Griffith's epic is not surprising. The film, Miller contends in the narration to his remix, "set the tone for how film portrayed history" for the next century and "hangs as a specter over the political process" even in the twenty-first century United States.[27]

According to Miller, we are entering "an era of multiplex consciousness." "Everything," he contends, "is completely open to revision and change." "How," he wonders, "do you live in a world where everything is edited, sequenced, spliced and diced?"[28] Drawing on hip hop and DJing as well as modernist

conceptions of collage, fracture, and appropriation, Miller revels in the possibilities of our postmodern moment. Images, sounds, and data have become
untethered from their original meaning and are now fodder for endless recon-
figuration, appropriation, and subversion. A student of French literature and
philosophy while an undergraduate at Bowdoin College, Miller wrote science
fiction before adopting the stage name The Subliminal Kid from a character
in William S. Burrough's novel *Nova Express*. His genre crossing is in keeping
with his penchant for postmodern cultural theory and artistic expression that
straddles the line between high and low art, aesthetics, and commodity. Miller
states baldly, "I don't really believe in the high/low distinction."[29]

Miller envisions himself a "memory artist" who is politically engaged in
"fighting stereotypes in patterns of thought." Describing American culture as
"a cut-and-paste culture" in which personal and collective identities have always been the product of "sampling," Miller intends his remix of *Birth of a
Nation* to emancipate us from the legacy of the source material: "It has been
said that those who don't learn from history are doomed to repeat it. But what
happens if we break the cycle?" "Stories," he affirms, "can be made as we go."[30]

Like Randall's *The Wind Done Gone* and Walker's silhouettes, Miller's *Rebirth of a Nation* confounds and inverts an icon of twentieth-century American mass culture. Although Miller's cinematic appropriation builds on a rich
tradition that extends back to Joseph Cornell's 1936 found-film montage, *Rose
Hobart,* Miller preserves the narrative structure of Griffith's film. He tightens
the narrative and manipulates film images in order to highlight particular
scenes and plot developments. But the recontextualization of the film is prin-
cipally achieved by projecting it as a triptych, with the center screen displaying the film in its proper sequence, though sampled, accelerated, and frozen
at Miller's discretion, with complementary flashbacks, flash-forwards, and images displayed on the two side screens. Through these multiple and simulta-
neous film narratives, Miller emphasizes underlying themes and contradic-
tions in *Birth of a Nation*. Miller augments Griffith's original film images with
filters, geometric designs that frame certain characters, and overlays of maps
and stylized circuit boards. Accompanying this visual remix is a soundtrack
that joins electronic beats, classical instrumentation, and early blues motifs
derived from bluesman Robert Johnson. Underscoring the contemporaneous
and endless possibilities of remixing, no two performances of *Rebirth* are the
same. Miller selects material in real time from the cuts and loops on his laptop
computer, matching them with elements from the soundtrack.

Miller's remix is less a revelation than a translation. Few contemporary filmgoers are likely to watch Griffith's lengthy silent movie with its melodramatic acting and unfamiliar intertitles between scenes. Miller's editing renders the film's pacing and acting far more accessible to contemporary viewers. Miller also uses his voiceover to insist on the film's continuing salience. Griffith's romantic portrayal of the Ku Klux Klan saving the nation's Aryans from the depredations of newly freed slaves, Miller contends, foreshadowed twentieth-century techniques of propaganda and historical revisionism. Miller even draws a connection between the sham history of D. W. Griffith's film and the spurious grounds for the U.S. invasion of Iraq in 2003.

In the end, however, Miller, like playwright Suzan-Lori Parks, displays an irreverence toward history. Like a mixmaster, he does not want us to be condemned to endless repetitions of the past. He insists that we reflect on the continuing grip of *Birth of a Nation* on the American imagination. But he seems unsure of how the influence of Griffith's film is manifest in contemporary life or how we can remix the past. Like many of his artistic peers who have taken on the historical memory of the Civil War, Miller is certain of the need for its revision. But he defers the responsibility to address what those revisions should entail. "I want people leaving with the idea of asking questions, not expecting answers," he explains.[31]

Kevin Willmott's ambition in his pseudo-documentary *C. S. A.* also seems to be to goad viewers into thinking anew about who really won the Civil War. His starting point is that "The South really didn't give up anything important after the Civil War. . . . They came to define black people in this country."[32] *C. S. A.* answers the question of what would have happened if the slave South had won the Civil War and the United States had been absorbed into the Confederate States of America. Using the pretext of the first airing of a controversial British documentary broadcast in the Confederate States, Willmott employs the technique of inversion to radically revise decisive events in the nation's history. Whereas in real life Confederate president Jefferson Davis was captured while disguised in a woman's shawl, Willmott's mockumentary explains recounts Abraham Lincoln's capture while fleeing, in blackface, on the Underground Railroad to Canada. Harriet Tubman, who assisted Lincoln, was also captured. She subsequently was tried and executed. Lincoln, after years in Confederate prisons, was exiled to Canada, where he died in obscurity and disrepute. Dedicated abolitionists fled to Canada, where abolitionism became a secret conspiracy, and by the mid-twentieth century a Cold War between the C. S. A. and Canada posed the greatest threat to the C. S. A. Lincoln's Emancipation Proclamation proves to be a historical curiosity in the face of the rapid revival of slavery across the continent. After accepting their defeat with relative equanimity, white northerners responded to tax incentives to invest in slaves. The C. S. A. even wedded slavery to Manifest Destiny and restored human bondage throughout the western hemisphere. The logical culmination of the Confederacy's ideology was the nation's decision to not only tolerate Hitler's rise—after all, his racial ideology complemented that of the C. S. A.—but also launch a sneak attack, on December 7, 1941, on Japan, the perceived source of an advancing Asian peril.

Willmott's artifice is that his counter-history is sufficiently plausible that it becomes eerily familiar. The footage of a Cold War–era African politico and slavery apologist could just as easily be of a pro-Western African dictator justifying his ruthless authoritarianism in the name of democracy. How different, Willmott implicitly asks, were the real-life 1960s urban riots in Detroit and Newark from the slave revolts in those cities depicted in *C. S. A.?* Even more telling, the faux commercials that interrupt the purported broadcast of the documentary expose the persistence of black stereotypes that graced advertisements for a century after the Civil War. Like Spike Lee, who includes alarmingly realistic advertisements in *Bamboozled*, Willmott is acutely aware of how Madison Avenue and Hollywood have fashioned the image of African Americans in the national imagination. And like the visual imagery of racial stereotypes that Kara Walker depicts in her silhouettes, advertisements, according to Willmott, filter representations of African Americans so as to render them grotesquely superficial and stereotypical.[33]

Willmott has acknowledged that, as for many of his peers, identity is a central theme of his art. "All my films deal with the complexities of African American identity and the lies that have to be broken down to arrive at a more secure self-definition of who we are."[34] A recurring talking head throughout *C. S. A.* is Ambrose Fauntroy, a descendant of distinguished Confederates, a present-day apologist for slavery and other "traditional" values, and an aspiring presidential candidate. Fauntroy's campaign is derailed and the candidate is driven to suicide after he is denounced by a slave who claims that Fauntroy is descended from black slaves. In this instance, the "lie" of Fauntroy's whiteness points up the absurdity of fixed racial identities; only by twisting history can white Confederates claim racial purity and superiority. Fauntroy's identity as a white man and as a purportedly selfless paternalist are a fiction that is preserved only as long as his human chattel are voiceless.

Fauntroy's exposure by a slave is one of the few instances when Willmott acknowledges African American agency in *C. S. A.* Seemingly underscoring Willmott's unmistakable pessimism about the possibilities for African American self-determination in the United States, Willmott devotes no time to exploring African American resistance to slavery. Instead the abolitionists exiled to Canada after the Civil War evolve into present-day freedom fighters/terrorists. Not only is there no civil rights struggle in the Willmott's counter-history, but there also is apparently no possibility of a W. E. B. Du Bois or a Martin Luther King Jr. Instead, Willmott depicts a history almost devoid of either black voices or black agency. *even in slavery - counter to much scholarship*

Like many of her creative peers, poet Natasha Trethewey uses her art to ponder what history is forgotten, what history is remembered, and how the recalled past weighs on us. But her orientation toward tradition is distinctive; rather than set out to satirize, explode, or scrap it, Trethewey engages respectfully with the inherited past. She seems to suggest that the weight of the past is not entirely an unwelcome burden. Trethewey is a Mississippian, born of a white father and a black mother in 1966, two years before the Supreme Court ruled miscegenation laws unconstitutional. Her heritage and identity as a biracial southerner inform her poetry and prompt her to question familiar or fixed conceptions of racial and regional identity. She is especially keen to expose the erasures—"things that aren't monumented or memorialized"—and to broaden the traditions from which she draws her inspiration.[35]

Trethewey, along with her post-soul peers, is adept at finding new uses for inherited artistic forms. In Trethewey's work, poetic forms and thematic concerns complement each other. Her Pulitzer Prize–winning collection, *Native Guard*, demonstrates her mastery of arcane forms that are almost certainly unfamiliar to many readers. In the collection she includes: a pantoon (pantoun), an uncommon Malaysian-derived poetic form rarely used in English; a villanelle, a form that consists of nineteen lines that use only two rhymes; a cancrizan, in which the second twelve lines repeat the first twelve lines but in reverse order; a ghazal, an Urdu poetic form associated with erotic love; and lyrical sonnets. By employing these diverse forms Trethewey displays poetic virtuosity and acknowledges the history of her craft; she also memorializes her subjects. She explains: "I used a lot of forms that had repetition or refrain, like the blues, the blues sonnet, or a pantoon, so that I could say the lines over and over again. It seemed to me that, in order to try to inscribe or reinscribe what is forgotten, I needed to say a thing and to say it again."[36]

The weight of and responsibility to the past—both welcome and unwelcome—is a recurring theme in her poems. While in Vicksburg, the narrator of "Pilgrimage" dreams that "the ghost of history lies down beside me, / rolls over, pins me beneath a heavy arm."[37] The poem "Southern History" explores how some versions of the past acquire authority and power while others are silenced or ignored. It recalls a "senior-year / history class." *"Before the war they were happy,* he said, / quoting our textbook . . . *The slaves were clothed, fed, / and better off under a master's care . . .* No one / raised a hand, disagreed. Not even me" (italics original).[38] In these lines Trethewey focuses on the silencing of counter-histories of slavery and the complicity of the students who remain silent when confronted with flagrant distortions of history. She draws attention to her own silence, which weighs on her because she is biracial and hence has both a unique perspective and authority to dissent from regional shibboleths. She also dwells on the silence created by the suppression of the past in "South." Pondering the unmarked and lost graves of "colored troops" who were left unburied at Port Hudson, Mississippi, Trethewey contrasts their anonymity—their "bodies swelled / and blackened beneath the sun . . . until earth's green sheet pulled over them"—with a contemporary landscape where "the roads, buildings, and monuments / are named to honor the Confederacy, / where that old flag still hangs."[39]

In the collection's title sequence, a group of unrhymed sonnets, Trethewey recalls the forgotten history of the Louisiana Native Guard, one of the Union army's first black regiments. "Elegy for the Native Guards" chronicles her visit to a Gulfport, Mississippi, historical site where the Native Guards were stationed but where their service has subsequently gone unacknowledged. The poem nods at Allen Tate's "Ode to the Confederate Dead" by borrowing its iambic rhythm, but otherwise Trethewey displays no fealty to Tate's Lost Cause verities or melancholic nostalgia. Her lament is not for a lost cause but for a lost memory. She closes her poem:

> The Daughters of the Confederacy
> has placed a plaque here, at the fort's entrance—
> each Confederate soldier's name raised hard
> in bronze; no names carved for the Native Guards—

2nd Regiment, Union Men, black phalanx.

What is monument to their legacy?[40]

For Trethewey, the telling of the history of the Native Guard is a restorative act that renders far more inclusive the region's and nation's history. While researching the Native Guard, she learned that "their colonel had confiscated a diary from a Confederate in Louisiana and took it for his own and began to cross write over what was there. That hit me as a perfect metaphor for what I was trying to say about our history of the South and the Americas; this cross-hatching a perfect intersection of north and south, black and white, that you can't separate."[41] Displaying less apparent pessimism than Walker, Trethewey implies that restorative acts of memory hold the promise not only to correct historical distortions but also to foster a deeper and more humane understanding of our intertwined histories.

In ways both obvious and subtle, Trethewey situates "Elegy for the Native Guard" in the canonical dialogue between Tate's "Ode to the Confederate Dead" and Robert Lowell's "For the Union Dead." Whether by adopting the same rhythm as Tate's poem, by invoking Lowell's imagery, or by implicitly contrasting the missing monument to the Native Guard with the Robert Gould Shaw monument that looms large in Lowell's poem, Trethewey engages with two of the most enduring literary meditations on the sacrifices made by warriors. Like fellow poet Kevin Young, whose 2007 collection *For the Confederate Dead* also grapples with Tate and Lowell, she betrays no apparent interest in displacing or replacing these canonical texts.[42] Rather her aim appears to be to broaden and enrich both of them by expanding the discussion of the Civil War's meaning to include the sacrifice of African Americans. Like other post-soul commentators on the Civil War, Trethewey has used repetition and inversion in her work, but parody has no place in her elegy. Befitting her subject and poetic form, her tone is reverent, quietly lyrical, and follows in a tradition that extends back through Lowell, Tate, and Lincoln to Pericles.

❧

In 1997, *The Spirit of Freedom*, a sculpture by Ed Hamilton memorializing black service during the Civil War, was unveiled at the corner of Vermont Avenue and U Street NW in Washington, DC. Depicting black infantrymen and sailors poised for combat, the monument is decorated with the names of the more than 200,000 African Americans who fought for the Union during the war.

The memorial has fulfilled the hopes of its funders, the Washington, DC, Commission on the Arts and Humanities, and has become a commemorative counterweight to the plethora of monuments to white soldiers that dot the capital's landscape. Now a favored site for rituals of memory, it hosted a Martin Luther King Day event in 2009 at which a crowd gathered to observe a wreath laying, sing spirituals, and watch a parade of African American reenactors in the guise of the celebrated all-black 54th Massachusetts Regiment. That anniversary took on additional meaning, preceding as it did by one day the inauguration of the nation's first African American president. Months later President Obama would send another wreath to the memorial to balance the traditional Memorial Day wreath laying at the monument to Confederate soldiers in Arlington Cemetery.[43]

The African American Civil War Memorial in Washington is a conspicuous example of the compensatory memory work undertaken by African Americans in the past quarter-century. They have intruded their reinterpretation of slavery and the Civil War era into public space and culture in a manner and to a degree that was previously unimaginable. No longer are African Americans shunted to the margins as historical agents during the era of the Civil War or as contemporary commentators on the legacy of the Civil War.

This recent memory work by African Americans, and artists especially, poses a profound challenge to earlier understandings of the Civil War and its legacy. It complicates any understanding of the conflict as a regrettable but heroic war that was the crucible for a great nation that would dominate the next century. It also precludes attempts to establish equivalency between the two contending nations in the conflict; African American artists and commentators consistently remind us that one side fought to preserve human slavery while the other (eventually) fought to destroy it.

The works by Randall, Walker, Parks, Miller, Willmott, Trethewey, and others go further and call into question the intelligibility of the past, including the nation's bloodiest conflict. Like Willie Levi Casey's identity as a Confederate reenactor, the past presented in these works is messy, contradictory, paradoxical, and irresolute. To a person, these artists suggest that history's lessons are obscure. No single reading of the past is adequate or even possible. The past is tenacious. It cannot be suppressed, evaded, or easily resolved. Although injustices can be discerned in the murk of the past, justice cannot. The nation's past, in short, is less a catalyst for action than a spur for reflection.

Recent African American reflection on the Civil War also undercuts the older African American certitude that history is purposeful and ultimately redemptive. Randall, Walker, and the other artists discussed in this essay share with earlier African American orators, activists, and artists the conviction that the past is neither exotically different nor obsolete. The lessons taught by the trying adjustments to freedom and enduring oppression of white racism have long encouraged blacks to see history as an unresolved, ongoing process. But in one important regard, the post-soul generation of artists diverges in their orientation toward the past. Despite the searing experience of slavery and the disappointments of freedom, for generations after the Civil War blacks found in their history cause for optimism. Their purposeful memory encouraged them to look to the future for the fulfillment of hopes that had been anticipated, inspired, and urged on by centuries of sacrifice. There is no comparable optimism in the art and memory work of the past twenty-five years. Walker's silhouettes suggest that we have yet to rid ourselves of centuries-old racist stereotypes; Willmott depicts a Confederate dystopia so as to shock us with its plausibility and even verisimilitude with aspects of contemporary American life; Parks leaves us with the unsettled prospect that we may struggle in vain to extract lessons from the past.

For all of their skepticism, even pessimism, the post-soul generation of black artists acknowledges little doubt about the important role that their art must play in dislodging deeply rooted stereotypes and historical myths. The goals of these artists are extraordinarily audacious. Randall, for instance, set out to reinterpret one of the most popular novels in the English language; Paul Miller to remix arguably one of the most influential films in cinema history. The extent to which these artists will succeed at their self-appointed task is impossible to discern at present. It is unlikely that any of these individual works will exert cultural influence comparable to *Gone With the Wind* or *Birth of a Nation*. The twentieth century was the golden age of popular mass culture. By refining and then translating well-established clichés to middlebrow fiction and spectacles of film and stage, Margaret Mitchell, D. W. Griffiths, and their ilk reached huge audiences. In contrast, most of the black artists discussed in this essay have affiliations with universities and have found their most receptive audiences among aesthetes and academics. Trethewey's arcane poetic forms or Parks' experimental dramatic style, to take two examples, are unlikely to gain vast audiences. The accelerating segmentation of American popular culture into ever smaller communities of consumption makes it difficult for artists, including even those who are steeped in contemporary popular culture, to reach audiences on a scale comparable to those common a half century earlier.

Perhaps the biggest challenge to these artists and self-appointed memory workers is the much-lamented penchant of Americans for cultural amnesia. With each passing year, the number of young Americans who have read *Gone With the Wind* or who have seen, let alone heard of, *Birth of a Nation* shrinks. While tropes inherited from these and other insidious cultural artifacts linger, few present-day Americans evince any interest in their sources. One wonders how resonant African American art that riffs and signifies on iconic works of twentieth-century white supremacy will be to generations who come of age in the United States after the election of Barack Obama.

War/Memory/History

Toward a Remixed Understanding

Kirk Savage

If "war is cruelty," as General Sherman told the townspeople of Atlanta after his capture of the city in 1864, civil wars must be the cruelest.[1] The terrible, continuing history of civil war in the postcolonial world could not possibly leave us with any illusions about its romance or valor. Yet the Civil War in the U.S. remains to this day a high point in national history, endlessly studied and celebrated for its passions, its glories, and its achievements. Even as the collective memory of the war changes in response to shifts in demography and the public sphere, it still functions as a cultural touchstone, a ruling metaphor of American nationality to which artists, politicians, and pundits inevitably return.

Will it be so forever? It is notoriously difficult to make sense of the currents of cultural memory and predict where they might be heading. One of the first to try was William Dean Howells, who bravely endeavored to sort out the lasting significance of the war barely a year after it had ended. He argued that the outpouring of proposals for soldier monuments in the immediate aftermath of the conflict was simply a passing "tumult, not a tendency of our civilization." "The pride which we felt in our army as a body, and in the men merely as soldiers, was an exultation which has already in a great part subsided."[2] The nation would rightly honor the moral outcome of the war, Howells predicted, but would soon enough forget the military and leave its stories of battle to "ignorant poets." Soldiers as mere soldiers, he thought, had no place in the landscape of national memory.

He could not have been more wrong, of course. One of the great legacies of the Civil War was the spread of the common-soldier monument and the glorification of "men merely as soldiers." Indeed, as fate would have it, the opposite universe that Howells glimpsed and then dismissed actually came into being. Today Americans live in a nation that expects its citizens to support their troops and take pride in their service regardless of the justice of the war's cause. Howells's failure to see this coming—whether wishful or not—is a warning to anyone trying to guess the future shape of national memory.

Yet other wars in the nation's history have been largely forgotten: the Mexican-American War, for example, or the many Indian wars, even though these conflicts were decisive in consolidating the territory of the U.S. and its identity as a white nation. In a profound sense these too were civil wars— violent struggles between different groups claiming the same land as their rightful inheritance. They are not remembered as civil wars because the nation stubbornly refuses to believe that it is driven by the sort of "tribalism" that is more typically thought to afflict peoples of color in the decolonized world.

Howells would surely have been happy that these wars were largely consigned to the dustbin, since they did not fit his idea of America's "immutable destiny, as God's agents, to give freedom to mankind." With that same faith in America's destiny he might not have been so surprised that the son of an African would one day become the president of the United States, using the rhetoric of Lincoln at the center of his campaign. But surely Howells would have found it unthinkable that almost one hundred and fifty years after Appomattox the governor of Virginia would proclaim the month of April, when Lee surrendered to Grant, to be Confederate History Month.[3] Even if neo-Confederates have lost much of their social status and institutional foothold in the South, as Tom Brown argues in the case of South Carolina, it is remarkable that they still have enough political traction to shape official memory practices.

Howells could not have anticipated how effectively the white South after 1865 would normalize the Confederacy, in large part by distancing the

Confederate cause from slavery. Even if all memory is "selective," the memory of the Lost Cause was egregiously so. The very constitution of the C. S. A., which the southern states had adopted in March 1861 as their founding document and then defended with their blood, enshrined "negro slavery" as a permanent, unalterable feature of its polity. That document specifically prohibited any "law denying or impairing the right of property in negro slaves" (Article 1, Section 9 [4]), and allowed the Confederacy to acquire new territory as long as "the institution of negro slavery, as it now exists in the Confederate States, shall be recognized and protected by Congress and by the Territorial government" (Article 4, Section 3 [3]).[4] Even as the Confederacy was collapsing under military reversals in 1864–65, southern statesmen clung to these principles. As late as March 1865, a month before Appomattox, the governor of Alabama issued a defiant proclamation declaring that "we must either become the slaves of Yankee masters, degrading us to equality with the Negroes or we must with the help of God, and our own strong arms and brave hearts, establish our freedom and independence."[5]

The brutal clarity of these documents stands in contrast to the long record of mystifications, evasions, and romanticizations of slavery that have marked the memory of the "Blue and the Gray" ever since. The near mystical rhetoric of "state sovereignty," the rise of the mammy myth, the erasure of the African American soldier from historical memory, have all worked to obscure not only the Confederate cause but also the larger history of slavery in North America, of which the Confederacy was a final chapter. When it becomes possible for some people to argue that Martin Luther King Jr. would have defended the Confederate flag flying over South Carolina's state house and for others to argue that Robert E. Lee would have opposed it, we know that we have reached a point where memory and history are almost impossible to untwine, where the counterfactual and the factual have become hopelessly confused. While the white South has always been most directly invested in this process of mystification, in order to readjust and reaffirm the system of racial privilege that undergirded slavery, the nation as a whole has been complicit. The core insight of the mockumentary *C. S. A.*—which imagines a world in which the Confederacy defeated the Union and slavery became the law of the land—is that the counterfactual fantasy of Confederate hegemony is uncomfortably close to the historical reality with its bitter legacy of Jim Crow segregation and continuing racial inequality. Despite Lincoln's optimistic vision at Gettysburg of "a new birth of freedom," the work of Civil War memory has never been free of a corrosive racial politics that has had very real, often disastrous effects on the lives of millions.

When President Barack Obama faced his first Memorial Day in office in 2009, his major political dilemma was whether to send a wreath to the Confederate Memorial in Arlington National Cemetery as every previous President since Woodrow Wilson had done.[6] Another sort of counterfactual, it seemed, had gone factual: a black President suddenly became in charge of a tradition steeped in white supremacy. The monument in question was no simple marker but a summation of Lost Cause self-justifications. Unlike most Confederate memorials that honored the "men merely as soldiers," to use Howells' words again, the Arlington memorial incorporated among other things a "mammy" image that pointed unmistakably to faithful slave mythology. A group of academics circulated a petition calling for Obama to make an official break with the Arlington memorial and with neo-Confederate politics in general. He decided to continue the tradition nevertheless but to send a second wreath to the African American Civil War Memorial in Washington, DC, an idea proposed by this author in a *Washington Post* editorial a few days beforehand. Whatever Obama's intentions were, he stayed silent on the issue.[7]

My own rationale for the dual-wreath solution was twofold. First, even though the Arlington memorial was clearly the product of white supremacist thinking and practice, the decision to stop sending a wreath there would have had the effect of singling out the ordinary soldiers of the Confederacy as beyond the moral pale. As I argued in the *Post*, "the crime of slavery was interwoven not only into the Confederacy but into the fabric of the American nation, into the Constitution, our economic system and wars of territorial expansion across the continent." If the Lost Cause worked by denying the Confederacy's institutional defense of slavery, the countermove of refusing to honor the Confederate soldier would not help promote a better understanding of slavery's pervasive impact on American history.

Second, I argued that two wreaths would send a common message that "the descendants of slaves and the descendants of slaveholders should recognize each other's humanity, and do the hard work of reckoning with the racial divide that is slavery's cruelest and most enduring legacy." The point was not to make a political compromise that permits separate "heritages" to be celebrated uncritically, but rather to use the occasion as an opportunity to cross the divide and reach a new self-understanding.

Several of my own ancestors in Alabama joined the Confederate army. A couple of them were true believers who later rode with the Ku Klux Klan. One actually switched sides and joined the legendary Union regiment 1st Alabama cavalry, which rode with Sherman on his march to the sea. Another avoided combat by enlisting in an engineering regiment and building bridges for Confederate railroads; seven months after Appomattox he named his new son, my great-grandfather, Ulysses Grant Fife. Grant, as he was called, proudly displayed his full name on his tombstone in rural western Alabama when he died in the mid-twentieth century.[8] One of the side effects of neo-Confederate politics and the debate over it is that these less visible and more complicated human stories of conflict, ambivalence, accommodation, and resistance get lost or passed over. Despite the romanticized cliché of "brother versus brother," Americans have in fact had immense difficulty facing up to the civil war within their own communities and even within their own hearts.

Collective memory is sometimes celebrated for its counterfactual tendencies, its defiance of the strictures of professional, archival history. If history aspires to neutrality and comprehensiveness, memory is frankly partisan and always selective, shaped by and in turn shaping the interests of many different social groups jostling for position in the public arena. All too often memory has become a playing field for hucksters, charlatans, demagogues, and tyrants. In the modern era, collective memory has been packaged and marketed, transformed by practices of "authentic reproduction," to use the term highlighted by Elizabeth Young. The tree stumps embedded with cannon shot that fill dusty old Civil War museums and veterans posts were manufactured by entrepreneurs for the battlefield tourist market.[9] Producer and consumer alike winked at the charade: who cared as long as these artifacts evoked authentic memories? The bricolages of contemporary artists such as Dario Robleto, with his "pain bullets" cast from lead salvaged from various battlefields or even from melted vinyl records, recall these material practices and recombine them in startlingly new ways. Kara Walker's disturbing pseudo-Victorian silhouettes of plantation fantasies gone wrong, or Paul Miller's unique remixes of *Rebirth of a Nation*, continue and warp this tradition of reproduction and mis-production. Such artists help us see the mystifications of memory through a new lens.

On a recent visit to Montgomery, Alabama, I sat with a group of black tourists in the modest basement of Dexter Avenue Church, where Martin Luther King Jr. and others organized the Montgomery bus boycott that changed the world; on one wall a long mural narrated the violent story of the civil rights movement in the visual language of Christian redemption. From there I took a short walk to the first White House of the Confederacy, still a shrine to Jefferson Davis and his family, where, surrounded by white tourists and guides, I made my way through the high-style period rooms with their family bibles, fancy furniture, elegant portraits of beautiful white ladies, and vitrines chock full of Confederate relics. Two separate worlds, two separate "heritages," still largely segregated, jostling together in one touristic landscape—a bricolage desperately in need of remixing.

So how can the sesquicentennial help tear down these walls and foster mutual understanding? How can it remix the established positions and contribute to a different awareness of the war and its place in history? I will advance two broad suggestions.

First, as my anecdote suggested, the sesquicentennial of the war and of emancipation should be remixed with the semicentennial of the decisive phase of the civil rights movement. In the early 1960s the Civil War centennial buried the legacy of Jim Crow beneath the self-congratulatory rhetoric of "reconciliation," even as the moral bankruptcy of this reconciliation was being exposed on the ground for all to see, in the violent suppression of a disciplined nonviolent movement to end racial segregation. History demands that we understand these as interconnected phenomena; never again should Americans use romantic nationalism as a cover for flagrant injustice.

But beyond that, the intermixing of these two phenomena provides a launching pad to think more seriously about what Theodore Parker in the 1850s and Martin Luther King Jr. a century later called "the arc of the moral universe." On March 25, 1865, Union forces decisively defeated Lee's army at Fort Stedman, leading to his surrender a few weeks later. On March 25, 1965, King stood on the steps of the Alabama state capitol after finally completing the third attempt to march from Selma, and declared—in a paraphrase of one of Parker's sermons—that "the arc of the moral universe is long, but it bends toward justice." To see the arc for what it is, we need to see the slave trade, the Confederacy, the war, emancipation, Reconstruction, and the civil rights movement all as various episodes on a complex, and sadly winding trajectory of history. Parker and King did not have simple romantic notions of historical progress in mind, nor should we. Despite the persistent refrain of American exceptionalism, echoed by Howells in his remarks of 1866, Americans are no more "God's agents" than are any other people, with an "immutable destiny . . . to give freedom to mankind." Like the rest of humanity, Americans of all stripes are agents with mixed motivations and a mixed history.

If we do not force the Civil War and civil rights movement into a simplistic narrative of national redemption, we will see their historical actors as the human beings they were. We will see their actions as part of a much longer arc that begins in the forced diaspora of African peoples to the New World and continues into the racial divide of today's world. By all means we must face up to the brutal reality of the Confederacy's institutionalizing of slavery. Moral honesty demands that any visitor to Montgomery's White House of the Confederacy should understand instantly that its vision of gracious white living is in fact built on "wealth piled by the bondsman's two hundred and fifty years of unrequited toil," to use Lincoln's memorable phrase in the second inaugural. But we must also see that the arc does not begin or end there, just as it doesn't begin or end with the martyrs of the civil rights movement. As appalling as neo-Confederate ideology still is, we all know that expunging it will not solve the problematic legacy of slavery. Lincoln, in the second inaugural, was careful to call it "American slavery" (rather than "negro slavery") and to say that both North and South were being punished for its offense. The offense of American slavery carried us into the civil rights era and sparked a national upheaval, yet it still carries on in the racial divisions that plague our schools, our prisons, our communities, and indeed our own hearts. I am not advocating for apologies but for analysis and action: a true historical accounting looks at everyone's pasts and asks us all how to bend the long arc toward justice.

Secondly, the Civil War should be remixed with the larger story of civil war in North America and across the globe in more recent times. The tragic romance of the Civil War has long rested on the notion of fratricide—white against white, brother against brother—in a fight for honor and principle, not for mere "tribal" interests. Slavery is one puncture point in that balloon. Another is the long history of civil warfare between Anglo-Americans and other inhabitants and settlers of the continent, whether we are talking about the many wars with Native Americans from the seventeenth century onward or violent conflicts between Anglo settlers and Mexican nationals beginning in Texas in the 1830s. Seen in this context, both the Union and the Confederacy shared in the spoils of past civil wars but diverged in their visions of how those spoils should be distributed and managed.

In the twentieth century the U.S. has continued to be involved in civil wars, but far from home—in the Philippines, Korea, Vietnam, and elsewhere. Although these interventions were justified as the defense of U.S. interests against much larger enemies (corrupt monarchies, international communism), they stoked local civil wars that might have been avoided in the first place. The "tribal" wars in postcolonial Africa are also stoked and shaped by larger geopolitical conflicts over resources. If the American Civil War was a geopolitical conflict over the expansion of slavery in North America, then it is high time to connect that distinctly American experience to other geopolitical conflicts that have shaped the ongoing history of civil war in the modern world.

Even here the arc continues to bend, we hope, toward justice. Justice is what demands that all these phenomena be interconnected. But how do we do so in a sesquicentennial, by its nature a celebratory event expected to honor battles and warriors? The answer probably does not lie in more monuments and museums but in rethinking and reconnecting those that already exist. This was the basic idea behind the two-wreaths gesture on Memorial Day, though in practice it has not moved beyond empty ceremony.[10] It would be interesting to foster more genuine collaborations, for example between Ford's Theatre in Washington, DC, and the Lorraine Motel in Memphis, or between Andersonville Prison in Georgia and the Civil Rights Institute in Birmingham. If it is too much to expect that Montgomery's White House of the Confederacy might be made over, as the Wilberforce Museum was during Britain's 2007 bicentennial of the abolition of the slave trade, perhaps it is not too much to ask that the Ladies of the White House Association sit down with the staff of the Southern Poverty Law Center's Civil Rights Memorial and talk through how their respective visitors might learn from each others' sites. Beyond that, why not strive for international collaborations, say between Gettysburg Battlefield and the War Remnants Museum in Ho Chi Minh City? Even if the collaborations failed to materialize, the efforts behind them might well draw attention to the geopolitical forces that drive civil wars across the globe. At the very least the attempt to think transnationally would help counter the pull of American exceptionalism, which is likely to be strong in any anniversary of this sort.[11]

In the end the sesquicentennial will have accomplished something if it ceases to promise reconciliation between a mythical North and a mythical South, and instead extends respect and understanding to the full range of humanity that was marked by that terrible war and by other such wars across the globe.

Acknowledgments

This book originated in a celebration of the Abraham Lincoln bicentennial in Charleston, South Carolina, a conjunction of purpose and location that illustrates some of the changes that have taken place in the United States since the last important round of Civil War anniversaries. The gathering in February 2009 was made possible by the strong support of Lacy K. Ford, then chair of the History Department at the University of South Carolina. The College of Arts and Sciences provided vital matching assistance under the leadership of Dean Mary Anne Fitzpatrick and Tim Mousseau, who was then associate dean of the college. The Halsey Institute of Contemporary Art and the School for the Arts at the College of Charleston co-sponsored the conference. Mark Sloan, director of the Halsey Institute, was an insightful collaborator in the planning process and a gracious, efficient local host with the able assistance of Roberta Sokolitz, Rebecca Silberman, and Michelle Strick. Georgette Mayo hospitably welcomed the meeting to the Avery Research Center for African American History and Culture. The South Carolina Humanities Council provided partial funding. Robert Rosen, Rodger Stroup, Radcliffe Bailey, Titus Kaphar, Deborah Luster, Bernard Powers, Cathy Stanton, and Gordon Jones helped to make the event possible and to make it memorable.

It has been an honor and a pleasure for the editor to work with this group of co-authors, each of whom has made a variety of contributions to the project and extended generous personal kindnesses to me. I am particularly grateful to Gerard Brown for his wise advice in planning the book and his patient forbearance in editorial dealings with his brother. An impressive set of artists and institutions responded with impressive courtesy to requests for images. James Gehrt provided skillful and speedy technical assistance in preparing the illustrations. Bob Ellis was once again a helpful and good friend. This project was extremely fortunate to have attracted the encouragement and aid of Robert J. Brugger at the Johns Hopkins University Press, where Julie McCarthy, Jen Malat, Helen Myers, Kara Reiter, Claire McCabe Tamberino, Josh

Tong, and Karen Willmes joined in expertly guiding the manuscript through the publication process.

For a historian whose research has focused mostly on the Civil War era, participation in a book about contemporary America has offered a fresh field of exploration, and I have benefited from much formal and informal guidance. The anonymous referee for the press was exceptionally thoughtful. Barry Miller of the University of North Carolina, Greensboro, invited me to test out some ideas for the introductory essay in a public lecture at which Mark Elliott and others in the audience showed gratifying enthusiasm and asked good questions. My department at the University of South Carolina devoted a useful colloquium to a draft of my essay about the Confederate battle flag. Students, colleagues, friends, and family members have indulged me in many conversations about recent outcroppings of the Civil War and pointed me toward rich material. Lucian and Veronica Brown charitably humored my effort to catch up with this century and provided me with valuable orientation in current popular culture. My parents supplied me with newspaper clippings and confidence. Doug and Kay Harrison were wonderfully supportive. By far my greatest debt is to Carol Harrison, who embraced the project from its inception and contributed in countless ways to its progress. For all of our mutual professional interest in the past, I have welcomed the opportunity to share with her in this attempt to attend carefully to the world in which we live together.

Notes

INTRODUCTION: The Undead War

1. Robert Penn Warren, *The Legacy of the Civil War: Meditations on the Centennial* (New York: Random House, 1961), 4, 6–7, 46, 49, 54.

2. Warren, *Legacy of the Civil War,* 83, 92.

3. For important examples from the Lincoln bicentennial, see "Lincoln Studies at the Bicentennial: A Roundtable," *Journal of American History* 96 (Sept. 2009): 417–61, and Sean Wilentz, "Who Lincoln Was," *The New Republic* (July 15, 2009). Drew Gilpin Faust, "'We Should Grow Too Fond of It': Why We Love the Civil War," *Civil War History* 50 (Dec. 2004): 368–83, offers thoughtful reflections on the growth of scholarly interest in the Civil War since the late 1980s.

4. Warren, *Legacy of the Civil War,* 1; Roy Rosenzweig and David Thelen, *The Presence of the Past: Popular Uses of History in American Life* (New York: Columbia University Press, 1998).

5. John Jakes, *North and South* (New York: Harcourt Brace Jovanovich, 1982); John Jakes, *Love and War* (San Diego, CA: Harcourt Brace Jovanovich, 1984); John Jakes, *Heaven and Hell* (San Diego, CA: Harcourt Brace Jovanovich, 1987); Gore Vidal, *Lincoln: A Novel* (New York: Random House, 1984); Alexandra Ripley, *Scarlett: The Sequel to Margaret Mitchell's* Gone With the Wind (New York: Warner Books, 1991); Charles Frazier, *Cold Mountain* (New York: Atlantic Monthly Press, 1997). All information about *New York Times* best-seller list is from www.hawes.com (accessed Aug. 30, 2010); references are to the hardcover best-seller lists. On the persistence of *Gone With the Wind*, see Helen Taylor, *Scarlett's Women:* Gone With the Wind *and Its Female Fans* (New Brunswick, NJ: Rutgers University Press, 1989).

6. Barry Schwartz, "Postmodernity and Historical Reputation: Abraham Lincoln in the Late Twentieth Century," *Social Forces* 77 (1998): 63–103. Schwartz has more recently elaborated on his conclusion in *Abraham Lincoln in the Post-Heroic Era: History and Memory in Twentieth-Century America* (Chicago: University of Chicago Press, 2009), in which he reports at 148–52 that during the 1950s the *New York Times* index averaged fifty references to Lincoln each year; in the 1990s, it averaged seven references to Lincoln per year. The *Congressional Record* index showed twenty-nine Lincoln entries per year in the 1950s and eight references per year in the 1990s. Compare Edward L. Ayers, "Worrying about the Civil War," in *Moral Problems in American Life: New Perspectives on Cultural History*, ed. Karen Halttunen and Lewis Perry (Ithaca, NY: Cornell University Press, 1998), 145–65, which opens with the assertion that "the Civil War has never been more popular."

7. Warren, *Legacy of the Civil War,* 83. "Top-selling" is defined here as the number of weeks that a book was included in the *New York Times* list of best-selling hardcover books. The works on the Revolution were David G. McCullough, *John Adams* (New York: Simon and Schuster, 2001) (sixty weeks); Joseph Ellis, *Founding Brothers: The Revolutionary Generation* (New York: Alfred A. Knopf, 2000) (forty-three weeks); David G. McCullough, *1776* (New York: Simon and Schuster, 2005) (thirty-four weeks); Walter Isaacson, *Benjamin Franklin: An American Life* (New York: Simon and Schuster, 2003) (twenty-six weeks); Joseph Ellis, *His Excellency: George Washington* (New York: Alfred A. Knopf, 2004) (fifteen weeks); Ron Chernow, *Alexander Hamilton* (New York: Penguin Press, 2004) (twelve weeks); Cokie Roberts, *Founding Mothers: The Women Who Raised Our Nation* (New York: William Morrow, 2004) (eleven weeks); and Joseph J. Ellis, *American Creation* (New York: Alfred A. Knopf, 2007) (nine weeks). The Civil War books were Doris Kearns Goodwin, *Team of Rivals: The Political Genius of Abraham Lincoln* (New York: Simon and Schuster, 2005) (twenty weeks) and James L. Swanson, *Manhunt: The Twelve-Day Chase for Lincoln's Killer* (New York: William Morrow, 2006) (thirteen weeks). The Revolution has also been the subject for more widely watched film treatments in the last decade, the 2008 Home Box Office miniseries based on McCullough's *John Adams* and the 2000 cinematic release *The Patriot.*

8. On *Glory*, see Martin H. Blatt, "*Glory*: Hollywood History, Popular Culture, and the Fifty-Fourth Massachusetts Regiment" and Thomas Cripps, "*Glory* as a Meditation on the Saint-Gaudens Monument," both in *Hope and Glory: Essays on the Legacy of the Fifty-Fourth Massachusetts Regiment*, ed. Martin H. Blatt, Thomas J. Brown, and Donald Yacovone (Amherst: University of Massachusetts Press, 2001), 215–74, which cite previous studies. On *The Civil War*, see especially Tara McPherson, *Reconstructing Dixie: Race, Gender, and Nostalgia in the Imagined South* (Durham, NC: Duke University Press, 2003), 115–27; David Glassberg, "Watching *The Civil War*," in *Sense of History: The Place of the Past in American Life* (Amherst: University of Massachusetts Press, 2001), 88–108; and Robert Brent Toplin, ed., *Ken Burns's* The Civil War*: Historians Respond* (New York: Oxford University Press, 1996). On the Civil War in more recent film, see Jenny Barrett, *Shooting the Civil War: Cinema, History, and American Identity* (London: I. B. Tauris & Co., 2009); Gary W. Gallager, *Causes Won, Lost, and Forgotten: How Hollywood and Popular Art Shape What We Know about the Civil War* (Chapel Hill: University of North Carolina Press, 2008); Bruce Chadwick, *The Reel Civil War: Mythmaking in American Film* (New York: Alfred A. Knopf, 2001). On popular music, the starting points are Will Kaufman, *The Civil War in American Culture* (Edinburgh: Edinburgh University Press, 2005), 80–84, and Andrew K. Smith and James E. Akenson, "The Civil War in Country Music Tradition," in *Country Music Goes to War*, ed. Charles K. Wolfe and James E. Akenson (Lexington: University Press of Kentucky, 2005), 1–25. The limited presence of the Civil War in recent film, music, and video games should caution specialists in the war not to exaggerate its cultural visibility.

9. Russell Banks, *Cloudsplitter: A Novel* (New York: HarperCollins, 1998); Geraldine Brooks, *March* (New York: Viking, 2005); E. L. Doctorow, *The March* (New York: Random House, 2005); Dara Horn, *All Other Nights: A Novel* (New York: W. W. Norton, 2009); Bruce Murkoff, *Red Rain* (New York: Alfred A. Knopf, 2010); Marilynne Robinson, *Gilead* (New York: Farrar, Straus and Giroux, 2004); Jane Smiley, *The All-True Travels and Adventures of Lidie Newton* (New York: Alfred A. Knopf, 1998); Stephen Wright, *The*

Amalgamation Polka (New York: Alfred A. Knopf, 2006). This distinguished list might be extended, particularly by including fiction in which the Civil War has an oblique but crucial significance. Michael Chabon "The Martian Agent, an Interplanetary Romance," in *McSweeney's Mammoth Treasury of Thrilling Tales*, ed. Michael Chabon (New York: Vintage Books, 2003), 447–76, includes Lincoln, John Brown, and Generals Philip Sheridan and George Custer among the key figures of a civil war in a steampunk nineteenth-century America. Michael Cunningham, *Specimen Days* (New York: Farrar, Straus & Giroux, 2005) never mentions the sectional conflict but places Walt Whitman at the center of three apocalyptic vignettes. As Cunningham indicates by borrowing the title of the wound-dresser's autobiographical compendium, *Specimen Days* looks toward the Civil War in attending to prophetic voices that rise over the carnage.

10. Roy Blount Jr., *Robert E. Lee: A Penguin Life* (New York: Lipper/Viking Books, 2003); Adam Gopnik, *Angels and Ages: A Short Book about Darwin, Lincoln, and Modern Life* (New York: Alfred A. Knopf, 2009).

11. Warren, *The Legacy of the Civil War,* 85.

12. Katharina Otto-Bernstein, *Absolute Wilson: The Biography* (Munich: Prestel, 2006), 145; see also Arthur Holmberg, *The Theatre of Robert Wilson* (New York: Cambridge University Press, 1997). Glass has since returned to the Civil War in *Appomattox*, an opera first produced at the San Francisco Opera in 2007. Merrill D. Peterson, *Lincoln in American Memory* (New York: Oxford University Press, 1994), 390, sniffs that *the CIVIL Wars* "had little to do with Lincoln or the Civil War. The palpable human being, if found anywhere, was found at last in Ken Burns's historical documentary film, *The Civil War.*"

13. McPherson, *Reconstructing Dixie,* 127–40, provides an insightful assessment of *Sherman's March,* which does not appear in any of the other three recent books about Civil War movies cited in n. 8. For a similar white southern sensibility, see Jim Cullen's discussion of singer-songwriter Randy Newman in *The Civil War in Popular Culture: A Reusable Past* (Washington, DC: Smithsonian Institution Press, 1995), 131–36.

14. John Updike, *Memories of the Ford Administration: A Novel* (New York: Alfred A. Knopf, 1992).

15. McPherson, *Reconstructing Dixie,* 35–37.

16. All references to *The Simpsons* are drawn from *The Simpsons Archive,* www.snpp .com, particularly the list of references to U.S. presidents (accessed Nov. 30, 2009). Schwartz, *Lincoln in the Post-Heroic Era,* 159–60, similarly notes that the original dust-jacket cover of Jon Stewart's *Naked Pictures of Famous People* (New York: William Morrow and Company, 1998) featured an image of Lincoln, the American embodiment of a famous person.

17. Schwartz, *Lincoln in the Post-Heroic Era,* 163, 292–94; Thomas Mallon, *Henry and Clara* (New York: Houghton Mifflin, 1994). The best-sellers are Swanson, *Manhunt,* and Jay Winik, *April 1865: The Month That Saved America* (New York: HarperCollins, 2001). Another widely distributed book on the topic was Michael W. Kauffman, *American Brutus: John Wilkes Booth and the Lincoln Conspiracies* (New York: Random House, 2004). The world-premiere production of the Eric Sawyer–John Shoptaw opera about the Lincoln assassination, *Our American Cousin,* took place at the Academy of Music Theatre in Northampton, Massachusetts, in 2008.

18. Sarah Vowell, *Assassination Vacation* (New York: Simon and Schuster, 2005).

19. Robert J. Cook, *Troubled Commemoration: The American Civil War Centennial, 1961–1965* (Baton Rouge: Louisiana State University Press, 2007), 126–31; Gordon L. Jones, "'Gut History': Civil War Reenacting and the Making of an American Past" (Ph.D. diss., Emory University, 2007), 173, 177.

20. Tony Horwitz, *Confederates in the Attic: Dispatches from the Unfinished Civil War* (New York: Pantheon, 1998); Elmore Leonard, *Tishomingo Blues* (New York: William Morrow, 2002).

21. In addition to Jones, "'Gut History,'" see Lisa A. Long, *Rehabilitating Bodies: Health, History, and the American Civil War* (Philadelphia: University of Pennsylvania Press, 2003), and Jim Weeks, *Gettysburg: Memory, Market, and an American Shrine* (Princeton, NJ: Princeton University Press, 2003), 171–225, for discussions of Civil War reenacting.

22. Andrew Ferguson, *Land of Lincoln: Adventures in Abe's America* (New York: Atlantic Monthly Press, 2007); "140-Yr.-Old Cannonball Kills Civil War Fan," www.cbsnews.com/stories/2008/05/02/national/main4068515.shtml (accessed April 27, 2010). See also "Civil War Buff a Loose Cannon," *Morning Edition,* Sept. 7, 2009, www.npr.org/templates/story.php?storyId=112615600 (accessed July 28, 2010).

23. Daniel Aaron, *The Unwritten War: American Writers and the Civil War* (New York: Alfred A. Knopf, 1973).

24. Prominent examples in recent movies and television include the ex-Confederate antihero of the movie, *Jonah Hex* (2010), adapted from the comic-book series of the same title, and the ex-Confederate vampire in the leading male role of the television series, *True Blood* (2008–), based on Charlaine Harris's *Southern Vampire Mysteries* series of novels. Additional examples widely anticipated at this writing include a film version of Seth Grahame Smith's *Abraham Lincoln, Vampire Hunter* (New York: Grand Central Publishing, 2010), to be produced by Tim Burton and Timur Bekmambetov, and director Andrew Stanton's *John Carter of Mars*, based on Edgar Rice Burrough's *Barsoom* series of novels about an undead Confederate veteran transported to Mars during a period of civil war.

25. See Charles E. Morris III, "My Old Kentucky Homo: Abraham Lincoln, Larry Kramer, and the Politics of Queer Memory," in *Queering Public Address: Sexualities in American Historical Discourse,* ed. Charles E. Morris III (Columbia: University of South Carolina Press, 2007), 93–120; Dinitia Smith, "Finding Homosexual Threads in Lincoln's Legend," *New York Times,* Dec. 16, 2004. Chad Jones, "San Francisco Playhouse Grooves with 'Abraham Lincoln's Big Gay Dance Party,'" *San Francisco Examiner,* Dec. 14, 2008, reports on the world-premiere production of Aaron Loeb's play on this theme.

26. Warren, *Legacy of the Civil War,* 58; Robert K. Sutton, *Rally on the High Ground: The National Park Service Symposium on the Civil War* (n.p.: Eastern National, 2001).

27. Wright, *The Amalgamation Polka* (New York: Alfred A. Knopf, 2006), 311. Robert Burgoyne, *Film Nation: Hollywood Looks at U.S. History* (Minneapolis: University of Minnesota Press, 1997), 16–37, offers a penetrating analysis of the malleability of race in *Glory.*

28. Warren, *Legacy of the Civil War,* 17, 65, 73, 93; C. Vann Woodward, *The Burden of Southern History* (Baton Rouge: Louisiana State University Press, 1960).

29. See, for example, James M. McPherson, "The War That Never Goes Away," in *Drawn with the Sword: Reflections on the Civil War* (New York: Oxford University Press, 1996), 55–65.

30. Drew Gilpin Faust, *This Republic of Suffering: Death and the American Civil War* (New York: Alfred A. Knopf, 2008); James M. McPherson, *Tried by War: Abraham Lincoln as Commander in Chief* (New York: Penguin Press HC, 2008); James M. McPherson, *Crossroads of Freedom: Antietam* (New York: Oxford University Press, 2002); Louis Menand, *The Metaphysical Club: A Story of Ideas in America* (New York: Farrar, Straus and Giroux, 2001).

31. Stephen Cushman, *Bloody Promenade: Reflections on a Civil War Battle* (Charlottesville: University Press of Virginia, 1999); Christopher Benfey, *A Summer of Hummingbirds: Love, Art, and Scandal in the Intersecting Worlds of Emily Dickinson, Mark Twain, Harriet Beecher Stowe, and Martin Johnson Heade* (New York: Penguin Press, 2008).

32. David W. Blight, *Race and Reunion: The Civil War in American Memory* (Cambridge, MA: Harvard University Press, 2001); Alice Fahs, *The Imagined Civil War: Popular Literature of the North and South, 1861–1865* (Chapel Hill: University of North Carolina Press, 2001); Nina Silber, *The Romance of Reunion: Northerners and the South, 1865–1900* (Chapel Hill: University of North Carolina Press, 1993); Amy Murrell Taylor, *The Divided Family in Civil War America* (Chapel Hill: University of North Carolina Press, 2005). For a fuller discussion of this scholarship, see Thomas J. Brown, "Civil War Remembrance as Reconstruction," in *Reconstructions: New Perspectives on the Postbellum United States*, ed. Thomas J. Brown (New York: Oxford University Press, 2006), 206–36.

CHAPTER 1: The Lincoln-Obama Moment

This chapter is a revised version of a paper presented at the conference, "Lincoln and the Civil War in Contemporary America," held at the College of Charleston's Avery Research Center for African American History and Culture, Feb. 6, 2009. My thanks to Thomas Brown for his many helpful comments, to my fellow panelists, and to W. Fitzhugh Brundage, Bernard Powers, and members of the audience for their stimulating comments and suggestions. The original presentation was accompanied by a slide show of images, which are described below.

1. "Full Text of Senator Barack Obama's Announcement for President," Feb. 10, 2007, www.barackobama.com/2007/02/10/remarks_of_senator_barack_obam_11.php. The date also coincided with the opening of the 2007 State of the Black Union conference in Jamestown, Virginia. Obama's absence from the 2008 conference, at which Hillary Clinton made an appearance, was criticized by conference organizer Tavis Smiley and other speakers.

2. Merrill D. Peterson, *Lincoln in American Memory* (New York: Oxford University Press, 1994), 26–27.

3. For Obama's political pragmatism and commitment to the prophetic tradition see David A. Frank, "The Prophetic Voice and the Face of the Other in Barack Obama's 'A More Perfect Union' Address, March 18, 2008," *Rhetoric & Public Affairs* 12 (Summer 2009): 167–94; Willie J. Harrell Jr., " 'The Reality of American Life Has Strayed from Its Myths': Barack Obama's *The Audacity of Hope* and the Discourse of the American Reclamation Jeremiad," *Journal of Black Studies* 41 (Sept. 2010): 164–83; Keith B. Jenkins and Grant Cos, "A Time for Change and a Candidate's Voice: Pragmatism and the Rhetoric of Inclusion in Barack Obama's 2008 Presidential Campaign," *American Behavioral*

Scientist 54 (2010): 184–202; Bart Schultz, "Obama's Political Philosophy: Pragmatism, Politics, and the University of Chicago," *Philosophy of the Social Sciences* 39 (June 2009): 127–73.

4. Daniel A. Berkowitz and Sarah Raaii, "Conjuring Abraham, Martin and John: Memory and News of the Obama Presidential Campaign," *Memory Studies* 3 (2010): 364–78.

5. Barry Schwartz, *Abraham Lincoln in the Post-Heroic Era: History and Memory in Late Twentieth-Century America* (Chicago: University of Chicago Press, 2008).

6. Barry Schwartz, *Abraham Lincoln and the Forge of National Memory* (Chicago: University of Chicago Press, 2000), 263–64.

7. YouTube—*Abraham Obama* Q&A, n.d., www.youtube.com/watch?v=wZCjyNamv 4Q; English quoted in Kathy Rose Garcia, "Artist Brings Abraham-Obama to Seoul," *Korea Times*, Oct. 16, 2009, www.koreatimes.co.kr/www/news/art/2009/10/148_53665 .html; John C. Drake, "Street Artist Inspires Too Much Enthusiasm," *Boston Globe*, July 8, 2009, www.boston.com/ae/theater_arts/articles/2008/07/08/street_artist_inspires_ too_much_enthusiasm/. A complete listing of interviews, videos, etc., relating to the Abraham Obama tour is available at English's website Popaganda: The Art and Crimes of Ron English, www.popaganda.com/articles/2008obamaEverything/.

8. Available through Democraticstuff.com, www.democraticstuff.com/Obama-08 -Abe-Lincoln-Button-p/bt21419.htm. I have not been able to establish the origins of this button.

9. Carl R. Weinberg, "'Abarack Lincoln' and Lincoln's Legacy through Political Cartooning," *OAH Magazine of History* 23 (Jan. 2009): 49–50; Daryl Cagle's PoliticalCartoons. com, www.politicalcartoons.com. Search on keyword "Lincoln." Cagle's cartoon distribution service features cartoonists for regional dailies, and totals do not reflect the output in national dailies, national magazines, or from cartoonists not subscribing to his service.

10. "Lincoln Likes Obama," editorial cartoon collection at Cagle.com, http://cagle .com/news/LincolnLikesObama/main.asp; Richard Crowson, "Fist Bump," editorial cartoon, *Wichita (KS) Eagle*, Aug. 29, 2008; R. J. Matson, "Backstage at the Democratic National Convention," *St. Louis Post-Dispatch*, Aug. 27, 2008, http://politicalcartoons.com/ cartoon/2e42a0ba-330b-471f-ae60-7a9615a287cc.html.

11. Bob Staake, "Reflection," *New Yorker*, Nov. 17, 2008, www.newyorker.com/maga zine/toc/2008/11/17/toc_20081110; *Newsweek*, Nov. 24, 2008, www.newsweek.com/id/ 169170/page/1.

12. "Point by Point," FOX21 [Colorado Springs] telecast, n.d. Available on YouTube, www.youtube.com/watch?v=SNhK8kna_h4.

13. "Messiah Abe Obama," from the Gateway Pundit, blog, June 3, 2008, http:// gatewaypundit.blogspot.com/2008/06/historic-primary-ends-dems-pick-far.html. As of Jan. 6, 2010, this link no longer works and the image appears to have been removed from the First Things website. Copy of digital image in author's collection.

14. Alexander Gardner, "Antietam, Md. Allan Pinkerton, President Lincoln, and Maj. Gen. John A. McClernand; another view," Oct. 3, 1862. Library of Congress Prints and Photographs Division, Washington, DC, Digital ID, http://hdl.loc.gov/loc.pnp/ cwpb.04326; modified image posted by "musicman," Dec. 23, 2008, to Freerepublic .com, www.freerepublic.com/focus/f-news/2153370/posts.

15. "Obama—New Declaration of Independence Needed," online discussion forum at castboolits.gunloads.com, Jan. 17, 2009, http://castboolits.gunloads.com/showthread .php?p=472375.

16. "Bush-Bashing Pumpkin Contest: Political Art for a Better World," TagYerit political website, wwwtagyerit.com/politics/. Another entry featured Republican vice presidential nominee Sarah Palin as the bride of Frankenstein.

17. Boz Vahkshori, "Lincoln-Obama T-shirt," digital image at RedBubble.com, www .redbubble.com/people/bozvakhshori/t-shirts/1448632-2-lincoln-obama; Walter Sem- kiw, "The Relationship Between Barack Obama and Abraham Lincoln," www.john adams.net/cases/samples/Obama-Trumbull/index.html; CafePress.com, www.cafepress .com/ObamaandLincoln. The ahsium.com website is no longer secure and readers are advised to use caution when accessing it.

18. Scott Sandage, "A Marble House Divided: The Lincoln Memorial, the Civil Rights Movement, and the Politics of Memory, 1939–1963," *Journal of American History* 80 (June 1993): 137; Peterson, *Lincoln in American Memory*, 363.

19. Sandage, "A Marble House Divided," 160.

20. Scott Jaschik, "Historians Team Up to Back Obama," *Inside Higher Ed*, Nov. 27, 2007, www.insidehighered.com/news/2007/11/27/obama.

21. Alec MacGillis, "Ken Burns Compares Obama to Lincoln," washingtonpost. com, Dec. 18, 2007, http://blog.washingtonpost.com/44/2007/12/18/ken_burns_com pares_obama_to_li.html.

22. Joseph J. Ellis, "'The better angels' side with Obama," *Los Angeles Times*, Jan. 19, 2008, www.latimes.com/news/printedition/asection/la-oe-ellis19jan19,0,5818078 .story.

23. Sean Wilentz, "Obama's Misuse of History," *Los Angeles Times*, Jan. 26, 2008, www.latimes.com/news/opinion/commentary/la-oe-wilentz26jan26,0,5561702.story. Regarding the authorship of *Profiles in Courage*, former Kennedy advisor Ted Sorensen defends Kennedy's authorship and credits him with the basic concept and organiza- tion of the work. But he also characterizes it as a collaborative effort in which he ap- pears to have done the bulk of the writing. *Ted Sorensen, Counselor: A Life at the Edge of History* (New York: HarperCollins, 2008), 144–50.

24. Todd Purdum, "Raising Obama," *Vanity Fair*, March 2008, www.vanityfair.com/ politics/features/2008/03/obama200803?currentPage=1; Jann S. Wenner, "A New Hope," *Rolling Stone*, March 20, 2008.

25. Tom Robbins, "Name-Dropping Lincoln at the Obama Speech," Runnin' Scared News Blog, *Village Voice*, March 27, 2008, http://blogs.villagevoice.com/runninscared/ archives/2008/03/namedropping_li.php. This is an early instance of commentary on the "Lincoln play."

26. "Clinton Challenges Obama to a 'Lincoln-Douglas' Debate," ABC News Political Radar Blog, April 26, 2008, http://blogs.abcnews.com/politicalradar/2008/04/clinton -chall-2.html.

27. Barack Obama, "A More Perfect Union," transcript as published in the *New York Times*, March 18, 2008, www.nytimes.com/2008/03/18/us/politics/18text-obama.html ?pagewanted=1&_r=1.

28. Garry Wills, "Two Speeches on Race," *New York Review of Books*, May 1, 2008, www.nybooks.com/articles/21290.

29. Al Gore, 2008, Democratic National Convention Speech, Aug. 28, 2008, Mile High Stadium, Denver, Colorado, www.americanrhetoric.com/speeches/convention 2008/algore2008dnc.htm (accessed Feb. 3, 2009).

30. DivinePattern, "Mysterious Obama & Lincoln Destiny," Feb. 7, 2009, www.you tube.com/user/DivinePattern#p/u/2/x-B6e6PyhpA.

31. Jack Tapper, "Will Obama's Team of Rivals Fare Better Than Lincoln's?" ABC News Political Punch Blog, Nov. 23, 2008, http://blogs.abcnews.com/politicalpunch/ 2008/11/will-obamas-tea.html (accessed Nov. 25, 2008).

32. Ed Hornick, "Can Lincoln's Playbook Help Obama in the Years Ahead?" CNN .com, Nov. 19, 2008, www.cnn.com/2008/POLITICS/11/18/obama.lincoln/index.html (accessed Feb. 24, 2009).

33. Joe Conason, "Not a Team of Rivals at All," *New York Observer*, Dec. 2, 2008, www.observer.com/2008/politics/not-team-rivals-all; Matthew Pinsker, "The Myth of 'Rivals,'" *Los Angeles Times*, Nov. 18, 2008, http://articles.latimes.com/2008/nov/18/ opinion/oe-pinsker18; Joseph Williams, "Will Obama's 'Team of Rivals' Play Today?" *Boston Globe*, Nov. 21, 2008, www.boston.com/news/politics/2008/articles/2008/11/ 21/will_lincolns_team_of_rivals_play_today/.

34. Jonah Goldberg, "Honestly, Another Abe?" *National Review*, Nov. 21, 2008, www .nationalreview.com/articles/226359/honestly-another-abe/jonah-goldberg?page=2.

35. Allen C. Guelzo, "Our Lincoln: Obama, He Was Not," *National Review*, Feb. 23, 2009, 25–28. Guelzo does not mention other aspects of Lincoln's conservatism, including his support for Whig Henry Clay and Clay's American System and his opposition to United States territorial aggression in the war with Mexico. Eric Foner, "Our Lincoln," *The Nation*, Jan. 26, 2009, www.thenation.com/doc/20090126/foner.

36. Guelzo, "Our Lincoln," 26.

37. Michael Knox Beran, "Obama's Lincoln," *National Review*, Jan. 20, 2009, www .nationalreview.com/articles/226720/obamas-lincoln/michael-knox-beran; Thomas Krannawitter, "Obama as Lincoln," *Washington Times*, Dec. 19, 2008, www.washington times.com/news/2008/dec/19/obama-as-lincoln/?page=1.

38. Thomas DiLorenzo, *The Real Lincoln: A New Look at Abraham Lincoln, His Agenda, and an Unnecessary War* (Roseville, CA: Prima Lifestyles, 2002); Lerone Bennett Jr., *Forced into Glory: Abraham Lincoln's White Dream* (Chicago: Johnson Publishing Company, 2000). See also Don E. Fehrenbacher, "The Anti-Lincoln Tradition," *Journal of the Abraham Lincoln Association (JALA)* 4 (1982), www.historycooperative.org/journals/ jala/4/fehrenbacher.html; Matthew D. Norman, "An Illinois Iconoclast: Edgar Lee Masters and the Anti-Lincoln Tradition," *JALA* 24 (Winter 2003), www.historycooperative .org/journals/jala/24.1/norman.html.

39. John A. Sellers, compiler, "Books for Lincoln's 200th Birthday," *Publishers Weekly*, Jan. 8, 2009, www.publishersweekly.com/article/CA6627419.html; Michael F. Bishop, "Abe's 200th: Dozens of New Books for Lincoln's Birthday," *Publishers Weekly*, Jan. 19, 2009, www.publishersweekly.com/article/CA6630343.html; "Four-Score and Seven New Books on Lincoln: A PW Reviews Roundup," *Publishers Weekly*, Jan. 12, 2009, www.publishersweekly.com/article/CA6581809.html.

40. Harold Holzer, interview with Rich Kelley for the Library of America e-News letter, n.d., www.loa.org/images/pdf/Holzer_interview_on_Lincoln.pdf (accessed Aug. 30, 2010).

41. Hans Nichols, "Obama Inaugural Strains Lincoln Comparisons While Inviting Them," *Bloomberg News*, Jan. 17, 2009, www.bloomberg.com/apps/news?pid=news archive&sid=az5HzIamy_NQ; the Lincoln theme was announced by Joint Congressional Committee on Inaugural Ceremonies (JCCIC) chairwoman Diane Feinstein soon after the election. "Senator Feinstein Announces 2009 Inaugural Theme 'A New Birth of Freedom,'" press release dated Nov. 5, 2008, http://inaugural.senate.gov/media/releases/release-11052008-inauguralwebsite.cfm.

42. Holzer, interview with Rich Kelley.

43. Schwartz, *Forge of National Memory*, 126–29.

44. For a critical appraisal of Reagan's use of the past see Harvey Kaye's *The Powers of the Past: Reflections on the Crisis and Promise of History* (Minneapolis: University of Minnesota Press, 1991). See also his more recent effort at reclaiming Thomas Paine from the Republican Party, *Thomas Paine and the Promise of America* (New York: Hill & Wang, 2005). For Reagan's rhetorical manipulation of collective memory see Denise M. Botsdorff and Steven R. Goldzwig, "History, Collective Memory, and the Appropriation of Martin Luther King Jr.: Reagan's Rhetorical Legacy," *Presidential Studies Quarterly* 35 (Dec. 2005): 661–90.

45. John Murphy, "Power and Authority in a Postmodern Presidency," in *The Prospect of Presidential Rhetoric*, ed. James Aune and Martin Medhurst (College Station: Texas A&M University Press, 2008). Murphy notes that epideictic rhetoric "relies on memoria, or recollection of a shared past, as a key source of invention," 35. See also Karlyn Campbell and Kathleen Hall Jamieson, *Deeds Done in Words: Presidential Rhetoric and the Genres of Governance* (Chicago: University of Chicago Press, 1990).

46. C. Wyatt Evans, "The Liberal Dilemma in American Politics," unpublished paper delivered at the Organization of American Historians' annual conference, April 2006. Using the acceptance speeches of Republican and Democratic nominees from 1992 to 2004, I charted their references to historical figures and events, and the "value words" and appeals to providence linked to these references. The greatest disparity between candidates was in 2000. John Kerry fared slightly better in 2004, as some commentators at the time noted, but was hamstrung by the controversy over his Vietnam record and his reluctance to use forceful appeals to providence.

47. For brevity's sake, several allied speech forms including the prophetic tradition, the black prophetic tradition, civil religious discourse, and the political jeremiad have been lumped together here under one heading. There are differences between these forms but all hold in common an appeal to America's past, its providential destiny, and the exhortation to listeners to abide by this destiny by doing their utmost to work for it. See Robert N. Bellah, "The American Civil Religion," *Daedalus* 96 (Feb. 1967): 1–21; Perry Miller, *Errand into the Wilderness* (Cambridge, MA: Harvard University Press, 1956); Sacvan Bercovitch, *The American Jeremiad* (Berkeley: University of California Press, 1978); Conrad Cherry, ed., *God's Chosen Nation*, rev. ed. (Chicago: University of Chicago Press, 1993).

48. George Lakoff, *Don't Think of an Elephant: Know Your Values and Frame the Debate* (White River Junction, VT: Chelsea Green, 2004).

49. Michael Kazin, *A Godly Hero: The Life of William Jennings Bryan* (New York: Alfred A. Knopf, 2006); E. J. Dionne Jr. "Faith Full—When the Religious Right Was Left," *New Republic Online*, Feb. 21, 2005, www.tnr.com/article/faith-full (accessed Sept. 6, 2010).

50. A partial sampling of the black community's views regarding Lincoln may be gleaned in the commentaries accompanying several YouTube videos from the State of the Black Union conference held in Feb. 2007. See "Bennett on Obama," www.youtube .com/watch?v=QgrGwQo7MaU (accessed Aug. 29, 2010). A recent critical yet balanced scholarly appraisal of Lincoln's attitudes and actions toward black Americans and civil rights is *Lincoln on Race and Slavery*, ed. Henry Louis Gates Jr. and Donald Yacavone (Princeton, NJ: Princeton University Press, 2009).

51. Sandage, "A Marble House Divided," 150.

52. Christopher Hayes, "Obama's Media Maven," *The Nation*, Feb. 19, 2007, www .thenation.com/doc/20070219/hayes.

53. Schwartz, *Abraham Lincoln in the Post-Heroic Era*, 21–41, 59–66.

54. David Montgomery, "Mary Rakovich's Small Protest against Stimulus Erupted into 'Tea Party' Movement," *Washington Post*, May 29, 2010, www.washingtonpost .com/wp-dyn/content/article/2010/05/28/AR2010052804673.html; "Santelli's Tea Party," CNBC.com, Feb. 19, 2009, www.cnbc.com/id/15840232?video=1039849853.

55. Critics have accused the movement of receiving substantial funding from wealthy conservative donors and special interests through FreedomWorks, a political action committee chaired by former U.S. Senate majority leader Dick Armey.

56. Jonathan Kay, "Black Helicopters over Nashville," *Newsweek*, Feb. 8, 2010, www .newsweek.com/2010/02/08/black-helicopters-over-nashville.html.

57. An extensive and referenced account of the Tea Party movement may be found at http://en.wikipedia.org/wiki/Tea_Party_movement. Organization web pages include www.teapartypatriots.org/, www.teapartyactivists.com/, and www.teaparty.org/.

58. Brian Montopoli, "Glenn Beck 'Restoring Honor' Crowd Estimate Explained," Political Hotsheet, CBS News, Aug. 31, 2010, www.cbsnews.com/8301-503544_162 -20015214-503544.html; "Beck's Accusations That Progressives Have 'Co-opted' Civil Rights Movement Rings Hollow," MediaMatters Blog, June 4, 2010, http://mediamatters .org/mobile/research/201006040004; Amy Gardner et al., "Beck, Palin, Tell Thousands to 'Restore America,'" *Washington Post*, Aug. 29, 2010, www.washingtonpost.com/wp -dyn/content/article/2010/08/28/AR2010082801106.html?sid%3DST2010082704942& sub=AR.

59. Dana Milbank, "Civil Rights' New 'Owner': Glenn Beck," *Washington Post*, Aug. 29, 2010, www.washingtonpost.com/wp-dyn/content/article/2010/08/27/AR2010082702359 .html.

60. Ronald White, *The Eloquent President: A Portrait of Lincoln through His Words* (New York: Random House, 2005), 123, 186.

61. Garry Wills, "Obama's Legacy: Afghanistan," NYR Blog, July 27, 2010, www .nybooks.com/blogs/nyrblog/2010/jul/27/obamas-legacy-afghanistan/ (accessed Sept. 1, 2010).

CHAPTER 2: The Confederate Battle Flag and the Desertion of the Lost Cause Tradition

1. Robert Olwell, *Masters, Slaves, and Subjects: The Culture of Power in the South Carolina Low Country, 1740–1790* (Ithaca, NY: Cornell University Press, 1998), 271–74; D. E. Huger Smith, "Wilton's Statue of Pitt," *South Carolina Historical and Genealogical Magazine*

15 (Jan. 1914): 34–35. The statue now decorates the entrance hall of the Charleston County courthouse, a few yards from its original position, embellished by a different quotation from Pitt about law as the guarantor of liberty.

2. Bill Swindell, "Hodges' Flag Plan Leads Pack," *Charleston Post and Courier* (hereafter *PC*), Feb. 16, 2000, a1.

3. Columbia *State* (hereafter *CS*), April 10, 1997, a16 (letter of William Higgins); J. Michael Martinez, William D. Richardson, and Ron McNinch-Su, eds., *Confederate Symbols in the Contemporary South* (Gainesville: University Press of Florida, 2000), 4; K. Michael Prince, *Rally 'round the Flag, Boys! South Carolina and the Confederate Flag* (Columbia: University of South Carolina Press, 2004), 53, 57; John Coski, *The Confederate Battle Flag: America's Most Embattled Emblem* (Cambridge, MA: Harvard University Press, 2005), 271. See also J. Michael Martinez, "The Georgia Confederate Flag Dispute," *Georgia Historical Quarterly* 92 (Sept. 2008): 200–228.

4. See Gerald R. Webster and Jonathan I. Leib, "Whose South Is It Anyway? Race and the Confederate Battle Flag in South Carolina," *Political Geography* 20 (March 2001): 271–99; Laura R. Woliver, Angela D. Ledford, and Chris J. Dolan, "The South Carolina Confederate Flag: The Politics of Race and Citizenship," *Politics & Policy* 29 (Dec. 2001): 708–30.

5. *CS*, June 10, 2000, a10 (letter of Gary Bunker); Rachel Graves, "Flag Could Obscure Other Legislative Issues," *PC*, Dec. 12, 1999. On the Walterboro incident, see "Colleton Request Illustrates Difference between Symbols," *CS*, Feb. 3, 1997, a8; Lisa Hofbauer, "Civil War Monument Issue Dies," *PC*, Feb. 4, 1997. This pattern, which should be distinguished from disputes over attempts to commission new government tributes to the Confederacy, has a few exceptions across the region. In 2000, for example, Richmond changed the names of two bridges that honored Stonewall Jackson and J. E. B. Stuart, substituting the names of local civil rights leaders. More common have been retreats from remembrance of slavery that related to or overlapped with Confederate commemoration, such as the renaming of New Orleans public schools that honored slaveholders. The most widespread retractions of public tributes to the Confederacy have occurred in high school and college athletics, the realm of recreation and consumption in which this essay situates the battle flag.

6. *CS*, June 12, 1996, a12 (letter of J. R. Owen Jr.). See also *CS*, April 17, 1995, a6 (letter of Duane J. Speight); *CS*, Feb. 5, 1998, a12 (letter of Bill Pierce); *CS*, Jan. 4, 2000, a8 (letter of Corry E. Mason).

7. Samuel W. Howell IV, "Flying Rebel Banner Does Honor to S.C.'s Confederate Veterans," *CS*, March 19, 1997, a13; Bryon Collier, "Tribute Paid to Confederate Dead at Exercises," *Charleston News and Courier*, May 11, 1952, b7.

8. Coski, *Confederate Battle Flag*, chaps. 4–8. On the flapper origins of *Gone With the Wind*, see Elizabeth Young, *Disarming the Nation: Women's Writing and the American Civil War* (Chicago: University of Chicago Press, 1999), 238–73.

9. Coski, *Confederate Battle Flag*, 86–87; Prince, *Rally 'round the Flag*, 28–32.

10. Coski, *Confederate Battle Flag*, 130, 166–67; "Confederate War Group Wins Yanks with Kindness," *Charleston News and Courier*, April 11, 1961, 1b. On commercialism in the Civil War centennial see Robert J. Cook, *Troubled Commemoration: The American Civil War Centennial* (Baton Rouge: Louisiana State University Press, 2007), 45–47.

11. Coski, *Confederate Battle Flag,* 106; "Traditions and Code for Correct Use of the Confederate Flags—How to Display and Respect Our Flags," *United Daughters of the Confederacy Magazine* 24 (Sept. 1961): 19. See also *United Daughters of the Confederacy Magazine* 24 (July 1961): 3; (Oct. 1961): 3; (Nov. 1961): 15.

12. John Hammond Moore, "Running Up the Flag, or How John Amasa May Thumbed His Nose at JFK," research file, South Carolina Political Collections, University of South Carolina. Moore's notes and photocopies remain valuable in clarifying details of the story later illuminated more broadly by Cook, *Troubled Commemoration;* Coski, *Confederate Battle Flag;* and Prince, *Rally 'round the Flag.*

13. Heidi Beirich, "The Struggle for the Sons of Confederate Veterans: A Return to White Supremacy in the Early Twenty-First Century?" in *Neo-Confederacy: A Critical Introduction,* ed. Euan Hague, Heidi Beirich, and Edward H. Sebesta (Austin: University of Texas Press, 2008), 284–85.

14. "Governor Hollings Gets Official Bid to Centennial Ceremonies," *CS,* April 7, 1961, c1, includes a photograph of May in the vest. *Charleston News and Courier,* April 12, 1961, a1 shows U.S. Senator Strom Thurmond wearing an identical vest at the Fort Sumter gathering.

15. "The 'Stars and Bars' Fly Again," *CS,* April 8, 1961; Cook, *Troubled Commemoration,* 88–119, 151; *Journal of the House of Representatives of the Second Session of the 94th General Assembly of the State of South Carolina, Being the Regular Session Beginning Tuesday, January 9, 1962* (Columbia: State Budget and Control Board, n.d.), 458–59; *Journal of the Senate of the Second Session of the 94th General Assembly of the State of South Carolina, Being the Regular Session Beginning Tuesday, January 9, 1962* (Columbia: State Budget and Control Board, n.d.), 316–17.

16. Albert Boime, *The Unveiling of the National Icons: A Plea for Patriotic Iconoclasm in a Nationalist Era* (Cambridge: Cambridge University Press, 1998), 46; Robert N. Bellah, "Religion in America," *Daedalus* 96 (Winter 1967): 1–21.

17. William E. Mahoney, "Pickens County's Sen. Morris Deplores 'Cheapening' Abuse of Confederate Flag," *Columbia Record* (hereafter *CR*), Dec. 2, 1965; "Morris: Dixie Flag Proposal Supported," unidentified clipping, SCL. On Confederate flags during and immediately after the Civil War, see Robert E. Bonner, *Colors and Blood: Flag Passions of the Confederate South* (Princeton, NJ: Princeton University Press, 2002).

18. "Flag-Burning Arrest Made," *CS,* Feb. 18, 1969, b1. The Supreme Court decision in *United States v. O'Brien,* 391 U.S. 367 (1968) clearly indicated that prosecution would be untenable. A narrow majority later ruled in *Texas v. Johnson,* 491 U.S. 397 (1989) that the First Amendment protects burning of the American flag, but the dissent in that case rested squarely on the uniqueness of the national flag.

19. Brian Hicks, "CSA Galleries Closing Its Doors," *PC,* Feb. 24, 2009, b1. Gary W. Gallagher, *Causes Won, Lost, and Forgotten: How Hollywood and Popular Art Shape What We Know about the Civil War* (Chapel Hill: University of North Carolina Press, 2008), 135–207, analyzes and provides many illustrations of prints in the vein sold by CSA Galleries.

20. Jim Weeks, *Memory, Market, and an American Shrine* (Princeton, NJ: Princeton University Press, 2003), 195–225, ably discusses Civil War reenactment.

21. Cindi Ross Scoppe, "House Unravels on Flag," *CS,* April 4, 1997; *CS,* April 30, 2000, d2 (letter of Joseph K. Taylor Jr.); "Be It Resolved . . . ," *CS,* March 29, 2000, a13.

Notable interventions by professional historians include Tom Terrill, "In Search of a Suitable Past," *CS,* Jan. 7, 1997, a9; Eric Foner, "Rebel Yell," *The Nation* 270 (Feb. 14, 2000): 4–5; Charles W. Joyner, "The Flag Controversy and the Causes of the Civil War: A Statement by Historians," *Callaloo* 24 (Winter 2001): 196–98. This issue of *Callaloo,* devoted to the Confederate flag, is a stimulating collection of southern intellectuals' reflections on the theme.

Not all disagreements over the flag were historical. The most common objection to the display on the capitol dome was that the site should be reserved for flags of governments with authority in South Carolina. This argument centered on the meaning of the dome rather than the meaning of the flag, as nobody supposed that the battle flag was the emblem of a current government.

22. Margaret O'Shea, "Flag Tug of War Focus," *CS,* July 19, 1972, b8; Neville Patterson, "Groups Request Flag's Removal," *CR,* July 18, 1972, b1.

23. *CS,* Dec. 25, 1999, a14 (letter of Bob Brown); *CS,* May 3, 1989, a13 (letter of Fred Boyd). For more examples of the several dozen letters and guest editorials on this theme, see *CS,* Jan. 24, 1988, b3 (letter of Elston Gunn); Oct. 25, 1993, a8 (letter of Sam Martin); Dec. 9, 1993, a15 (letter of Vincent Cox); July 2, 1994, a9 (letter of Charles O'Neal); March 6, 1996, a10 (letter of Greg Putnam); Nov. 22, 1996, a13 (letter of Susan Wolfe); Dec. 11, 1996, a16 (letter of Jeannette M. Smith); July 27, 1999, a8 (letter of Toni Letempt); and J. Mark Taylor, "Flag Represents Prideful Defiance," *CS,* Jan. 10, 1997, a9. The only contribution to point even vaguely to the importance of the centennial controversy was *CS,* Nov. 22, 1999, a8 (letter of John Hammond Moore). On Alabama and Georgia, see Coski, *Confederate Battle Flag,* 238, 252–55.

24. Coski, *Confederate Battle Flag,* 255–56; Clark Surratt, "Flag Flap," *CS,* Feb. 22, 1987; "Patterson Suggests Flying Stars and Bars over Capitol," *CR,* June 17, 1987; *CS,* Nov. 20, 1999, a1.

25. Prince, *Rally 'round the Flag,* 180.

26. Bryan Hicks, "Dixie Divided: Trip Ends in Fla. City as Divided as S.C. over Flag," *PC,* March 16, 2000, a1. See also *CS,* Dec. 23, 1994, a16 (letter of P. Payne).

27. The narrative of the civil rights movement suggested by the flag protest was in these respects much like several commemorative initiatives discussed in Renee C. Romano and Leigh Raiford, eds., *The Civil Rights Movement in American Memory* (Athens: University of Georgia Press, 2006).

28. Kenneth A. Harris, "Civil Rights Veterans Greet New Generation," *CS,* Jan. 18, 2000, a1; Kathryn Winiarski, "Columbia Marcher Remembers Segregation," *CS,* April 5, 2000, b1. See also *CS,* Jan. 28, 1996, d2 (letter of Eileen Hajdu); Aug. 18, 1999, a12 (letter of Steve Osheyack); Feb. 7, 2000, a10 (letter of Viron K. Jones).

29. *CS,* May 13, 2000, a13 (letter of Coy Bayne); Cindi Ross Scoppe, "House Unravels on Flag," *CS,* April 4, 1997, a10. See also *CS,* May 28, 1991, a8 (letter of William G. Carter); July 8, 1994, a9 (letter of Nick W. Hille); Sept. 7, 1999, a12 (letter of Jill Coffman); Oct. 24, 1999, d2 (letter of Joan Martin); Feb. 2, 2000, a10 (letter of Thomas Daniels).

30. Wayne Wall, "With Common Heritage, We Face Common Enemy," *CS,* March 13, 2000, a9; Nina Brook, "Flag Compromise Support Grows," *CS,* Oct. 16, 1993, a8 (Courson); *CS,* May 28, 1989, a8 (letter of Glenn McConnell); *CS,* June 11, 1991, a10 (letter of Keith A. Edwards) (King); Feb. 17, 1996, a10 (letter of J. Dale Weaver). Other vivid examples of this position include *CS,* Feb. 11, 1991, a12 (letter of Robert Whitaker);

Aug. 24, 1991, a8 (letter of Ursula E. Slimp); Nov. 23, 1996, a10 (letter of Marshall T. Mays); Dec. 2, 1999, a12 (letter of John W. Kimbrell); Glenn McConnell, "No Need for Another Battle over the Flag," *CS,* April 21, 2007, a11.

31. Thomas J. Brown, "Civil War Remembrance as Reconstruction," in *Reconstructions: New Perspectives on the Postbellum United States,* ed. Thomas J. Brown (New York: Oxford University Press, 2006), 215–17, surveys the leading scholarship, to which should be added Caroline E. Janney, *Burying the Dead but Not the Past: Ladies' Memorial Associations and the Lost Cause* (Chapel Hill: University of North Carolina, 2008).

32. *CS,* July 15, 1992, a14 (letter of Catherine D. McDonald); May 21, 1994, a9 (letter of Felicia Forman Dryden).

33. Warren Bolton, "Shhh! No Debating the Flag While the Legislature Is In Session!" *CS,* May 12, 1999, a12; April Simun, "Why a Mom Fights the Flag," *CS,* Dec. 17, 1999, a1.

34. Anna Griffin, "Southerners Line Up to Defend Heritage," *CS,* April 20, 1997, b1; Joseph S. Stroud, "Flag Losing Favor with S.C. Voters," *CS,* Sept. 27, 1999, a1; June Murray Wells, "Talk at South Carolina State House, January 8, 2000" and "Update, January 29, 2000," www.electricscotland.com/escgi (accessed Aug. 4, 2009); Susan Hill Smith, "June Wells: Preserving History of Confederacy Is Her Life's Work," *PC,* Feb. 26, 2000, d1. Of the 931 individuals who contributed more than 1100 letters and guest editorials on the flag issue to *The State* from January 1991 through July 2000, contributors' names provide a strong basis for identification of the gender of 815 contributors. Women constituted 204 individuals in this group, or almost exactly one-fourth of the total. Women contributed twenty-six of the forty-three letters or guest editorials from contributors identifiable by gender that explicitly called for relocation of the flag to a museum or elsewhere entirely removed from the capitol grounds.

35. Lee Bandy, "Beasley Seeks Truce on Flag," *CS,* Nov. 12, 1996, a1; Bill Swindell and Rachel Graves, "McConnell Offers Flag Plan with 'Healing Pool,'" *PC,* March 30, 2000, a1. See also Robert L. Brown, "Keep It Flying," *CS,* May 30, 1993, d1; *CS,* July 21, 1992, a6 (letter of Herbert O. Chambers III); Dec. 21, 1999, a10 (letter of Ed Fetner).

36. *CS,* June 11, 1989, d3 (letter of Teddy Spencer).

37. See, e.g., *CS,* April 8, 1993, a14 (letter of Herbert O. Chambers III); Dec. 9, 1993, a15 (letter of Jason B. Owen); Jan. 8, 1997, a8 (letter of William Rush); March 27, 2000, a8 (letter of Gene Graj).

38. Joseph S. Stroud, "Flag Supporter Rallies His Forces," *CS,* Jan. 6, 2000, a1 (quoting Daniel B. Verdin III); Kenneth A. Harris and Churck Carroll, "Flag's Battle Lines Redrawn," *CS,* Jan. 21, 2000, a1; "S.C. House Votes to Move Flag," *CS,* May 11, 2000, a17. Rebecca Bridges Watts, *Contemporary Southern Identity: Community through Controversy* (Jackson: University Press of Mississippi, 2008), 110–11, offers more examples.

39. Brown, "Civil War Remembrance as Reconstruction," 208–12, summarizes the scholarship on these themes.

40. "Confederate Battle Flag Should Be Moved in '93," *CS,* June 17, 1992, a14; "Debating the Flag: Three Views," *CS,* Dec. 1, 1996, d4.

41. *CS,* Dec. 14, 1999, a16 (letter of J. Wesley Peace); David Broder, "Confederate Banner Controversy Tests GOP Unity in SC," *CS,* Jan. 15, 1997, a8; Lewis F. Galloway, "Living Together in Peace Must Be Our Goal," *CS,* Jan. 16, 1997, a11; "A Statement from South Carolina Religious Leaders Concerning the Confederate Battle Flag," *CS,* Jan. 19,

1997, d8. Vivid examples include *CS*, Aug. 6, 1994, a11 (letter of Harry McGirt); Dec. 3, 1996, a10 (letter of Ned Crosby); Dec. 6, 1996, a8 (letter of Daniel Dix); Sept. 25, 1999, a14 (letter of Debra Majo-Steading); Nov. 14, 1999, d2 (letter of Joby Stafford Robinson); Dec. 8, 1999, a12 (letter of Guy E. Miller); Jan. 20, 2000, a14 (letter of Thomas Nunn); Jan. 21, 2000, a12 (letter of Whit Plowden); July 24, 2000, a8 (letter of Brian Cooney).

42. "Voices of the Flag," *CS*, Dec. 22, 1996, d4; Brad Warthen, "It Seems the Romans Had this Dispute over 'Heritage' . . . ," *CS*, Jan. 14, 1997, a8; *CS*, Sept. 25, 1997, a14 (letter of Rev. Bobby Eubanks); Jan. 28, 2000, a12 (letter of Rev. Ronald E. Lee); May 17, 2000, a12 (letter of Rev. L. Carroll Pope Jr.); and the guest editorials of Wayne Wall, "The Flag Flap: A More Excellent Way," *CS*, Aug. 6, 1999, a16; "Our Flag and Our Culture: Compromise or Capitulation," *CS*, Jan. 5, 2000, a9; "With Common Heritage, We Face Common Enemy," *CS*, March 13, 2000, a9.

43. "The Sun Rises on the Evil and the Good," *CS*, Jan. 26, 1997, d4 (quoting Ravenel); *CS*, April 25, 1989, a13 (letter of W. Randolph Bass); Nov. 18, 1996, a9 (letter of Richard Towell Hines). See also *CS*, Dec. 27, 1990, a8 (letter of Stephen Brown); July 16, 1994, a9 (letter of Johnny Gardner); Nov. 23, 1996, a10 (letter of Robert W. Whitaker); Dec. 29, 1996, d2 (letter of Jamie Brown); Jan. 10, 1997, a8 (letter of Rusty Rentz); Sept. 13, 1999, a14 (letter of E. Meetze); Dec. 8, 1999, a12 (letter of Julius M. Price); May 10, 2000, a14 (letter of Sam Johnson). William B. DePass Jr., "Hiding Behind Bible Is Worst Part of Debate about Flag," *CS*, Jan. 30, 1997, a9, expresses this view from the standpoint of a Republican flag admirer who supported the Heritage Act despite opposition to Beasley's sacralization of the issue.

44. "Debating the Flag: Three Views"; see also E. Wayne Wall, "The Flag Flap: A More Excellent Way"; *CS*, Nov. 7, 1993, d2 (letter of Chip G. Bunce); Dec. 27, 1996, a6 (letter of John Sanders); March 23, 1997, d2 (letter of Louise B. Tisdale).

45. Brown, "Civil War Remembrance as Reconstruction," 212–14.

46. Lee Bandy, "Flag Still Flies, but the Winds Are Shifting," *CS*, Dec. 8, 1996, d4; Michael Graham, "Southern Hospitality," Columbia *Free Times*, March 30–April 12, 1994. See also *CS*, Jan. 24, 1988, b3 (letter of Elston Gunn); Tom Teepen, "In Politics, Confederate Flag Means Defiance," *CS*, Jan. 18, 1993, a9; *CS*, Jan. 13, 1997, a7 (letter of Edwin Coulter); March 6, 1997, a11 (letter of Linda Kraska).

47. Nina Brook and Cindi Ross Scoppe, "Campbell Could Call for Flag Session Soon," *CS*, June 25, 1994, a1. The legislature thwarted the lawsuit by enacting clear authorization for the display.

48. Sonny DuBose, "Confederate Flag Issue Is Turning into Three-Ring Circus," *CS*, March 21, 1994, a9; David G. Ellison Jr., "Confederate Leaders Themselves Signaled Furling Wartime Banner," *CS*, Jan. 30, 1997, a9; *CS*, July 2, 1994, a8 (letter of William A. Byrd); Nov. 22, 1996, a13 (letter of Mary Pinckney Powell); Dec. 23, 1996, a12 (letter of Gail Richards Dunn); Jan. 4, 1997, a7 (letter of Virginia Baker); April 2, 1997, a11 (letter of Elizabeth Beard); Feb. 10, 2000, a14 (letter of Ann H. Brown). The only partial exception is *CS*, Feb. 7, 1994, a6 (letter of R. B. Dunovant Jr.), a letter from the grandson of a signer of the Ordinance of Secession who noted that he did not need to look up to the dome for a reminder of his southern heritage and anticipated further attacks on white southern symbols after removal of the flag.

49. Ellison, "Confederate Leaders"; Robert N. Rosen, "Lower the Flag in Honor of Southern Icon, Robert E. Lee," *CS*, Dec. 12, 1999, d3; Mary Foster Dillard, "South

Represents Gentility, Grace, Not Hatred," *CS*, Feb. 27, 2000, d3; *CS*, Oct. 23, 1995, a8 (letter of Kenneth Emory Bell); March 27, 1997, a20 (letter of Kevin Lewis); Jan. 25, 2000, a8 (letter of John Jay Jones); May 6, 2000, a11 (letter of Bill Rogers). Other notable examples include Graham, "Southern Hospitality"; Ann I. Furr, "Mind Your Manners; Furl Flag," *CS*, Sept 30, 1999, a15; *CS*, Aug. 30, 1999, a8 (letter of Shane Edge); Dec. 6, 1999, a8 (letter of Robert G. Garvin). On Lee, see especially *CS*, Sept. 15, 1999, a14 (letter of Genevieve Peterkin); Jan. 10, 2000, a8 (letter of Jean F. Smurthwaite); Jan. 16, 2000, d2 (letter of Chip McPheeters).

50. *CS*, July 27, 1972, a26 (letter of Clif Judy Jr.); April 22, 1994, a11 (letter of William Carter). See also *CS*, Dec. 4, 1993, a10 (letter of Reid Hearn); Dec. 5, 1993, d2 (letter of George Bell); April 20, 1994, a11 (letter of Robert Bentley).

51. Rachel Graves, "Flag Could Obscure Other Legislative Issues," *PC*, Dec. 12, 1999, a1; W. Thomas Smith Jr., "Compromising Colors," *Free Times*, May 17–23, 2000. See also *CS*, Nov. 16, 1994, a12 (letter of Charles A. Carson Sr.); Dec. 21, 1996, a10 (letter of Herbert O. Chambers III); Aug. 30, 1999, a8 (letter of Duane J. Speight); Dec. 16, 1999, a16 (letter of Dick Clarke); June 12, 2000, a8 (letter of Ursula Slimp).

52. Steve Piacente, "Ravenel Stepped Outside 'Civility,' Clyburn Says," *PC*, Jan. 15, 2000, a1; "Debating the Flag: Three Views."

53. "Debating the Flag." For the standard estimate that 45.8 percent of white South Carolina families owned slaves in 1860, see Walter Edgar, *South Carolina: A History* (Columbia: University of South Carolina Press, 1998), 311. See also *CS*, Jan. 29, 1988, a22 (letter of Dan Henderson); June 3, 1989, a8 (letter of Rusty Rentz); July 1, 1990, d2 (letter of Will Culbreath); July 21, 1992, a6 (letter of Lewis C. Thornton Jr.); Jan. 4, 1993, a6 (letter of Pauline Hatchell); Jan. 23, 1994, d2 (letter of Danny B. Robbins); April 7, 1994, a10 (letter of Vincent Simonowicz); Feb. 12, 1996, a8 (letter of Wesley B. Anderson); Jan. 22, 1997, a8 (letter of Polly Jernigan); Jan. 19, 2000, a10 (letter of Wesley Pittman).

54. Clyde Wilson, "Southern Commitment to Self-Government Was Main Cause of War between the States," *CS*, Jan. 11, 1997, a9; Fred Hobson, *But Now I See: The White Southern Racial Conversion Narrative* (Baton Rouge: Louisiana State University Press, 1999); *CS*, June 18, 1993, a12 (letter of Eugene E. Downs Jr.); Simvin, "Why a Mom Fights the Flag." Other outstanding examples include *CS*, Oct. 25, 1993, a8 (letter of Sam Martin); May 16, 1995 (letter of Catherine C. Gross); Dec. 14, 1996, a10 (letter of Andrew B. Jones); Bill McDonald, "Flag Debate Hits Home," *CS*, May 15, 1994, e1; Tom Turnipseed, "Southerners Must Have Courage to Break Racist Traditions," *CS*, March 23, 1996, a11.

55. Schuyler Knopf, "Two Lawmakers Push Full Acceptance of Confederate Holiday," *PC*, May 11, 2006, b1.

56. "Confederate Memorial Day," *New York Times*, April 27, 1878; Robert S. Seigler, *A Guide to Confederate Monuments in South Carolina: "Passing the Silent Cup"* (Columbia: South Carolina Department of Archives and History, 1997), 23, 57, 358, 408; see also 65, 89, 110, 266, 298, 344, 469, 474, 486, 489, 494, 510. *CS*, Aug. 23, 1999, a8 (letter of Lawrence B. Glickman) uniquely emphasized this point in the millennial debate.

57. *An Address by Sen. John D. Long of Union County on The Confederate Battle Flag to the Senate of South Carolina, Tuesday, January 22, 1957* (n.p., 1957?), 5. For recent scholarship on sectional reconciliation see Brown, "Civil War Remembrance as Reconstruction," 218–27.

58. See, e.g., *CS,* June 11, 1989, d3 (letter of Gary Graves); Feb. 26, 1990, a6 (letter of Pamela Prettyman); March 23, 1991, a6 (letter of Tim Livingston); March 27, 1991, a12 (letter of Marsha DeLain); June 20, 1991, a8 (letter of Steve Coleman); May 15, 1993, a15 (letter of Bill Chao); Oct. 25, 1993, a8 (letter of Sam Martin); April 5, 1995, a10 (letter of Marcus A. Manos); Aug. 5, 1997, a6 (letter of Tim Monaco); July 1, 1998, a18 (letter of Leah Verona); Aug. 23, 1999, a8 (letter of Richard Irwin); Sept. 7, 1999, a12 (letter of Willie Fuller); Nov. 27, 1999, a20 (letter of Barbara Harper); Dec. 20, 1999, a14 (letter of Pat Jobe); March 25, 2000, a14 (letter of W. D. Leonhardt).

59. *CS,* Aug. 31, 1991, a8 (letter of C. W. Otto).

60. "Debating the Flag"; Rachel Graves, "Flag Deal Offered, Rejected," *PC,* Jan. 19, 2000, a1. See also John Courson, "We Must Honor Each Other's Heroes," *CS,* May 15, 1993, a10. Flag defenders took the suggestion that elites had influenced those ordinary soldiers as an insult to the intelligence and independence of the yeomanry. An officer in the Sons of Confederate Veterans deemed it "absurd" to suppose that "thousands of working-class southerners" had endangered themselves to preserve slavery. *PC,* April 24, 2007, a11 (letter of Bill Norris).

61. Patrick Hagopian, *The Vietnam War in American Memory: Veterans, Memorials, and the Politics of Healing* (Amherst: University of Massachusetts Press, 2009).

62. Unidentified newspaper clipping, Confederate Flag vertical file, Richland County Public Library.

63. *CS,* June 13, 1994, a9 (letter of Linda L. McCall); March 22, 1996, a6 (letter of Jane D. Floyd); Aug. 30, 1999, a8 (letter of J. Stuart Torrey); *PC,* Aug. 19, 2006, a10 (letter of Barry Barrineau).

64. *PC,* Nov. 8, 2003, a12 (letter of Sandy Priester); *Address by Sen. John D. Long,* 3; *CS,* May 2, 2000, a6 (letter of John F. Cantey); Bill Swindell and Rachel Graves, "McConnell Offers Flag Plan with 'Healing Pool,'" *PC,* March 30, 2000, a1. On the Vietnam Veterans Memorial as a therapeutic monument, see Kirk Savage, *Monument Wars: Washington, D.C., the National Mall, and the Transformation of the Memorial Landscape* (Berkeley: University of California Press, 2009), 261–84. See also Gaines M. Foster, "Coming to Terms with Defeat: Post-Vietnam America and the Post-Civil War South," *Virginia Quarterly Review* 66 (Winter 1990): 17–35.

65. Seigler, *Guide to Confederate Monuments,* 216–17; W. H. Trescot to Isabella D. Martin, Feb. 14, 1879, Martin MSS., South Caroliniana Library, University of South Carolina.

66. *PC,* April 9, 2003, a12 (letter of Kenneth S. Anderson Jr.). Meili Steele, *Hiding from History: Politics and Public Imagination* (Ithaca, NY: Cornell University Press, 2005), 1–4, similarly treats the flag debate as a revealing example of the privatization of values in contemporary political dialogue.

67. Clauda Smith Brinson, "Flag Furor Dialogue Was Unique in S.C. History," *CS,* July 1, 2001, a1.

68. Valerie Bauerlein, "Change Waves Red Flag," *CS,* Dec. 7, 2001, a1.

69. Brian Hicks, "Politics Spices Barbecue Brothers' Conflicts," *PC,* Jan. 14, 2001, a1. See also "Maurice's Owner Flies New Confederate Flag," *CS,* Oct. 27, 2007, b3, reporting that Bessinger had substituted the stars and bars for the southern cross at half of his restaurants.

70. "Spurrier: Take Down That Flag," *CS,* April 14, 2007, a1.

71. Kenneth A. Harris, "Flag on Capitol Grounds Torched," *CS,* April 18, 2002, a1; Roddie A. Burris, "Methodist Ministers Lead Protest against Flag," *CS,* May 2, 2007, b1; Wiley B. Cooper, "Called to Stand against the Flag," *CS,* May 25, 2007. John O'Connor, "Compromise Holds, for Now," *CS,* July 1, 2010, b1, offers an overview of the issue on the tenth anniversary of the removal of the flag from the capitol dome.

72. See Boime, *Unveiling of the National Icons,* 52–81; Lonn Taylor, Kathleen M. Kendrick, and Jeffrey L. Brodie, *The Star-Spangled Banner: The Making of an American Icon* (New York: Smithsonian Institution, 2008).

73. Bonner, *Colors and Blood,* 96–103.

74. Wylma Wates, *A Flag Worthy of Your State and People,* 2nd ed. (Columbia: South Carolina Department of Archives and History, 1990); Susan Hill Smith, "The Other Flag: Retailers and Buyers Just Can't Get Enough of the Simple and Striking Design of the South Carolina Flag," *PC,* March 11, 2001, g1.

75. Ernest Renan, "What Is a Nation?" in *Becoming National: A Reader,* ed. Geoff Eley and Ronald Grigor Suny (New York: Oxford University Press, 1996), 52.

CHAPTER 3: Celebrating Freedom

1. Brian R. Ballou, "Juneteenth to Have Its Day—Mass. To Observe Date Marking Final End Of Slavery," *Boston Globe,* June 17, 2007; Juneteenth World Wide Celebration! www.juneteenth.com (accessed Jan. 24, 2009). This website does not explicitly call for a national holiday, though it is campaigning for the U.S. Postal Service to issue a Juneteenth commemorative stamp. The affiliated web site, The National Association of Juneteenth Lineage, www.juneteenth.com/najl.htm, also claims Juneteenth as "the oldest African American holiday," but does not promote a national holiday. It concentrates its efforts on supporting cultural awareness and commemorating the cultural heritage of the African American people.

2. *Huntsville (AL) Gazette,* June 18, 25, 1881; June 23, 1883; June 13, 1885.

3. Anna-Lisa Cox, *A Stronger Kinship: One Town's Extraordinary Story of Hope and Faith* (Boston: Little Brown, 2006), 137.

4. The range of dates celebrated during the nineteenth century and occasional efforts to reach consensus on a single date are documented in Mitch Kachun, *Festivals of Freedom: Memory and Meaning in African American Emancipation Celebrations, 1808–1915* (Amherst: University of Massachusetts Press, 2003), 117–21, 138–45, 183–88, 196–99.

5. One effort by blacks in Richmond, Virginia, to establish a national holiday is described in Ellen M. Litwicki, *America's Public Holidays, 1865–1920* (Washington, DC: Smithsonian Institution Press, 2000), chap. 2.

6. "The New Emancipation," *AME Church Review* 29, no. 3 (Jan. 1913): 260–64.

7. *Journal and Guide* editorial, as reprinted in Chicago *Whip,* in Tuskegee Institute Newspaper Clipping File (hereafter TCF), reel 240, frame 889.

8. *Gary American,* Jan. 4, 1929, in TCF, reel 240, frame 925; unattributed 1922 editorial, TCF, reel 240, frame 887; *Atlanta Independent,* Jan. 2, 1930, TCF, reel 240, frame 930.

9. Biographical information on Wright from Rayford W. Logan and Michael R. Winston, eds., *Dictionary of American Negro Biography* (New York: W. W. Norton, 1982),

674; Elizabeth Ross Haynes, *The Black Boy of Atlanta* (Boston: House of Edinboro, 1952); Plummer, *Rising Wind*, 19; Florence Murray, ed., *The Negro Handbook* (New York: Wendell Malliet and Co., 1949), 354; Webb Waldron, "Black Banker," *Negro Digest* (May 1945): 11–15; "Banker," *The New Yorker* 23 (July 5, 1947): 16–17. Obituaries include the following: "Major Wright Left Record of Achievement," *St. Louis Argus*, July 11, 1947, cited in TCF, reel 238, frame 643; "Major R. R. Wright," *Atlanta Daily World*, July 6, 1947, TCF, reel 238, frame 642; "Veteran Financier Laid to Rest in Philadelphia, Pa.," *Nashville Globe and Independent*, July 11, 1947, TCF, reel 238, frame 643; "Tell Them We Are Rising," *Los Angeles Tribune*, July 12, 1947, TCF, reel 238, frame 645; "Noted Leader Passes in Philadelphia," *St. Louis Argus*, July 11, 1947, TCF, reel 238, frame 645; "Major Wright Left $36,000 Pa. Estate," *Baltimore Afro-American*, n.d., TCF, reel 238, frame 647; "Maj. R. R. Wright, 92, Dies on Eve of Trip," *Baltimore Afro-American*, July 11, 1947, TCF, reel 238, frame 647; "Major R. R. Wright, Banker, Dies at 92," *Pittsburgh Courier*, July 12, 1947, TCF, reel 238, frame 648.

10. Major Wright's commemorative zeal and his role in the creation of National Freedom Day receive detailed attention in Mitch Kachun, "'A beacon to oppressed peoples everywhere': Major Richard R. Wright Sr., National Freedom Day, and the Rhetoric of Freedom in the 1940s," *Pennsylvania Magazine of History and Biography* 128 (July 2004): 279–306.

11. Haynes, *Black Boy of Atlanta;* various newspaper articles on the sesquicentennial, TCF, reel 240, frames 908, 910; Ilene D. Lieberman, "Race and Remembrance: Philadelphia's All Wars Memorial to Colored Soldiers and Sailors and the Politics of Place," *American Art Journal* 29, nos. 1–2 (1998): 18–51.

12. Details of Michaeux's and Wright Jr.'s financial arrangements in "League Spends $90,000 to Get Colored Votes for Roosevelt," *Washington Post*, Oct. 30, 1936, x1, 3.

13. "Says Special Stamp Distorts History; Has Political Move [*sic*]," *Washington Tribune*, Oct. 26, 1940, TCF, reel 240, frame 998; "Charges Post Office Department Is Playing Politics and Distorts History in Special Stamp Issue," *New York Age*, Oct. 26, 1940, TCF, reel 240, frame 1010.

14. One exception worth noting, however, is that National Freedom Day has been a regular part of the annual Hilton Head Island Gullah Celebration, held every February. The year 2009 marked the thirteenth annual event. I am curious about how and why this tradition came to be transplanted there. Perhaps it has something to do with Major Wright's regional roots; from the 1890s to 1920 he served as the president of the State College of Industry for Colored Youth in Savannah (which is now Savannah State College). "Schedule of Events," Annual Hilton Head Island Gullah Celebration, www.gullahcelebration.com/images/calendarofevents.pdf (accessed Jan. 24, 2009).

15. On the early history of Washington, DC, celebrations, see Kachun, *Festivals of Freedom,* chap. 6.

16. "State of Tennessee, Public Acts 2007, House Bill No. 207," www.state.tn.us/sos/acts/105/pub/pc0015.pdf (accessed July 15, 2009). On nineteenth-century traditions of politicized emancipation commemorations, see Kachun, *Festivals of Freedom*. A thoughtful essay on Tennessee's Eighth of August tradition is George White Jr., "'We held out our eyes delirious with grace': The Meanings and Significance of August 8th," *Soul Photo Net*, www.soulphoto.net/index.php/site/we_held_out_our_eyes_delirious_with_grace_the_meanings_and_significance_of/ (accessed July 15, 2009).

17. Emancipation Committee of Upson County, ecupson.org/Home.html (accessed Jan. 31, 2009); "Emancipation Committee Plans MLK Celebration," *The Thomaston Times* (online), www.thomastontimes.com/pages/full_story?article-Emancipation-Committee -Plans-MLK-Celebration%20=&page_label=home_top_stories_news&id=1661576 -Emancipation-Committee-Plans-MLK-Celebration&widget=push&instance=secondary _news_left_column&open=& (accessed Jan. 31, 2009).

18. "Gallipolis, Ohio," *American Profile*, www.americanprofile.com/spotlights/article/ 1403.html (accessed Jan. 31, 2009). On nineteenth-century regional celebrations, see Kachun, *Festivals of Freedom*, 77–79, 122–31, 192–97.

19. William A. Blair, "Celebrating Freedom: The Problem of Emancipation in Public Commemoration," in *Lincoln's Proclamation: Emancipation Reconsidered*, ed. William A. Blair and Karen Fisher Younger (Chapel Hill: University of North Carolina Press, 2009), 204–8.

20. Blair, "Celebrating Freedom," 209; Askia Muhammad, "Juneteenth, Slavery, and the Race Debate," *Washington (DC) Informer*, 32, no. 38 (July 2, 1997): 16.

21. John Nichols, "MLK, LBJ, Clinton, Obama and the Politics of Memory," *The Nation* (Blogs, The Beat), Jan. 14, 2008, www.thenation.com/blogs/thebeat/270210 (accessed July 16, 2009).

22. Kachun, "'A beacon to oppressed peoples everywhere.'"

23. John McWhorter, "Why Juneteenth's Not My Thing," *The Root*, www.theroot .com/id/46902 (accessed Jan. 29, 2009).

24. A very few examples include, John Hope Franklin and Loren Schweninger, *Runaway Slaves: Rebels on the Plantation* (New York: Oxford University Press, 1999); Patrick Rael, *Black Identity and Black Protest in the Antebellum North* (Chapel Hill: University of North Carolina Press, 1999); Steven Hahn, *A Nation under Our Feet: Black Political Struggles in the Rural South from Slavery to the Great Migration* (Cambridge, MA: Harvard University Press, 2003); John David Smith, ed., *Black Soldiers in Blue: African American Troops in the Civil War Era* (Chapel Hill: University of North Carolina Press, 2003).

25. See *19th of June*, www.19thofjune.com and Juneteenth.us, www.juneteenth.us (both accessed Jan. 24, 2009).

26. Hahn, *A Nation under Our Feet*, 362; "Exodus of 1879," *Handbook of Texas Online*, www.tshaonline.org/handbook/online/articles/EE/ume2.html (accessed July 17, 2009); Alwyn Barr, *Black Texans: A History of African Americans in Texas, 1528–1995*, 2nd ed. (Norman: University of Oklahoma Press, 1996), 145–46, 154; "The Twentieth Century Experience: An Introduction" in *The African American Experience in Texas: An Anthology*, ed. Bruce A. Glasrud and James M. Smallwood (Lubbock: Texas Tech University Press, 2007), 173–82; William H. Wiggins Jr., "From Galveston to Washington: Charting June-teenth's Freedom Trail," in *Jubilation! African American Celebrations in the Southeast*, ed. William H. Wiggins Jr. and Douglas DeNatale (Columbia: University of South Carolina Press, 1994), 62–64.

27. Ashley Luthern, "Juneteenth: A New Birth of Freedom," *Around the Mall: Scenes and Sightings from the Smithsonian Museums and Beyond*, June 19, 2009, http://blogs .smithsonianmag.com/aroundthemall/2009/06/juneteenth-a-new-birth-of-freedom/ (accessed July 18, 2009); William H. Wiggins Jr., "Juneteenth: Tracking the Progress of an Emancipation Celebration," *American Visions* 8 (June/July 1993): 28–31.

28. "Group Requests the Attention of Clinton to Observe Juneteenth," *Tri-State Defender* (Memphis) Sept. 4, 1996, 45, no. 35: 5A; "Mississippi Based Group Presses for Second Independence Day," *Tri-State Defender,* June 16, 1999.

29. "Message from the NAJL President," *The National Association of Juneteenth Lineage Inc.,* www.juneteenth.com/najl.htm (accessed July 20, 2009).

30. "Mississippi Based Group Presses for Second Independence Day," *Tri-State Defender,* June 16, 1999.

31. Kathy Williamson, "Effort Underway to Establish National Juneteenth Holiday," *Los Angeles Sentinel,* June 21, 2000; Kathy Williamson, "Congressman Hall Continues Push for Apology for Slavery: Effort Supported by National Juneteenth Crusade," *Los Angeles Sentinel,* Aug. 30, 2000; "Juneteenth Leaders Dismayed with President Bush," *Oakland (CA) Post,* Aug. 12, 2001; Virginia L. Porter, "Leaders up in Arms over Bush Stand on Juneteenth," *Tri-State Defender,* Aug. 22, 2001.

32. U.S. Senate, 110th Congress, 2nd session, "untitled," Resolution no. 584, available through *Lexis-Nexis Congressional* (accessed July 25, 2009). The House of Representatives passed an identical resolution (House res. 1237). Similar bills were passed by the House and Senate in 2001, 2005, 2006, 2007, and 2009.

33. House of Representatives, 111th Congress, 1st session, "untitled," Concurrent resolution no. 26, available through *Lexis-Nexis Congressional* (accessed July 25, 2009); "Obama on Juneteenth," Letters to the Editor, *St. Louis (MO) American,* July 3, 2009; Rev. Ronald V. Myers Sr., MD, "Response to President Obama's 2010 Junteenth Statement," www.juneteenth.us/obama3.html (accessed Aug. 2, 2010; italics and bold font in original).

34. Valerie Wesley, *Freedom's Gifts: A Juneteenth Story* (New York: Simon and Schuster, 1997); Muriel Miller Branch, *Juneteenth: Freedom Day* (New York: Cobblehill Books, 1999); "Press Release," *19th of June,* www.njclc.com/pressreleaseII.htm (accessed Aug. 2, 2010); June Preszler, *Juneteenth: Jubilee for Freedom* (Mankato, MN: Capsone, 2007); Angela Leeper, *Juneteenth: A Day to Celebrate Freedom from Slavery* (Berkeley Heights, NJ: Enslow Elementary, 2004); Carole Boston Weatherford, *Juneteenth Jamboree* (New York: Lee and Low Books, 1997); Carole Boston Weatherford and Eida de la Vega, trans., *Celebremos Juneteenth* (New York: Lee and Low Books, 1997); Laura Krauss Melmed, *Heart of Texas: A Lone Star ABC* (New York: HarperCollins, 2009). A search for "Juneteenth" on the Amazon.com websites will turn up these and many other titles.

35. Ralph Ellison, *Juneteenth: A Novel,* ed. John F. Callahan (New York: Random House, 1999); Ralph Ellison, "Juneteenth," *Quarterly Review of Literature* 14 (1965): 262–76.

36. Ellison, *Juneteenth,* 114–40, quoted at 114, 115, 117.

37. There is a range of opinions on whether we should continue having a Black History Month.

38. Several examples will suffice: in July 2009 black Harvard professor Henry Louis Gates was arrested in his home by a white police officer, which prompted the "beer summit" at the White House with those two parties and President Obama; Virginia Governor Bob McDonnell declared April 2010 as "Confederate History Month," while avoiding any mention of slavery as a cause of the Civil War, prompting much criticism and eventually an apology from McDonnell; U.S. Department of Agriculture official Shirley Sherrod was fired in the summer of 2010 after a right-wing pundit misrepresented her

statements about racial bias to suggest her own (and by implication, the Obama administration's) purported discrimination against whites.

CHAPTER 4: The Civil War and Contemporary Southern Literature

1. Tony Horwitz, *Confederates in the Attic: Dispatches from the Unfinished Civil War* (New York: Vintage, 1999), 5–6.

2. David Goldfield, *Still Fighting the Civil War: The American South and Southern History* (Baton Rouge: Louisiana State University Press, 2002), 1.

3. Rick Bass, "Government Bears," in *The Watch* (New York: W. W. Norton, 1999), 172–73.

4. Craig A. Warner works with this idea in examining the Civil War fiction of Howard Bahr. See Craig A. Warner, *Scars to Prove It: The Civil War Soldier and American Fiction* (Kent: Kent State University Press, 2009), 162–69.

5. Allen Tate, "Ode to the Confederate Dead," in *Collected Poems, 1919–1976* (New York: Farrar Straus Giroux, 1977), 21.

6. Alice Randall, *The Wind Done Gone* (Boston: Houghton Mifflin, 2001), 175. For this work and those that follow, further citations are given parenthetically in the text.

7. Quoted in Horwitz, 52.

8. Edward P. Jones, *The Known World* (New York: HarperCollins, 2003), 42.

9. Toni Morrison, *Beloved* (New York: Knopf, 1992), 36.

10. Ishmael Reed, "The Neo-HooDoo Aesthetic," in *Conjure: Selected Poems, 1963–1970* (Amherst: University of Massachusetts Press, 1972), 26.

11. Quoted in Paul K. Saint-Amour, *The Copywrights: Intellectual Property and the Literary Imagination* (Ithaca: Cornell University Press, 2003), 208.

12. For a good discussion of the earlier generation of southern writers, see Louis D. Rubin Jr., "The Image of an Army: The Civil War in Southern Fiction," in *Southern Writers: Appraisals in Our Time*, ed. R. C. Simonini Jr. (Charlottesville: University Press of Virginia, 1964), 50–70.

13. Newt Gingrich and William Forstchen, *Never Call Retreat, Lee and Grant, The Final Victory* (New York: Thomas Dunne, 2007), xi.

14. Charles Frazier, *Thirteen Moons* (New York: Random House, 2006), 357.

15. Madison Smartt Bell, *Devil's Dream* (New York: Pantheon, 2009), 254.

16. Allan Gurganus, *The Oldest Living Confederate Widow Tells All* (New York: Alfred A. Knopf, 1989), 52.

17. Kaye Gibbons, *On the Occasion of My Last Afternoon* (New York: Putnam, 1998), 236.

18. Charles Frazier, *Cold Mountain* (New York: Atlantic Monthly Press, 1997), 16.

19. Josephine Humphreys, *Nowhere Else on Earth* (New York: Viking, 2000), 30.

20. Howard Bahr, *The Judas Field* (New York: Henry Holt, 2006), 165.

21. David Madden, *Sharpshooter* (Knoxville: University of Tennessee Press, 1996), 6–7.

22. Bobbie Ann Mason, "Shiloh," in *Shiloh and Other Stories* (New York: Harper & Row, 1982), 13.

23. Barry Hannah, *Ray* (New York: Alfred A. Knopf, 1980), 45.

24. Amanda C. Gable, *The Confederate General Rides North* (New York: Scribner, 2009), 270.

25. Ron Rash, *The World Made Straight* (New York: Henry Holt, 2006), 162.

26. Judy Budnitz, "The Kindest Cut," in *Nice Big American Baby* (New York: Alfred A. Knopf, 2005), 238.

27. Natasha Trethewey, "Native Guard," in *Native Guard* (Boston: Houghton Mifflin, 2006), 26.

28. In the image of the overwritten diaries, Trethewey draws from the similarly written diary of Colonel Nathan W. Daniels, the white commander of the 2nd Louisiana Native Guard Volunteers. Daniels wrote his diary over the confiscated diary of a cotton merchant in New Orleans. Trethewey uses an image of Nathan's cross-written diary on the front cover of *Native Guard*. See C. P. Weaver, ed., *Thank God My Regiment an African One: The Civil War Diary of Colonel Nathan W. Daniels* (Baton Rouge: Louisiana State University Press, 1998).

29. Robert Penn Warren, *The Legacy of the Civil War: Meditations on the Centennial* (New York: Random House, 1961), 3.

30. Trethewey's recasting of Southern mythology about the war resembles the type of revisioning for which Tara McPerson calls. See Tara McPherson, *Reconstructing Dixie: Race, Gender, and Nostalgia in the Imagined South* (Durham, NC: Duke University Press, 2003).

CHAPTER 5: Lincoln and the Civil War in Twenty-First-Century Photography

1. For overviews of Civil War battlefield photography, see Michael L. Carlebach, *The Origins of Photojournalism in America* (Washington, DC: Smithsonian Institution Press, 1992), 62–101; Keith F. Davis, " 'A Terrible Distinctness': Photography of the Civil War Era," in *Photography in Nineteenth-Century America,* ed. Martha A. Sandweiss (Fort Worth, TX: Amon Carter Museum, 1991), 130–79; and Bob Zeller, *The Blue and Gray in Black and White: A History of Civil War Photography* (Westport, CT: Praeger, 2005). For overviews of Lincoln photography, see Charles Hamilton and Lloyd Ostendorf, *Lincoln in Photographs: An Album of Every Known Pose,* rev. ed. (Dayton, OH: Morningside, 1985); Harold Holzer, Gabor S. Boritt, and Mark E. Neely Jr., *The Lincoln Image: Abraham Lincoln and the Popular Print* (Urbana: University of Illinois Press, 2001); and Philip B. Kunhardt III, Peter W. Kunhardt, and Peter W. Kunhardt Jr., *Looking for Lincoln: The Making of an American Icon* (New York: Alfred A. Knopf, 2008).

2. Greta Pratt, *Using History* (Göttingen: Steidl, 2005), n.p. More of her Lincoln photographs are reproduced in Pratt, "Playing President," *New York Times,* Feb. 16, 2009, a19. For more information on the artist, see www.gretapratt.com. For discussion of Lincoln reenactors, see Andrew Ferguson, *Land of Lincoln: Adventures in Abe's America* (New York: Grove Press, 2007), 152–66.

3. For influential discussions of photography and postmodernism, see Douglas Crimp, "The Photographic Activity of Postmodernism," *On the Museum's Ruins* (Cambridge, MA: MIT Press, 1993), 108–25, and Abigail Solomon-Godeau, "Photography after Art Photography," *Photography at the Dock: Essays on Photographic History, Institutions, and*

Practices (Minneapolis: University of Minnesota Press, 1991), 103–23. Interpretations of serial form in Warhol include Ernst Beyeler et al., *Andy Warhol: Series and Singles* (Riehen/ Basle: Fondation Beyeler, 2000), and William V. Ganis, *Andy Warhol's Serial Photography* (Cambridge: Cambridge University Press, 2004).

4. These images are reproduced in Hamilton and Ostendorf, *Lincoln in Photographs,* 260–61, 270, which includes the fullest dossier of altered Lincoln photographs, 256–82.

5. Harold Holzer, "Visualizing Lincoln: Abraham Lincoln as Student, Subject, and Patron of the Visual Arts," in *Our Lincoln: New Perspectives on Lincoln and His World,* ed. Eric Foner (New York: W. W. Norton, 2008), 105.

6. Ostendorf and Hamilton term this image a "composite photograph" *(Lincoln in Photographs),* 275. On the history of this image, see Nell Irvin Painter, *Sojourner Truth: A Life, A Symbol* (New York: W. W. Norton, 1996), 260. On Truth's shaping of her photographs, see Carla L. Peterson, *"Doers of the Word": African-American Women Speakers and Writers in the North (1830–1880)* (New York: Oxford University Press, 1995), 40–44. I am grateful to Edward Blum for drawing my attention to the relevance of this image for this project.

7. On the representation of Lincoln in a variety of visual media, see Harold Holzer and Gabor Boritt, "Epilogue: Lincoln in 'Modern' Art," in *The Lincoln Enigma: The Changing Faces of an American Icon,* ed. Gabor Boritt (New York: Oxford University Press, 2001), 146–277; Gary L. Bunker, *From Rail-Splitter to Icon: Lincoln's Image in Illustrated Periodicals, 1860–1865* (Kent, OH: Kent State University Press, 2001); Cara A. Finnegan, "Recognizing Lincoln: Image Vernaculars in Nineteenth-Century Visual Culture," *Rhetoric & Public Affairs* 8, no. 1 (2005): 31–58; and Harold Holzer, *Lincoln Seen and Heard* (Lawrence: University Press of Kansas, 2000). On Lincoln in the context of Civil War art, see Gary Gallagher, *Causes Won, Lost and Forgotten: How Hollywood and Popular Art Shape What We Know about the Civil War* (Chapel Hill: University of North Carolina Press, 2008); Harold Holzer and Mark E. Neely Jr., *Mine Eyes Have Seen the Glory: The Civil War in Art* (New York: Orion, 1993); Mark E. Neely Jr., Harold Holzer, and Gabor S. Boritt, *The Confederate Image: Prints of the Lost Cause* (Chapel Hill: University of North Carolina Press, 1987); Neely and Holzer, *The Union Image: Popular Prints of the Civil War North* (Chapel Hill: University of North Carolina Press, 2000); and Shirley Samuels, *Facing America: Iconography and the Civil War* (New York: Oxford University Press, 2004). On Lincoln's image in more general terms, see Merrill D. Peterson, *Lincoln in American Memory* (New York: Oxford University Press, 1994); Barry Schwartz, *Abraham Lincoln and the Forge of National Memory* (Chicago: University of Chicago Press, 2000); and Schwartz, *Abraham Lincoln in the Post-Heroic Era: History and Memory in Late Twentieth-Century America* (Chicago: University of Chicago Press, 2008).

8. Oliver Wendell Holmes, "Doings of the Sunbeam," *Atlantic Monthly* 12 (July 1863): 11.

9. On battlefield photographs, see Brooks Johnson, ed., *An Enduring Interest: The Photographs of Alexander Gardner* (Norfolk, VA: Chrysler Museum, 1991); D. Mark Katz, *Witness to an Era: The Life and Photographs of Alexander Gardner* (Nashville, TN: Rutledge Hill Press, 1991); Geoffrey Klingsporn, "Icon of Real War: *A Harvest of Death* and American War Photography," *Velvet Light Trap* 45 (Spring 2000): 4–19; Franny Nudelman, *John Brown's Body: Slavery, Violence, and the Culture of War* (Chapel Hill: University of North Carolina Press, 2004), 103–31; Anthony W. Lee and Elizabeth Young, *On Alexander*

Gardner's "Photographic Sketch Book" of the Civil War (Berkeley: University of California Press, 2007); Mary Panzer, *Mathew Brady and the Image of History* (Washington, DC: Smithsonian Institution Press, 1997); Timothy Sweet, *Traces of War: Poetry, Photography, and the Crisis of the Union* (Baltimore: Johns Hopkins University Press, 1990); Alan Trachtenberg, *Reading American Photographs: Images as History, Mathew Brady to Walker Evans* (New York: Hill & Wang, 1989), 71–118; and Megan Rowley Williams, *Through the Negative: The Photographic Image and the Written Word in Nineteenth-Century American Literature* (New York: Routledge, 2003), 61–97.

10. Sweet, *Traces of War*, 107–37.

11. This restaging was first documented by William A. Frassanito in *Gettysburg: A Journey in Time* (New York: Scribner's, 1975).

12. Sally Mann, *What Remains* (Boston: Bulfinch, 2003), 79–99.

13. For an earlier photographic series that suggests a more oblique reenactment of Gardner, see Cindy Sherman's *Civil War* (1991–92), which features lurid, stylized close-ups of dismembered body parts on dirty ground. This series implicitly mimics the staged quality of Gardner's bodies, a mimicry consistent with Sherman's emphasis on staging in her famous self-portraiture. Images from this underanalyzed series are reproduced in Régis Durand et al., *Cindy Sherman* (Paris: Flammarion, 2006), and Rosalind Krauss, *Cindy Sherman, 1975–1993* (New York: Rizzoli, 1993), 196–201; for discussion, see Durand, "Introduction," *Cindy Sherman*, 260.

14. William Earle Williams, *Unsung Heroes: African American Soldiers in the Civil War, Contact Sheet #140* (Syracuse, NY: Light Work, 2007). On Williams's work in the context of African American photography, see Deborah Willis, *Reflections in Black: A History of Black Photographers, 1840 to the Present* (New York: W. W. Norton, 2000), 194, 322.

15. See Kirk Savage, *Standing Soldiers, Kneeling Slaves: Race, War, and Monument in Nineteenth-Century America* (Princeton, NJ: Princeton University Press, 1997). On the erasure of racial conflict from the history of the war, see David W. Blight, *Race and Reunion: The Civil War in American Memory* (Cambridge, MA: Harvard University Press, 2001).

16. On photographs of black soldiers, see Gwendolyn DuBois Shaw and Emily K. Shubert, "Portraits of a People," in *Portraits of a People: Picturing African Americans in the Nineteenth Century*, ed. Shaw (Andover, MA: Addison Gallery of Art, 2006), 132–35. On the Saint-Gaudens monument, see Martin H. Blatt, Thomas J. Brown, and Donald Yacovone, eds., *Hope and Glory: Essays on the Legacy of the Fifty-Fourth Massachusetts Regiment* (Amherst: University of Massachusetts Press, 2001). On *Glory*, see Jim Cullen, *The Civil War in Popular Culture: A Reusable Past* (Washington, DC: Smithsonian Institution Press, 1995), 139–71.

17. Williams, *Unsung Heroes*, 46.

18. W. J. T. Mitchell, "Imperial Landscape," in *Landscape and Power*, ed. Mitchell (Chicago: University of Chicago Press, 1994), 5.

19. John Huddleston, *Killing Ground: Photographs of the Civil War and the Changing American Landscape* (Baltimore: Johns Hopkins University Press, 2002). All subsequent citations to this text will be given parenthetically in the text; I refer to photographic pairings by the name of the battlefield in the caption under the left-side image, except as noted.

20. See Mark Klett et al., *Second View: The Rephotographic Survey Project* (Albuquerque: University of New Mexico Press, 1984), and Klett et al., *Third Views, Second Sights: A Rephotographic Survey of the American West* (Santa Fe: Museum of New Mexico Press, 2004). For discussion of this project, see William L. Fox, *View Finder: Mark Klett, Photography, and the Reinvention of Landscape* (Albuquerque: University of New Mexico Press, 2001).

21. This pairing appears in the volume on 108–9, where Huddleston describes the contemporary image as follows: "In the early afternoon of the first day, the Confederates forced the Federals to retreat from this position just north of the college" (109). For an assessment of Huddleston's work in relation to rephotography, see Chad Randl, review of *Killing Ground,* in *CRM: The Journal of Heritage Stewardship* 3, no. 2 (Summer 2006), http://crmjournal.cr.nps.gov/07_rbook_sub.cfm?issue=Volume%203%20Number%202%20Summer%202006&seq=7. Huddleston resists the characterization of his work as "rephotographic in that precise sense of duplicating the view of an earlier photograph. I wanted to be free in responding to the modern landscape and its meanings" ("Killing Ground, Healing Ground: An Interview with Photographer John Huddleston," *Identity Theory,* May 1, 2008, www.identitytheory.com/visual/huddleston.php).

22. *Killing Ground* moves around in the chronology of Civil War battle, which Huddleston also summarizes in an appendix, 167–74.

23. Petersburg is listed as both "private and national park" (175), the Kmart presumably standing on private ground.

24. Five other pairings in the volume also reverse chronology, with the new image on the left (26–27, 48–49, 84–85, 112–13, and 142–43). In three pairings from this project published earlier in *DoubleTake,* the Kmart image was printed on the right-hand side ("Killing Ground: John Huddleston," *DoubleTake* 2, no. 1 [Winter 1996]: 32–37).

25. Other photographs involving amputation appear in the volume on 24, 34, 52, 110, and 113. For analysis of Civil War medical photographs, see J. T. H. Connor and Michael G. Rhode, "Shooting Soldiers: Civil War Medical Images, Memory, and Identity in America," *Invisible Culture: An Electronic Journal for Visual Culture* 5 (2003), www.rochester.edu/in_visible_culture/Issue_5/ConnorRhode/ConnorRhode.html; Kathy Newman, "Wounds and Wounding in the American Civil War: A (Visual) History," *Yale Journal of Criticism* 6, no. 2 (Fall 1993): 63–86; and Samuels, *Facing America,* 62–70.

26. See, for example, Bontecou's photograph of a pile of amputated feet, in Stanley B. Burns, *A Morning's Work: Medical Photographs from the Burns Archive & Collection, 1843–1939* (Santa Fe: Twin Palms, 1998), n.p. (plate 23).

27. On the racial dynamics of this photograph, see Lee and Young, *On Alexander Gardner's "Photographic Sketch Book" of the Civil War,* 43–47, 87–90.

28. On postcards and other visual representations of lynching, see James Allen et al., *Without Sanctuary: Lynching Photography in America* (Santa Fe: Twin Palms, 2000); Dora Apel and Shawn Michelle Smith, *Lynching Photographs* (Berkeley: University of California Press, 2007); Jacqueline Goldsby, *A Spectacular Secret: Lynching in American Life and Literature* (Chicago: University of Chicago Press, 2006); and Amy Louise Wood, *Lynching and Spectacle: Witnessing Racial Violence in America, 1890–1940* (Chapel Hill: University of North Carolina Press, 2009).

29. *Harper's Weekly*, Aug. 1, 1863, 484. On the lynching of William Jones, see Barnet Schecter, *The Devil's Own Work: The Civil War Draft Riots and the Fight to Reconstruct America* (New York: Walker, 2005), 157, 170.

30. On the visual dimensions of this episode, see Elizabeth Alexander, "'Can you be BLACK and look at this?': Reading the Rodney King Video(s)," in *Black Male: Representations of Masculinity in Contemporary American Art,* ed. Thelma Golden (New York: Whitney Museum of American Art, 1994), 91–110, and Robert Gooding-Williams, ed., *Reading Rodney King/Reading Urban Uprising* (New York: Routledge, 1993).

31. Ken Gonzales-Day, *Lynching in the West, 1850–1935* (Durham, NC: Duke University Press, 2006), 29.

32. Paul Laurence Dunbar, "The Haunted Oak," in *The Collected Poetry of Paul Laurence Dunbar,* ed. Joanne Braxton (Charlottesville: University Press of Virginia, 1993), 219.

33. For discussion of lynching photographs in the context of *A Harvest of Death*, see Goldsby, *Spectacular Secret*, 232–36.

34. Sonya Clark, "Artist's Statement," *Political Craft* exhibition (Boston: Society of Arts & Crafts, Boston, 2008), n.p. For more information on Clark, see www.sonyaclark.com.

35. Suzan-Lori Parks, *The America Play*, in *The America Play, and Other Works* (New York: Theatre Communications Group, 1995), and Parks, *Topdog/Underdog* (New York: Theatre Communications Group, 2001).

36. Clark, "Artist's Statement."

37. On the Lincoln-Obama connection, see Wyatt Evans, "The Lincoln-Obama Moment," chap. 1 in this volume. On *Abraham Obama* and English's "popaganda," see the artist's websites at www.popaganda.com and www.abrahamobama.net and Dan Goede and Ron English, eds., *Abraham Obama: A Guerilla Tour through Art and Politics* (San Francisco: Last Gasp of San Francisco, 2009). An important analysis of this work appears in Alexandre Borrell, "Peut-on greffer le visage d'une icône? *Abraham Obama*," *Parlement(s), Revue d'histoire politique,* 13 (Jan. 2010): 117–29, www.cairn.info/revue-parlements-2010-1-page-117.html (translations from this essay are my own). On *Abraham Obama* and *Hope*, see Shepard Fairey and Jennifer Gross, eds., *Art for Obama: Designing "Manifest Hope" and the Campaign for Change* (New York: Abrams, 2009). On the visual culture of Obama, see "The Obama Issue," *Journal of Visual Culture* 8, no. 2 (August 2009). The form of *Abraham Obama* is described in different ways; the term "digitized print mural" is that of Mark Favermann, "*Abraham Obama* Morphes Art and Politics: Ephemeral Public Art in a Time of Angst," in *Abraham Obama,* ed. Goede and English, 13. My interpretation is based on viewing the original installation of *Abraham Obama* at Gallery XIV in Boston in July 2008.

38. "Warholian pop style" is in English, "Introduction," *Abraham Obama,* ed. Goede and English, 3; "postmodern visual statement" is used by Favermann, "*Abraham Obama* Morphes Art and Politics," in *Abraham Obama,* 11.

39. English describes this process in a 2009 CNN interview with Emmanuel Tambakakis, "Two Faces, One Man," www.cnn.com/video/?/video/living/2009/02/11/lif.abraham.obama.

40. See English, "Introduction," *Abraham Obama,* 1–5, on his support for Obama. Carlo McCormick characterizes English's usual approach as "deviant mimicry, mediated appropriation, and grotesque parody" ("Myth & Metaphor," in *Abraham Obama,* 84).

41. See S. J. Ferris, *Washington and Lincoln (Apotheosis)* (1865) and Otto Knirsch, *National Picture* (1865). On visual representations of the links between Lincoln and Washington, see Holzer, "Visualizing Lincoln," 80–83, and Holzer, *Washington and Lincoln Portrayed: National Icons in Popular Prints* (Jefferson, NC: McFarland, 1993).

42. This connection was brought full circle in a cover image of *The New Yorker* that portrayed Obama as Washington (Drew Friedman, "The First," *New Yorker*, Jan. 26, 2009).

43. See Borelle, "Peut-on greffer le visage d'une icône" ["Can one graft the face of an icon"]: "Cette greffe . . . est assurément une réussite esthétique, quoi que les attributs de Lincoln phagocytent un peu les traits d'Obama. . . . Au vu du 'poids' respectif des deux personnages, largement favorable à l'aîné, la greffe est inversée: c'est à Obama qu'on a greffé les attributs de Lincoln" ["This graft is an esthetic success, in which the attributes of Lincoln absorb the traits of Obama. . . . In relation to the respective 'weight' of the two men, which largely favors the older one, the graft is reversed: it is onto Obama that the traits of Lincoln have been grafted"] (128).

44. P. S. Duval, *Emancipation Proclamations. / Allegorical Portrait of Abraham Lincoln.* This image is reproduced and discussed in Holzer, Boritt, and Neely, *Lincoln Image,* 96–97.

45. For discussion of the Great Emancipator iconography, see Peterson, *Lincoln in American Memory,* 29–30, 348–58, and Schwartz, *Abraham Lincoln in the Post-Heroic Era,* 116–21, 131–45, 166–70, 228–35; on the Bennett essay, see Peterson, 357–58, and Schwartz, 166.

46. The complete text of the caption is as follows. Man at left: "It's no use old fellow! You can't pull that wool over my eyes, for I can see 'the Nigger' peeping through the rails." Greeley: "I assure you my friend, that you can safely vote our ticket, for we have no connection with the Abolition party, but our Platform is composed entirely of rails, split by our Candidate." Lincoln: "Little did I think when I split these rails, that they would be the means of elevating me to my present position." This image is reprinted and discussed in Holzer, Boritt, and Neely, *Lincoln Image,* 37. On Lincoln's rail-splitter image, see Bunker, *From Rail-Splitter to Icon.*

47. Other figures in this complex image lampoon specific politicians; for explication, see Bernard F. Reilly Jr., *American Political Prints, 1766–1876* (Boston: G. K. Hall, 1991), 536–39. On the racial meanings of *Othello* in America, see Tilden G. Edelstein, "*Othello* in America: The Drama of Racial Intermarriage," in *Interracialism: Black-White Intermarriage in American History, Literature, and Law,* ed. Werner Sollors (Oxford: Oxford University Press, 2000), 356–68; and Francesca T. Royster, "Playing with (a) Difference: Early Black Shakespearean Actors, Blackface and Whiteface," in *Shakespeare in American Life,* ed. Virginia Mason Vaughan and Alden T. Vaughan (Washington, DC: Folger Shakespeare Library, 2007), 35–47. On minstrelsy, see Eric Lott, *Love and Theft: Blackface Minstrelsy and the American Working Class* (New York: Oxford University Press, 1993); on Lincoln and minstrelsy, see Mark E. Neely Jr., *The Boundaries of American Political Culture in the Civil War Era* (Chapel Hill: University of North Carolina Press, 2005), 97–127.

48. This image is reproduced and discussed in John H. Rhodehamel and Thomas F. Schwartz, *The Last Best Hope of Earth: Abraham Lincoln and the Promise of America* (San Marino, CA: Huntington Library, 1993), 62.

49. This image was based on the character of "Mokanna" in Thomas Moore's Romantic poem *Lalla Rookh* (1817). It is reproduced and discussed in Lucy Shelton Caswell, "Drawing Swords: War in American Editorial Cartoons," *American Journalism* 21, no. 2 (Spring 2004): 25–27. On Volck, see also Neely, Holzer, and Boritt, *Confederate Image*, 44–54.

50. The best-known of these images is *Miscegenation or The Millennium of Abolitionism* (1864), reproduced and discussed in Elise Lemire, *"Miscegenation": Making Race in America* (Philadelphia: University of Pennsylvania Press, 2002), 118–21.

51. See Shawn Michelle Smith, "Obama's Whiteness," in "The Obama Issue," *Journal of Visual Culture*, 129–33.

52. For related assessments of the racial politics of the work, see Favermann: "The mural's Warholian shifts in color and value suggest racial undertones and nuances. There is a black-and-white unspoken reference in the color. Obama is of mixed race. All this is significantly and inherently stated in the mural" (*"Abraham Obama* Morphes Art and Politics," 14), and Borrell, "La juxtaposition de tirages colorisés forme un arc-en-ciel qui résout et dépasse, sur le plan esthétique, la question politique de la couleur de peau" ["The juxtaposition of colorized prints forms a rainbow that resolves and exceeds, on an esthetic plane, the political question of skin color"] ("Peut-on griffer le visage d'une icône," 119). Numerous black-and-white versions of *Abraham Obama* have also appeared and merit their own analysis; I focus on the color version, which remains the best known.

53. For a discussion of how to analyze political content in Warhol, see Thomas Crow, "Saturday Disasters: Trace and Reference in Early Warhol," in *Andy Warhol*, ed. Annette Michelson (Cambridge, MA: MIT Press, 2001), 49–66; for an interpretation focused on race in one Warhol work, see Anne M. Wagner, "Warhol Paints History, or Race in America," *Representations* 55 (Summer 1996): 98–119.

54. Other defaced images appear in Goede and English, *Abraham Obama*, 29, 31, 62–64.

55. David Freedberg, "Idolatry and Iconoclasm," *The Power of Images: Studies in the History and Theory of Response* (Chicago: University of Chicago Press, 1989), 415.

CHAPTER 6: Reenactment and Relic

1. Other exhibitions that have highlighted the Civil War include *Confronting History: Contemporary Artists Envision the Past,* hosted by the Middlebury College Museum of Art in 2008, and *Places with a Past: New Site-Specific Art in Charleston,* organized by the Spoleto Festival USA in 1991.

2. Ian Berry, "Medicine on the Spoon: A Dialogue with Dario Robleto," in Elizabeth Dunbar, *Alloy of Love: Dario Robleto* (Saratoga Springs, NY: The Frances Young Tang Teaching Museum and Art Gallery, 2008), 259.

3. Gary W. Gallagher, *Causes Won, Lost, and Forgotten: How Hollywood and Popular Art Shape What We Know about the Civil War* (Chapel Hill: University of North Carolina Press, 2008), 135–207.

4. On photography, see Elizabeth Young's essay, chap. 5 in this volume. On Kara Walker, see W. Fitzhugh Brundage's essay, chap. 7 in this volume. On Leo Twiggs, see Marilyn Laufer and Frank Martin, *Myths and Metaphors: The Art of Leo Twiggs* (Athens:

Georgia Museum of Art, 2004). For a broad sample of work related to slavery and emancipation, including contributions from Glenn Ligon and Whitfield Lovell, see Lowery Stokes Sims, Kathleen Hulser, and Cynthia R. Copeland, *Legacies: Contemporary Artists Reflect on Slavery* (New York: New York Historical Society, 2006). Another strand of recent art has concentrated on the image of Abraham Lincoln. See Gabor Boritt and Harold Holzer, "Epilogue: Lincoln in 'Modern' Art," in *The Lincoln Enigma: The Changing Faces of an American Icon,* ed. Gabor Boritt (New York: Oxford University Press, 2001), 146–277, and the Lincoln bicentennial anniversary project *21st Century Abe,* www.21stcenturyabe.com (accessed Aug. 27, 2010).

5. Toby Kamps, *The Old, Weird America: Folk Themes in Contemporary Art* (Houston: Contemporary Arts Museum Houston, 2008), 68–73.

6. On farbs and hardcores, see Tony Horwitz, *Confederates in the Attic: Dispatches from the Unfinished Civil War* (New York: Vintage, 1998). Jim Weeks, *Gettysburg: Memory, Market, and an American Shrine* (Princeton, NJ: Princeton University Press, 2003), 169–225, discusses the quest for authenticity. On gender relations in Civil War reenactment, see Cathy Stanton and Stephen Belyea, " 'Their Time Will Yet Come': The African American Presence in Civil War Reenactment," in *Hope and Glory: Essays on the Legacy of the 54th Massachusetts Regiment,* ed. Martin H. Blatt, Thomas J. Brown, and Donald Yacovone (Amherst: University of Massachusetts Press, 2001), 266–270. Jim Leonard's play, *Battle Hymn,* produced by the Circle X Theatre in Los Angeles in 2009, is another recent examination of the lasting martial shadow of the Civil War.

7. Joan M. Zenzen, *Battling for Manassas: The Fifty-Year Preservation Struggle at Manassas National Battlefield Park* (University Park: Pennsylvania State University Press, 1998), 177, 180.

8. Ariella Budick, "Enlisting in the Army of Art," *Newsday,* May 12, 2005, www .bellwethergallery.com (accessed Nov. 9, 2009).

9. *Victory Hall,* press release, May 26–June 25, 2005, www.bellwethergallery.com (accessed Oct. 21, 2010); *Hobby Horse,* www.allisonsmithstudio.com (accessed Nov. 9, 2009). Smith has also taken up the Civil War politics of race and slavery in *The Donkey, the Jackass, and the Mule,* commissioned by the Indianapolis Museum of Art in 2008. See Rebecca Uchill, ed., *On Procession: Art on Parade* (Indianapolis: Indianapolis Museum of Art, 2009).

10. Tom Eccles, "History in the Making" and Allison Smith, "Call to Arms," in Allison Smith, *Allison Smith: The Muster* (New York: Public Art Fund, 2007), 33–41, 42–45; *Armory,* www.allisonsmithstudio.com (accessed Nov. 9, 2009). See also www.themuster .com (accessed Nov. 9, 2009).

11. Allison Smith, "A Tour through the Encampment," in Smith, *The Muster,* 50, 52, 56, 61.

12. Smith, "A Tour through the Encampment," 51.

13. Smith, "Call to Arms," 45.

14. Smith, "A Tour through the Encampment," 71–72.

15. Smith, "A Tour through the Encampment," 67–68, 75–76; James Trainor, "Allison Smith Fights the Good Fight," in Smith, *The Muster,* 89–90.

16. Paul Monette, "Mustering," in *Last Watch of the Night: Essays Too Personal and Otherwise* (New York: Harcourt Brace & Co., 1994), 136, 140, 148, 150.

17. Smith, "Call to Arms," 44–45. The episode of the television comedy *South Park* entitled "The Red Badge of Gayness" (1999) similarly identifies reenactment with gay culture. See episode summary at www.wikipedia.org (accessed Nov. 30, 2009).

18. *Public Address*, www.allisonsmithstudio.com (accessed Nov. 9, 2009). Matt Wolf and Allison Smith, "Re-enacting Stonewall, Jackson That Is," *Journal of Aesthetics and Protest* 1, no. 4 (2005), observes that "*The Muster* functions as a dramatic commemoration of the Stonewall Rebellion, while claiming Stonewall Jackson's Civil War secessionist ethos," www.joaap.org/4/issue4.html (accessed Nov. 9, 2009).

19. *Victory Hall,* www.allisonsmithstudio.com (accessed Nov. 9, 2009).

20. Smith, *The Muster,* 20–21, and "A Tour through the Encampment," 55, 63–66.

21. Smith, "A Tour through the Encampment," 61.

22. Berry, "Medicine on the Spoon," 266–69.

23. Dunbar, *Alloy of Love,* 9–15.

24. Berry, "Medicine on the Spoon," 271.

25. Berry, "Medicine on the Spoon," 273; Dunbar, *Alloy of Love,* 19; Dunbar, "The Reconstructionist," in Dunbar, *Alloy of Love,* 211.

26. Dunbar, *Alloy of Love,* 24, 26, 44–45, 48; see also *When Your Heartstrings Break I Can Mend Them Back (The Supreme Solution),* in *Alloy of Love,* 42–43.

27. Dunbar, *Alloy of Love,* 20–21, 27, 32–33, 36–39, 52–55, 58–59.

28. Ibid., 16–17, 47, 55, 63, 68, 69, 73–75; Dunbar, "The Reconstructionist," 219.

29. Dunbar, *Alloy of Love,* 28–29, 76–77, 102–3; Dunbar, "The Reconstructionist," 221.

30. Dunbar, *Alloy of Love,* 100–101; Dunbar, "The Reconstructionist," 222–23.

31. Berry, "Medicine on the Spoon," 258.

32. See Lisa Marie Herschbach, "Fragmentation and Reunion: Medicine, Memory and Body in the American Civil War" (Ph.D. diss., Harvard University, 1997); Lisa A. Long, *Rehabilitating Bodies: Health, History, and the American Civil War* (Philadelphia: University of Pennsylvania Press, 2003), chap. 1.

33. Dunbar, *Alloy of Love,* 128–30, 142–43.

34. Ibid., 141–42; see also *A Sadness Silence Can't Touch* (2005–2006), in *Alloy of Love,* 166–67.

35. Dunbar, *Alloy of Love,* 112–13.

36. Ibid., *Alloy of Love,* 150–57, 162–65, 172–73, 178–81.

37. Ibid., *Alloy of Love,* 188–91, 196–97.

38. Alice Fahs, *The Imagined Civil War: Popular Literature of the North and South, 1861–1865* (Chapel Hill: University of North Carolina Press, 2001), chaps. 3–4; Judith Ann Giesberg, *Civil War Sisterhood: The U.S. Sanitary Commission and Women's Politics in Transition* (Boston: Northeastern University Press, 2000). See also Xandra Eden, "The Benevolent Efforts of Dario Robleto," in *Dario Robleto: Chrysanthemum Anthems* (Greensboro, NC: Witherspoon Art Museum, 2006), n.p., which identifies Mary Louise Kete, *Sentimental Collaborations: Mourning and Middle-Class Identity in Nineteenth-Century America* (Durham, NC: Duke University Press, 1999) as a scholarly complement to Robleto's art.

39. Dunbar, *Alloy of Love,* 100–101, 108–11, 116–17, 120–23; Drew Gilpin Faust, *This Republic of Suffering: Death and the American Civil War* (New York: Alfred A. Knopf, 2008), 144–70. See also Long, *Rehabilitating Bodies,* chap. 2.

40. Daniel J. Sherman, *The Construction of Memory in Interwar France* (Chicago: University of Chicago Press, 1999).

41. Leah Dickerman, *"Merz* and Memory: On Kurt Schwitters," in *The Dada Seminars,* ed. Leah Dickerman and Matthew S. Witkovsky (Washington, DC: National Gallery of Art, 2005). See also Leah Dickerman, ed., *Dada: Zurich, Berlin, Hannover, Cologne, New York, Paris* (Washington, DC: National Gallery of Art, 2005), 9, 97, 288–91.

42. Dunbar, *Alloy of Love,* 156–57.

43. Oliver Wendell Holmes, "The Soldier's Faith," in *Speeches* (Boston: Little, Brown and Company, 1913), 58.

CHAPTER 7: African American Artists Interpret the Civil War in a Post-Soul Age

1. Fredericksburg *Free Lance-Star,* June 30, 2002.

2. William Faulkner, *Requiem for a Nun* (New York: Random House, 1951).

3. Edmund Wilson, *Patriotic Gore: Studies in the Literature of the American Civil War* (New York: Oxford University Press, 1962).

4. David W. Blight, *Race and Reunion: The Civil War in American Memory* (Cambridge, MA: Harvard University Press, 2001); Robert Cook, *Troubled Commemoration: The American Civil War Centennial, 1961–1965* (Baton Rouge: Louisiana State University Press, 2007); David R. Goldfield, *Still Fighting the Civil War: The American South and Southern History* (Baton Rouge: Louisiana State University Press, 2002); Peter Novick, *That Noble Dream: The "Objectivity Question" and the American Historical Profession* (Cambridge: Cambridge University Press, 1988).

5. Blight, *Race and Reunion;* Kirk Savage, *Standing Soldiers, Kneeling Slaves: Race, War, and Monument in Nineteenth-Century America* (Princeton, NJ: Princeton University Press, 1997).

6. Daniel Aaron, *The Unwritten War: American Writers and the Civil War* (New York: Alfred A. Knopf, 1973).

7. W. Fitzhugh Brundage, *The Southern Past: A Clash of Race and Memory* (Cambridge, MA: Harvard University Press, 2005); Mark Anthony Neal, *Soul Babies: Black Popular Culture and the Post-Soul Aesthetic* (New York: Routledge, 2002).

8. Trey Ellis, "The New Black Aesthetic," *Callaloo* 38 (1989): 233–43; Nelson George, *Buppies, B-Boys, Baps, and Bohos: Notes on Post-Soul Black Culture* (Cambridge, MA: Da Capo, 2001); Neal, *Soul Babies.*

9. Suzan-Lori Parks, "An Equation for Black People Onstage," in *The America Play* (New York: Theatre Communications Group, 1995), 21.

10. Suzan-Lori Parks, "Commencement Speech to the Mount Holyoke College Class of 2001 Held on May 27, 2001," www.mtholyoke.edu/offices/comm/oped/loriparks .shtml (accessed Sept. 30, 2009).

11. On signifying, see Henry Louis Gates Jr., *The Signifying Monkey: A Theory of Afro-American Literary Criticism* (New York: Oxford University Press, 1988); and Gena Dagel Caponi, *Signifyin(g), Sanctifyin', & Slam Dunking: A Reader in African American Expressive Culture* (Amherst: University of Massachusetts Press, 1999).

12. Alice Randall, *The Wind Done Gone* (Boston: Houghton Mifflin, 2001).

13. For catalogs of Walker's art, see Kara Walker, *Pictures from Another Time* (Ann Arbor: University of Michigan Museum of Art, 2002); Kara Walker, *Narratives of a Negress* (Cambridge, MA: MIT Press, 2003); Kara Walker, *My Complement, My Enemy, My Oppressor, My Love* (Minneapolis: Walker Art Center, 2007); and Kara Walker, *Bureau of Refugees* (Milan: Charta, 2008).

14. Darby English, "'This Is Not about the Past': Silhouettes in the Work of Kara Walker," in Walker, *Narratives of a Negress,* 159–62; Victor I. Stoichita, *A Short History of the Shadow* (London: Reaktion Books, 1997), chap. 5; Anne M. Wagner, "Silhouette," in Walker, *Narrative of a Negress,* 91–101.

15. Han-Ulrich Obrist, "Interview with Kara Walker," in Johanes Schlebrugge, ed., *Safety Curtain: Kara Walker* (Vienna: Museum in Progress in Cooperation with Vienna State Opera House and P. S. Wien, 2000), 12.

16. Interview by Alexander Alberro in Gary Garrels and Alexander Alberro, *Kara Walker, Upon My Many Masters—an Outline* (San Francisco: San Francisco Museum of Modern Art, 1997), n.p.

17. For images of the "Battle of Atlanta" silhouettes, see Walker, *Narratives of a Negress,* 43; Walker, *Pictures from Another Time,* 15, 52, 56, 57, 58.

18. Walker, *My Complement, My Enemy, My Oppressor, My Love,* 321, 322, 324.

19. Robert Blakeslee Gilpin, "Monster and Martyr: America's Long Reckoning with Race, Violence, and John Brown" (Ph.D. diss., Yale, 2009).

20. On the evolving depictions of Brown in art, see Gwendolyn DuBois Shaw, *Seeing the Unspeakable: The Art of Kara Walker* (Durham, NC: Duke University Press, 2004), 69–76, 77–83.

21. Gilpin, "Monster and Martyr," 262–327; Shaw, *Seeing the Unspeakable,* 94–98.

22. For a reproduction of Walker's John Brown painting, see Walker, *My Complement, My Enemy, My Oppressor, My Love,* 164.

23. Shaw, *Seeing the Unspeakable,* 101.

24. Ken Collins and Victor Wishna, "Suzan-Lori Parks," in *In Their Company: Portraits of American Playwrights* (New York: Umbrage Editions, 2006), 186–89.

25. Suzan-Lori Parks, *"Possession,"* in *The America Play and Other Works* (New York: Theatre Communications Group, 1995), 5.

26. Parks, *"The America Play,"* in *The America Play,* 182, 183, passim.

27. Miller discusses his career in Carol Becker, Romi Crawford, and Paul D. Miller, "An Interview with Paul D. Miller a.k.a. DJ Spooky—That Subliminal Kid," *Art Journal* 61 (Spring 2002): 82–91.

28. Alex Williams, "Spooky's Splice of Life," Sydney *Daily Telegraph,* Dec. 17, 2004, 67.

29. Becker, et al., "Interview with Paul D. Miller," 84.

30. Matthew Davis, "Remixing the Past," Wellington *Dominion Post,* Feb. 8, 2006, Entertainment, 3.

31. Williams, "Splice of Life."

32. Jeff Loeb, "A Conversation with Kevin Willmott," *African American Review* 35 (n.d.): 253.

33. Ibid., 258.

34. Ibid., 253.

35. Interview on PBS "NewsHour," April 25, 2007, www.pbs.org/newshour/bb/entertainment/jan-june07/trethewey_04-25.html (accessed Oct. 1, 2009).

36. Ibid.

37. Natasha D. Trethewey, *Native Guard* (Boston: Houghton Mifflin, 2006), 20.

38. Ibid., 38.

39. Ibid., 46.

40. Ibid., 44.

41. "An Interview with Natasha Trethewey," BookSlut Blog, Feb. 2008, www.bookslut.com/features/2008_02_012353.php (accessed Oct. 1, 2009).

42. Kevin Young, *For the Confederate Dead* (New York: Alfred A. Knopf, 2007).

43. Darryl Pinckney, "What He Really Said," *New York Review of Books* 56 (Feb. 26, 2009).

AFTERWORD: War/Memory/History

I would like to thank the editor Tom Brown for his perceptive comments on earlier drafts of this essay.

1. Letter of William T. Sherman to James M. Calhoun, Mayor, E. E. Pawson and S. C. Wells, representing City Council of Atlanta, Sept. 12, 1864, at www.sagehistory.net/civilwar/docs/ShermanAtl.htm (accessed April 10, 2010).

2. William Dean Howells, "Question of Monuments," *Atlantic Monthly* (May 1866): 647.

3. "McDonnell Admits a 'Major Omission,'" *Washington Post*, April 8, 2010, a1.

4. *Constitution of the Confederate States, March 11, 1861,* at http://avalon.law.yale.edu/19th_century/csa_csa.asp (accessed April 10, 2010). The official declarations of the various secession conventions also make the same point, as Drew Gilpin Faust demonstrated in her now classic study, *The Creation of Confederate Nationalism: Ideology and Identity in the Civil War South* (Baton Rouge: Louisiana State University Press, 1988).

5. Quoted in James Pickett Jones, *Yankee Blitzkrieg: Wilson's Raid through Alabama and Georgia* (Lexington: University of Kentucky Press, 2000), 49.

6. "Correction," *Time*, Jan. 23, 2003, www.time.com/time/nation/article/0,8599,410965,00.html (accessed July 18, 2010). It had been reported that George Herbert Walker Bush had discontinued the tradition in 1990, but he had only changed the date (from Jefferson Davis's birthday to Memorial Day); the practice continued to be observed by Presidents Clinton and Bush.

7. Kirk Savage, "The President and the Confederacy," *Washington Post*, May 23, 2009, www.washingtonpost.com/wp-dyn/content/article/2009/05/22/AR2009052202999.html (accessed April 10, 2010). James W. Loewen, "Separate but Equal Wreaths Are Not a Permanent Solution to the Memorial Day Conundrum," http://hnn.us/articles/87913.html (accessed April 10, 2010).

8. Recorded interview between Mark Savage and Dean and Bertha Savage, August 1974, in author's possession; Temple F. Savage, listed in the National Park System's online "Civil War Soldiers and Sailors System," www.itd.nps.gov/cwss/soldiers.cfm (accessed March 4, 2011); gravestone in old Elmore Baptist Cemetery, Gordo, Alabama.

9. Conversation with Michael Kraus, curator of the Allegheny County Soldiers and Sailors Memorial, Feb. 2, 2010.

10. Obama sent both wreaths again in 2010, again without comment.

11. For a searing critique of British exceptionalism and self-congratulation during the 2007 bicentennial of the abolition of the slave trade, see Marcus Wood, *The Horrible Gift of Freedom: Atlantic Slavery and the Representation of Emancipation* (Athens: University of Georgia Press, 2010).

Contributors

Robert H. Brinkmeyer Jr. is the Emily Brown Jefferies Professor of English and Professor of Southern Studies at the University of South Carolina. His most recent book, *The Fourth Ghost: White Southern Writers and European Fascism, 1930–1950* (Louisiana State University Press, 2009), received the Warren-Brooks Award for Excellence in Literary Criticism and the PROSE Award, presented by the Association for American Publishers, for the most outstanding new book published in literature, language, and linguistics. He is the author of four previous books on modern southern literature, including *Remapping Southern Literature: Contemporary American Writers and the West* (University of Georgia Press, 2000), originally presented as the forty-second annual Lamar Lectures at Mercer University.

Gerard Brown is an assistant professor of art and chair of the Foundations Department at Tyler School of Art, Temple University. His art criticism has appeared in the *Philadelphia Weekly, Ceramics: Art and Perception,* and *Juxtapoz.*

Thomas J. Brown is an associate professor of history at the University of South Carolina. He is the author of *Dorothea Dix, New England Reformer* (Harvard University Press, 1998), the co-editor of *Hope and Glory: Essays on the Legacy of the 54th Massachusetts Regiment* (University of Massachusetts Press, 2001), and the editor of *The Public Art of Civil War Commemoration* (Bedford/St. Martin's, 2004) and *Reconstructions: New Perspectives on the Postbellum United States* (Oxford University Press, 2006).

W. Fitzhugh Brundage is the William B. Umstead Professor of History at the University of North Carolina, Chapel Hill. He is the author of three prize-winning books on southern history, including *The Southern Past: A Clash of Race and Memory* (Harvard University Press, 2005), which received the Lillian Smith Book Award of the Southern Regional Council and the Charles S. Sydnor Award of the Southern Historical Association. He is also the editor of several books, including *Where These Memories Grow: History, Memory, and Regional Identity in the American South* (University of North Carolina Press, 2000). Most recently, he is the editor of and a contributor to *Beyond Blackface: African Americans and the Creation of American Popular Culture, 1890–1930* (University of North Carolina Press, 2011).

C. Wyatt Evans is an associate professor of history at Drew University, where he also directs the graduate program in history and culture. His book, *The Legend of John Wilkes Booth: Myth, Memory, and a Mummy* (University Press of Kansas, 2004), received the Avery O. Craven Award, presented by the Organization of American Historians, as the outstanding new book on the Civil War era. He is a distinguished lecturer for the OAH, and his topics include Civil War refugees, domestic security, teaching the Civil War, and the uses of memory in contemporary politics. He is completing a book on the wartime career of Union chief detective Lafayette Baker and is starting a second, based in part on the essay included in this volume and tentatively titled *Drinking Tea with Lincoln*.

Mitch Kachun is an associate professor and director of graduate studies in the History Department at Western Michigan University, specializing in African American history, historical memory, and public commemorations. He is the author of *Festivals of Freedom: Memory and Meaning in African American Emancipation Celebrations, 1808–1915* (University of Massachusetts Press, 2003) and co-editor of *The Curse of Caste; or, the Slave Bride, a Rediscovered African American Novel by Julia C. Collins* (Oxford University Press, 2006). His current book project, tentatively entitled *First Martyr of Liberty*, examines Crispus Attucks's place in American history and memory. He lives with his family in Grand Rapids, Michigan.

Kirk Savage is a professor and chair of the Department of the History of Art and Architecture at the University of Pittsburgh. His *Standing Soldiers, Kneeling Slaves: Race, War, and Monument in Nineteenth-Century America* (Princeton University Press, 1997) received the John Hope Franklin Prize of the American Studies Association for the outstanding book of the year. His most recent book, *Monument Wars: Washington, D.C., the National Mall, and the Transformation of the Memorial Landscape* (University of California Press, 2009), received the Charles C. Eldredge Prize for Distinguished Scholarship awarded by the Smithsonian American Art Museum.

Elizabeth Young is the Carl M. and Elsie A. Small Professor of English at Mount Holyoke College. She is the author of *Disarming the Nation: Women's Writing and the American Civil War* (University of Chicago Press, 1999) and the co-author of *On Alexander Gardner's "Photographic Sketch Book" of the Civil War* (University of California Press, 2007). Her most recent book is *Black Frankenstein: The Making of an American Metaphor* (New York University Press, 2008).

Index

? hubristic self-delusion " (1)

· what does Brown mean by "remix"?